BEYOND

FIRST
FLIGHT

VOL. **7**

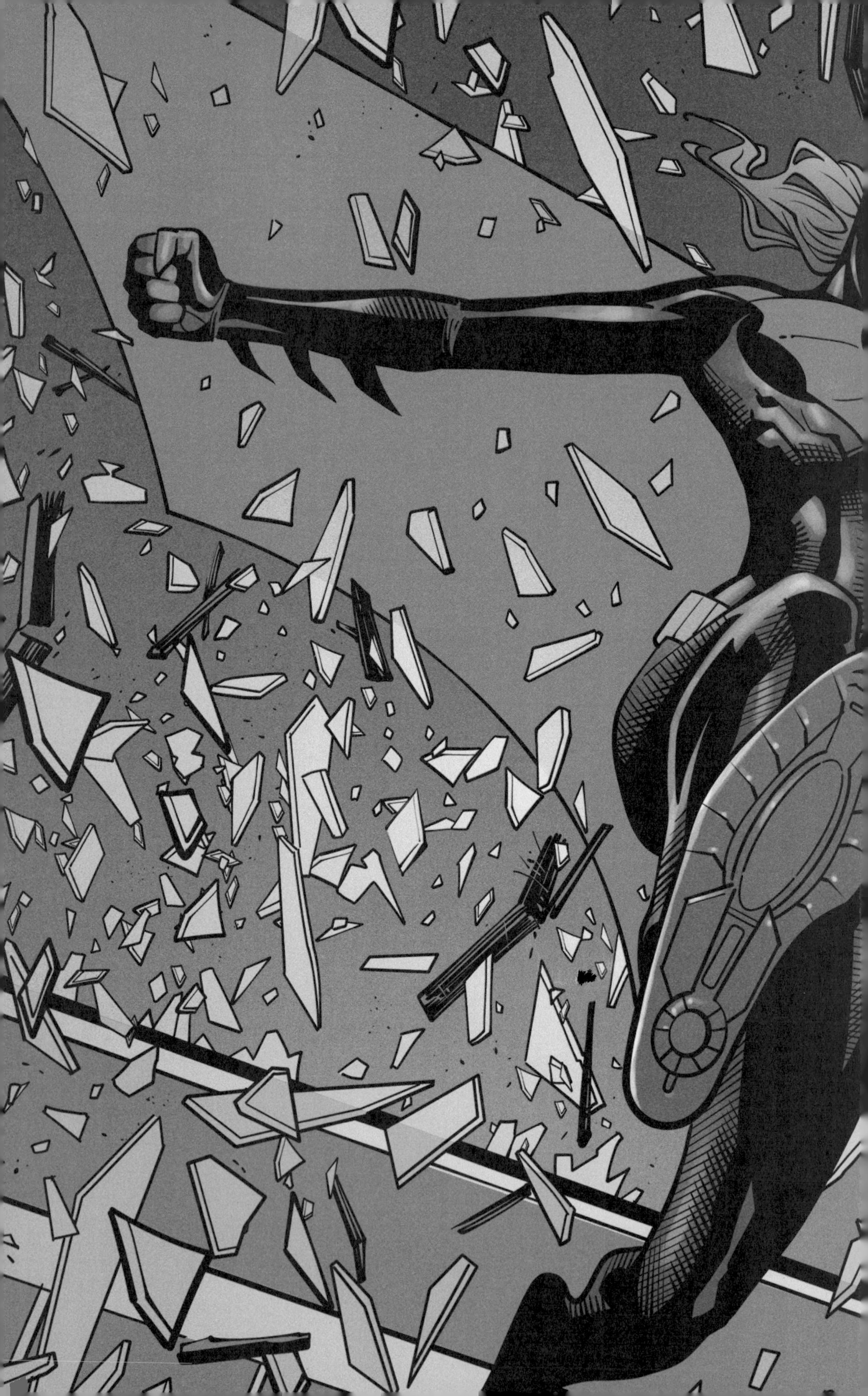

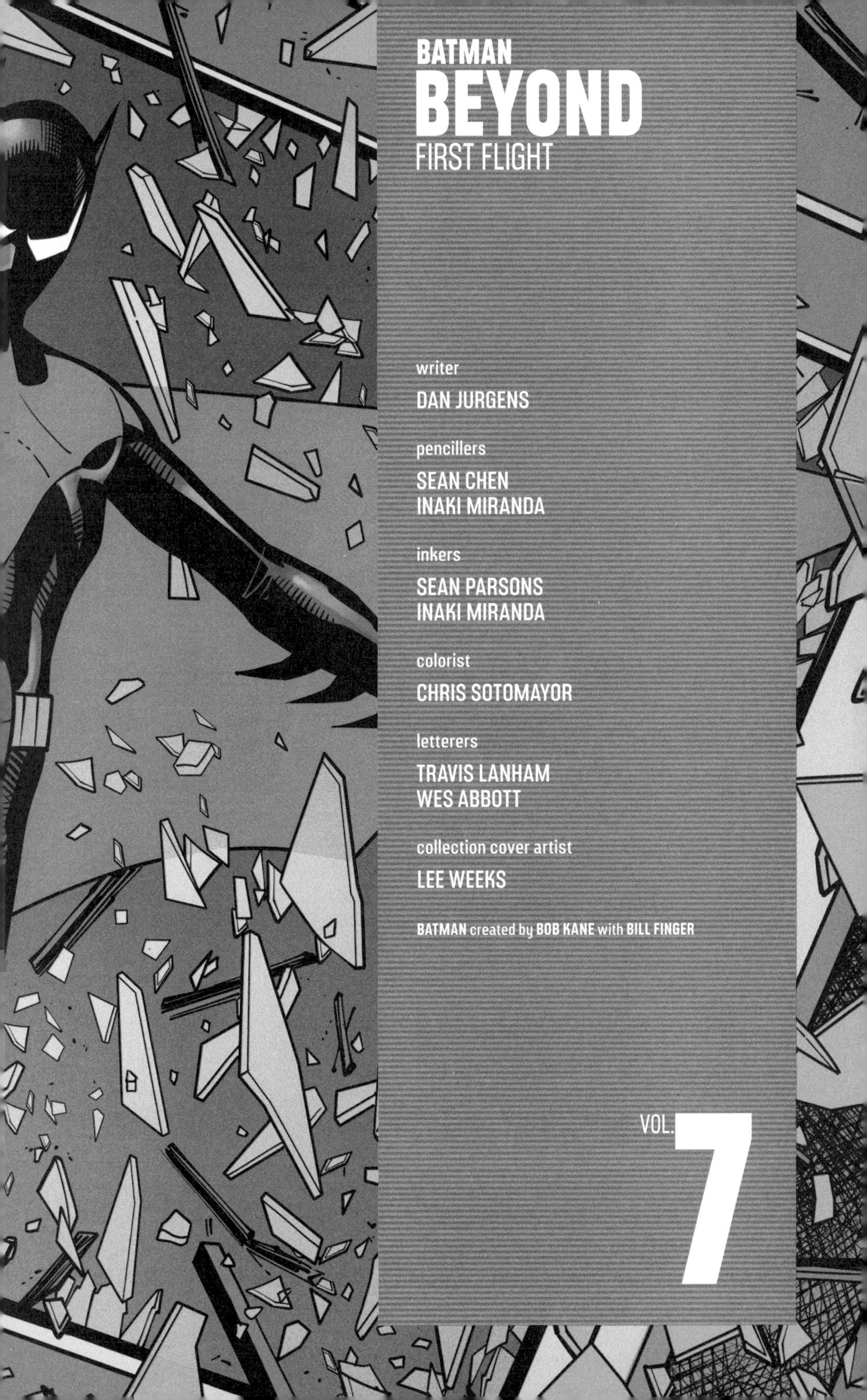

BATMAN BEYOND
FIRST FLIGHT

writer

DAN JURGENS

pencillers

SEAN CHEN
INAKI MIRANDA

inkers

SEAN PARSONS
INAKI MIRANDA

colorist

CHRIS SOTOMAYOR

letterers

TRAVIS LANHAM
WES ABBOTT

collection cover artist

LEE WEEKS

BATMAN created by **BOB KANE** with **BILL FINGER**

VOL. 7

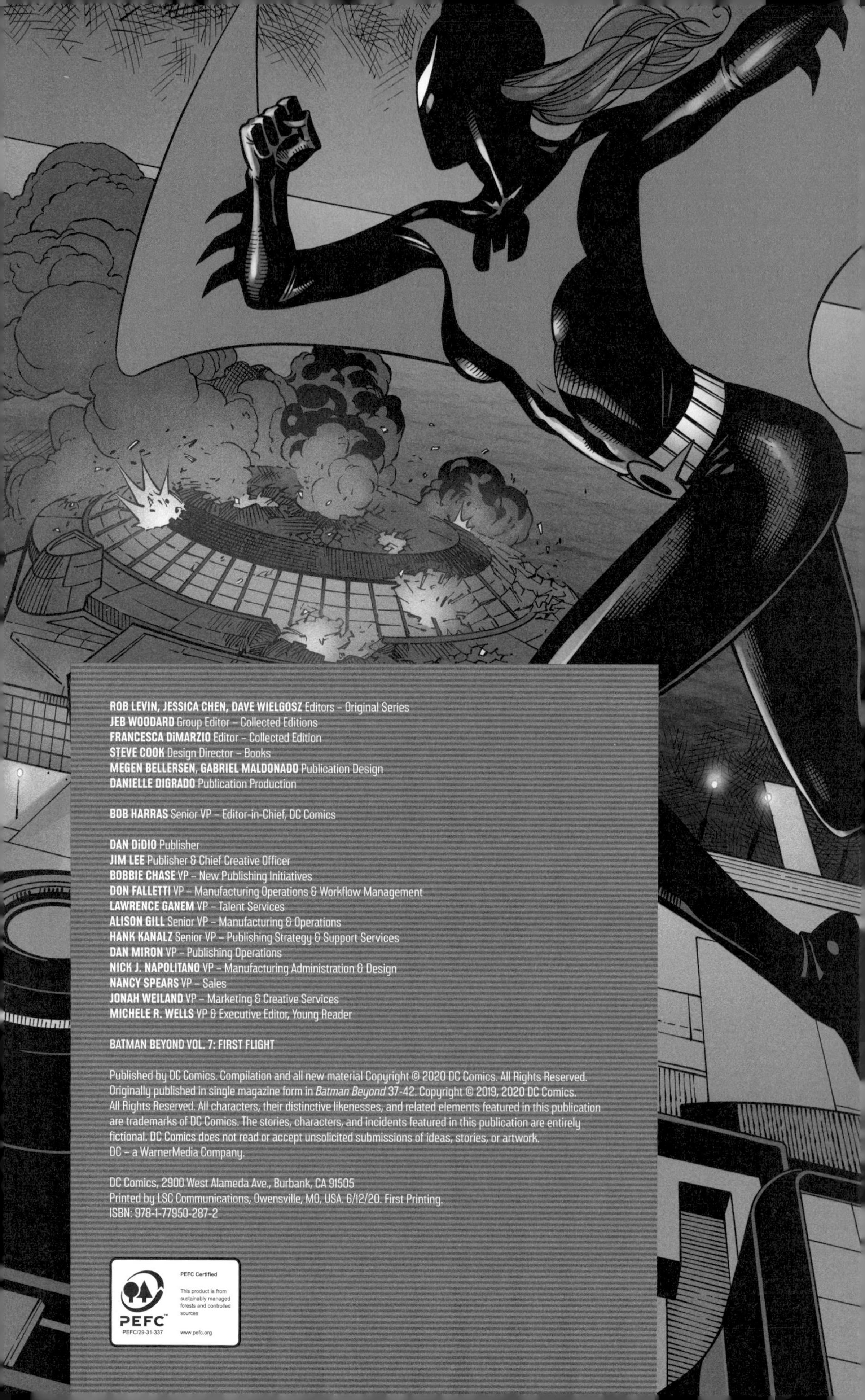

ROB LEVIN, JESSICA CHEN, DAVE WIELGOSZ Editors – Original Series
JEB WOODARD Group Editor – Collected Editions
FRANCESCA DiMARZIO Editor – Collected Edition
STEVE COOK Design Director – Books
MEGEN BELLERSEN, GABRIEL MALDONADO Publication Design
DANIELLE DIGRADO Publication Production

BOB HARRAS Senior VP – Editor-in-Chief, DC Comics

DAN DiDIO Publisher
JIM LEE Publisher & Chief Creative Officer
BOBBIE CHASE VP – New Publishing Initiatives
DON FALLETTI VP – Manufacturing Operations & Workflow Management
LAWRENCE GANEM VP – Talent Services
ALISON GILL Senior VP – Manufacturing & Operations
HANK KANALZ Senior VP – Publishing Strategy & Support Services
DAN MIRON VP – Publishing Operations
NICK J. NAPOLITANO VP – Manufacturing Administration & Design
NANCY SPEARS VP – Sales
JONAH WEILAND VP – Marketing & Creative Services
MICHELE R. WELLS VP & Executive Editor, Young Reader

BATMAN BEYOND VOL. 7: FIRST FLIGHT

DC Comics, 2900 West Alameda Ave., Burbank, CA 91505
Printed by LSC Communications, Owensville, MO, USA. 6/12/20. First Printing.
ISBN: 978-1-77950-287-2

PEFC Certified
This product is from sustainably managed forests and controlled sources
PEFC
PEFC/29-31-337
www.pefc.org

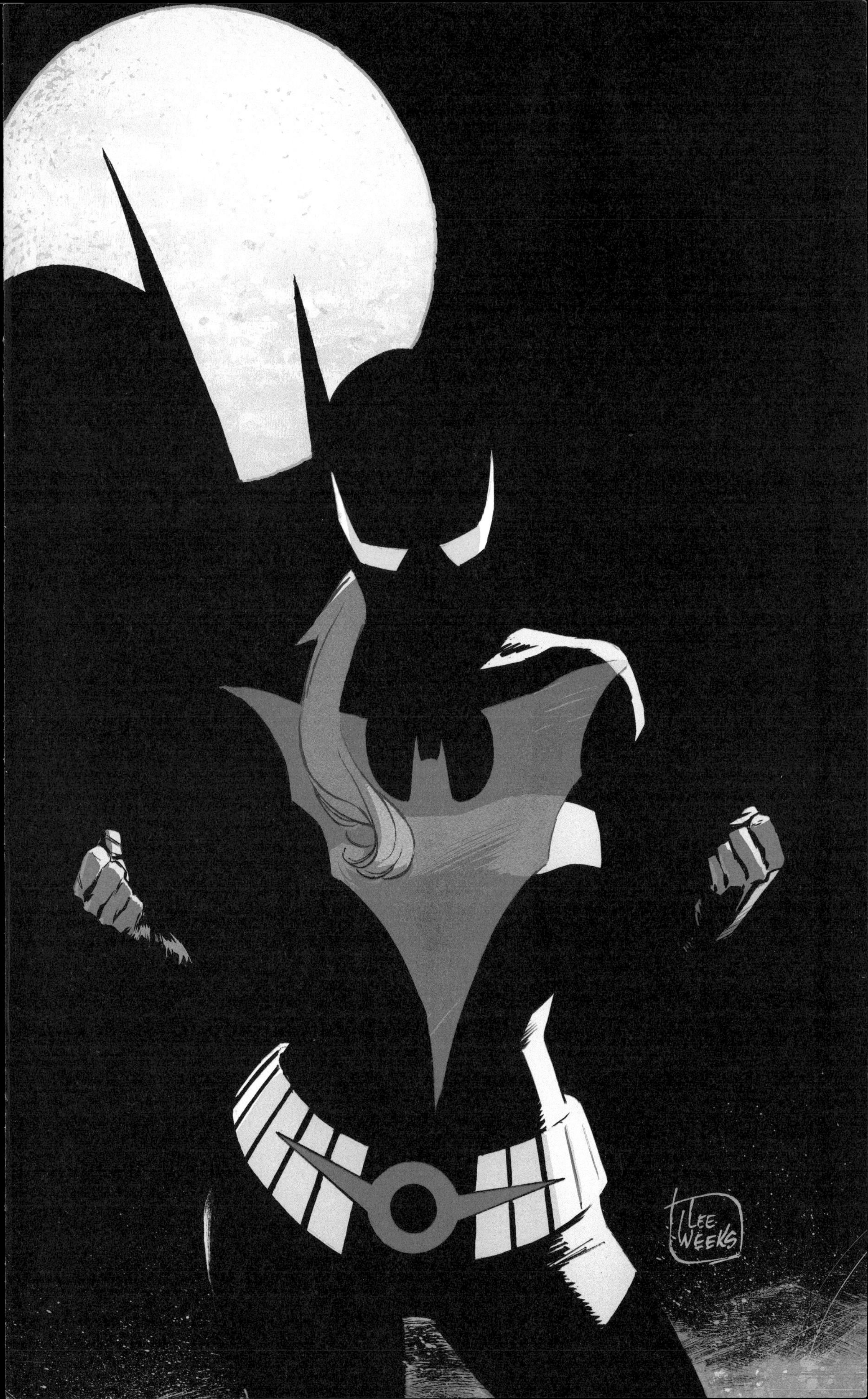
LEE WEEKS

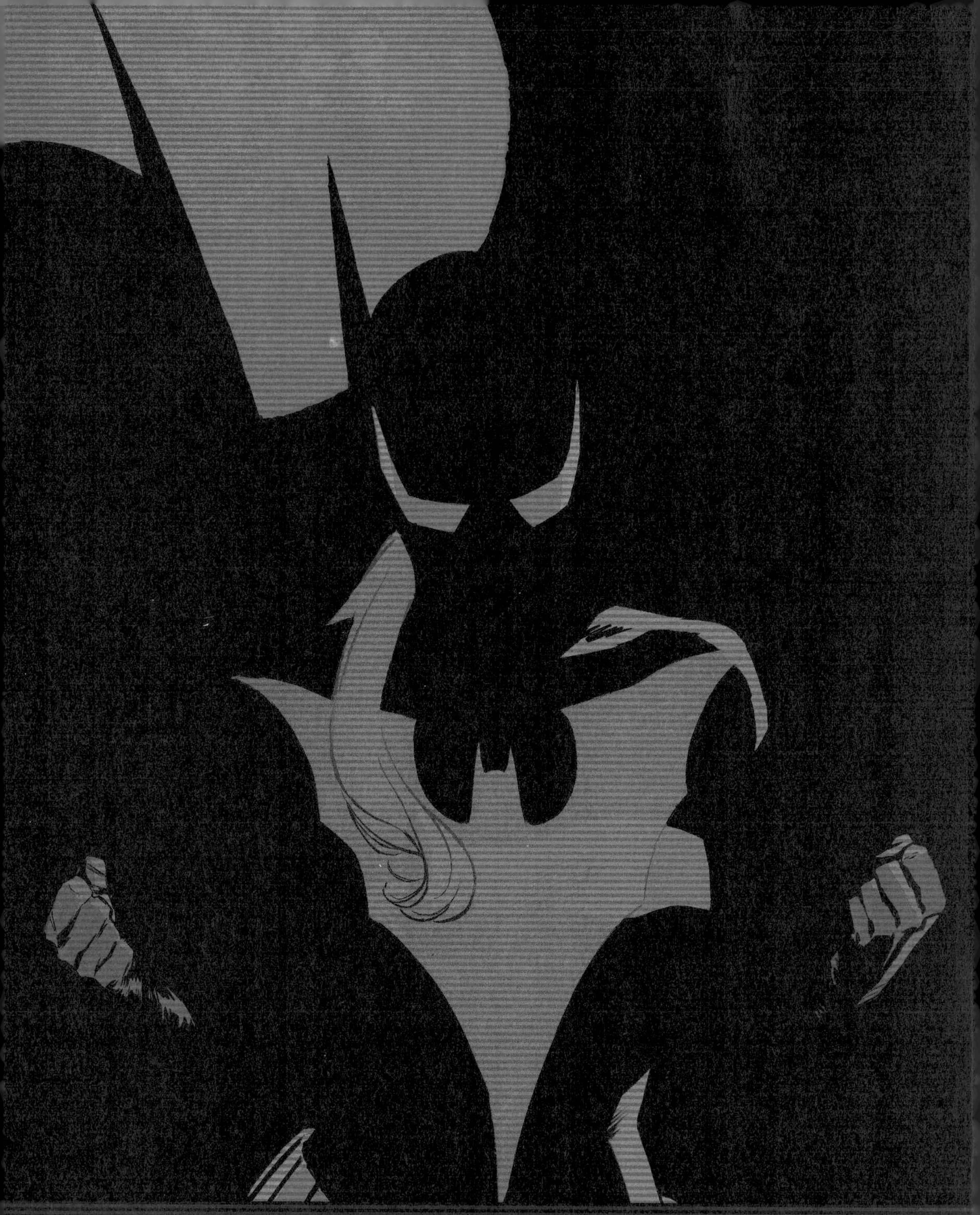

BATMAN
BEYOND
#37

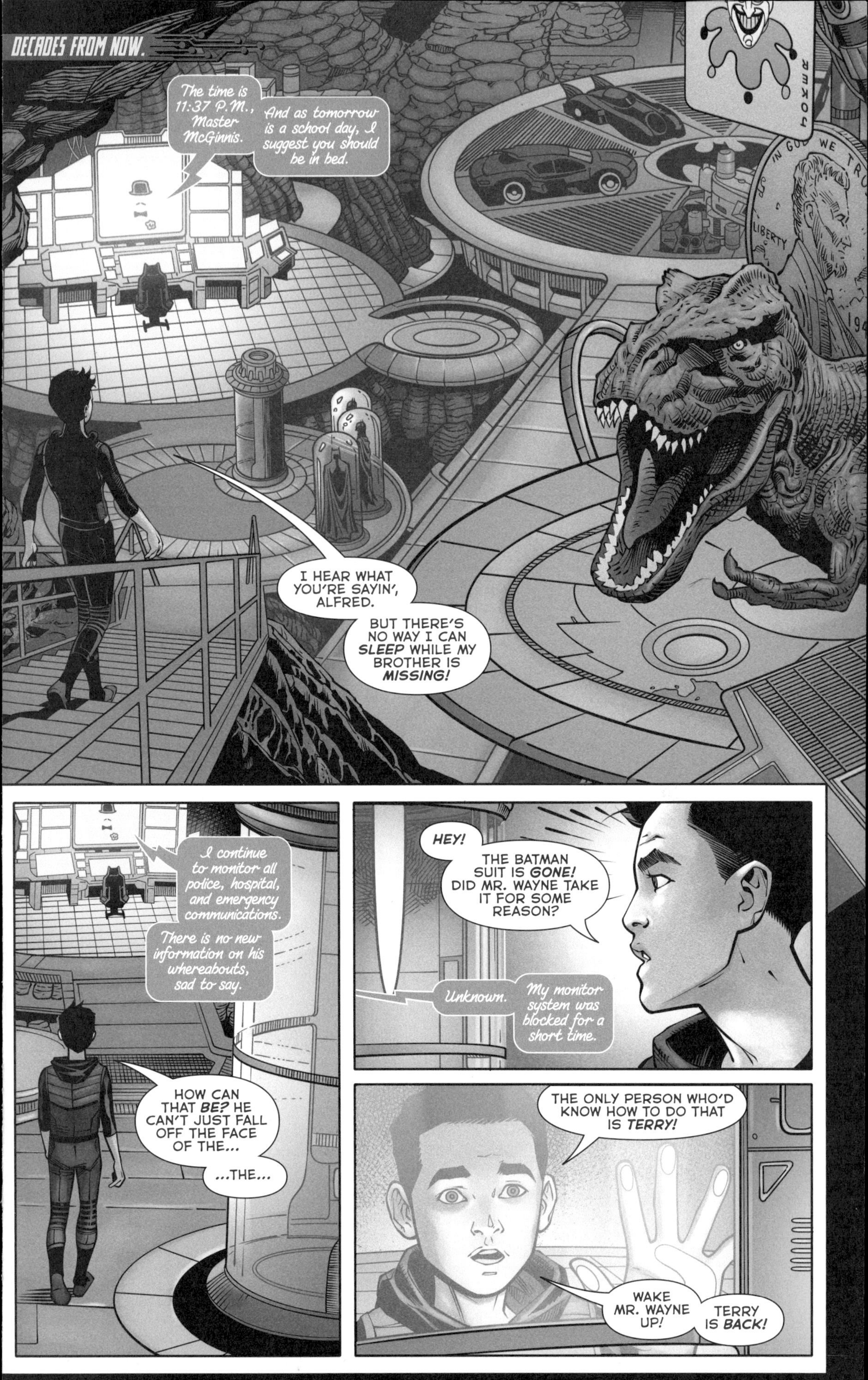
DECADES FROM NOW.
JOKER
IN GOD WE TR
LIBERTY
The time is 11:37 P.M., Master McGinnis.
And as tomorrow is a school day, I suggest you should be in bed.
I HEAR WHAT YOU'RE SAYIN', ALFRED.
BUT THERE'S NO WAY I CAN SLEEP WHILE MY BROTHER IS MISSING!
I continue to monitor all police, hospital, and emergency communications.
There is no new information on his whereabouts, sad to say.
HOW CAN THAT BE? HE CAN'T JUST FALL OFF THE FACE OF THE...
...THE...
HEY!
THE BATMAN SUIT IS GONE! DID MR. WAYNE TAKE IT FOR SOME REASON?
Unknown.
My monitor system was blocked for a short time.
THE ONLY PERSON WHO'D KNOW HOW TO DO THAT IS TERRY!
WAKE MR. WAYNE UP!
TERRY IS BACK!

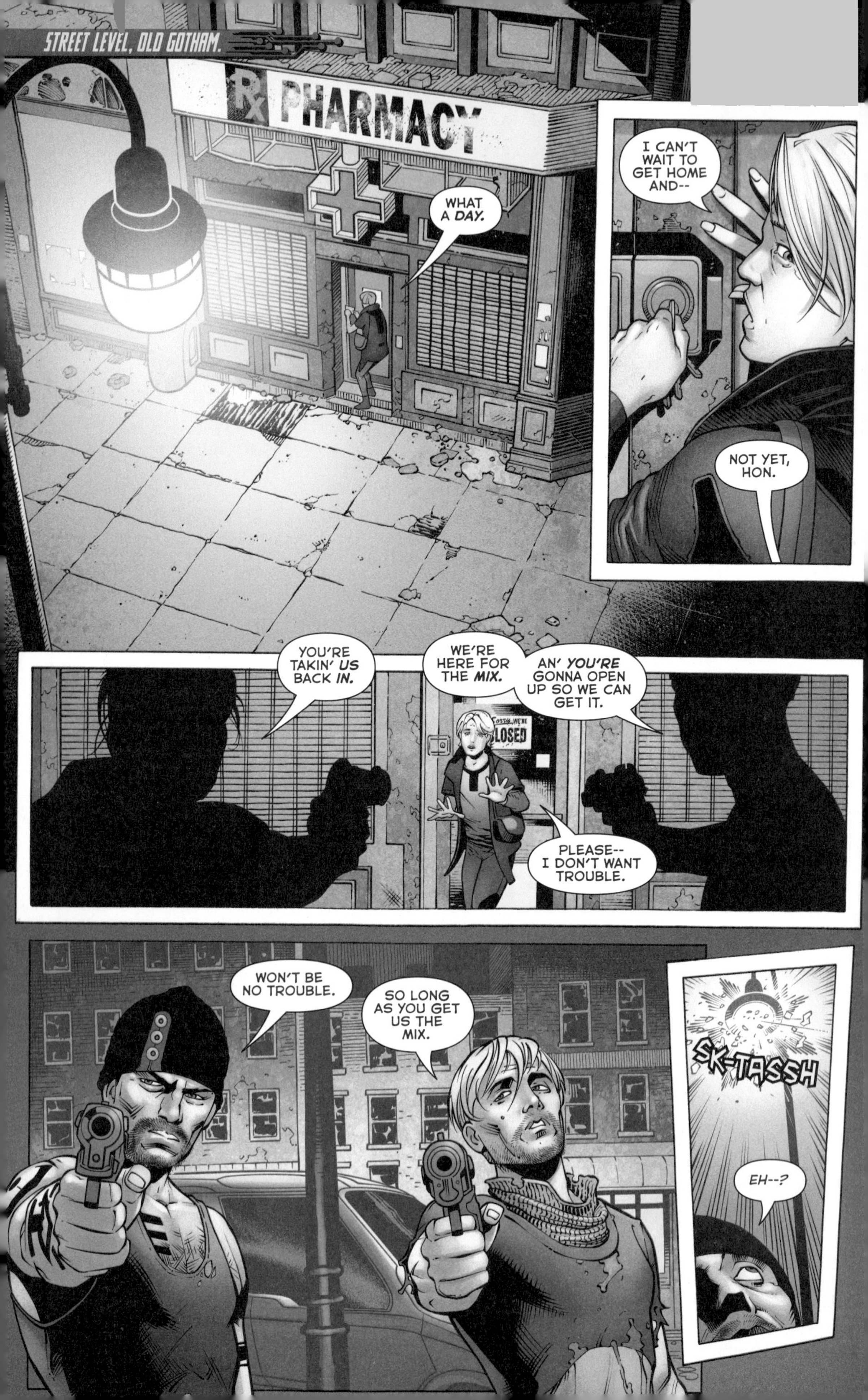
STREET LEVEL, OLD GOTHAM.
Rx PHARMACY
WHAT A DAY.
I CAN'T WAIT TO GET HOME AND--
NOT YET, HON.
YOU'RE TAKIN' US BACK IN.
WE'RE HERE FOR THE MIX.
AN' YOU'RE GONNA OPEN UP SO WE CAN GET IT.
PLEASE-- I DON'T WANT TROUBLE.
WON'T BE NO TROUBLE.
SO LONG AS YOU GET US THE MIX.
SK-TASSH
EH--?

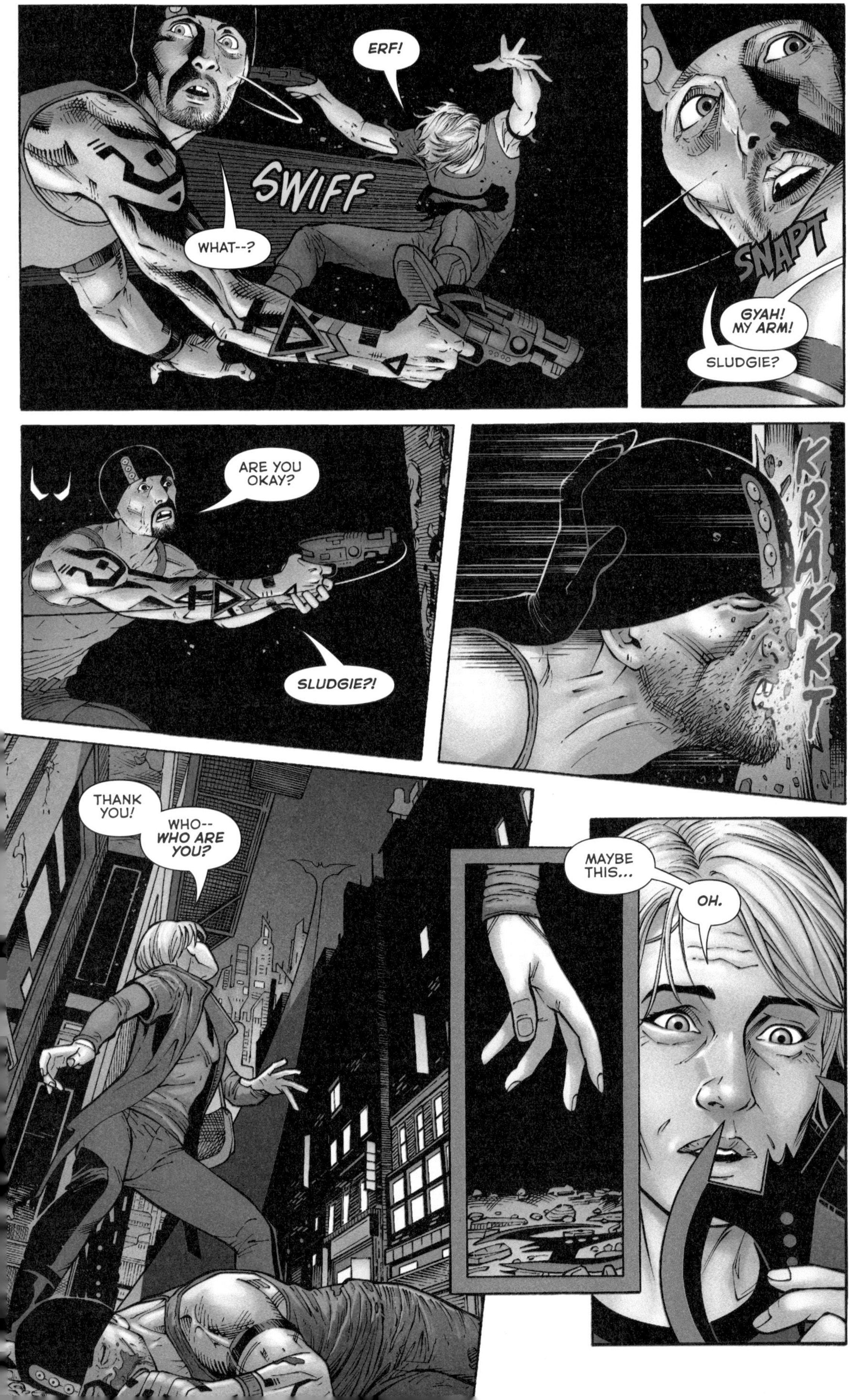
ERF!
SWIFF
WHAT--?
SNAPT
GYAH! MY ARM!
SLUDGIE?
ARE YOU OKAY?
SLUDGIE?!
KRAKKT
THANK YOU!
WHO-- WHO ARE YOU?
MAYBE THIS...
OH.

FIRST FLIGHT PART ONE

DAN JURGENS writer · SEAN CHEN penciller · SEAN PARSONS inker · CHRIS SOTOMAYOR colorist · TRAVIS LANHAM letterer · LEE WEEKS cover · ROB LEVIN editor · JAMIE S. RICH group editor

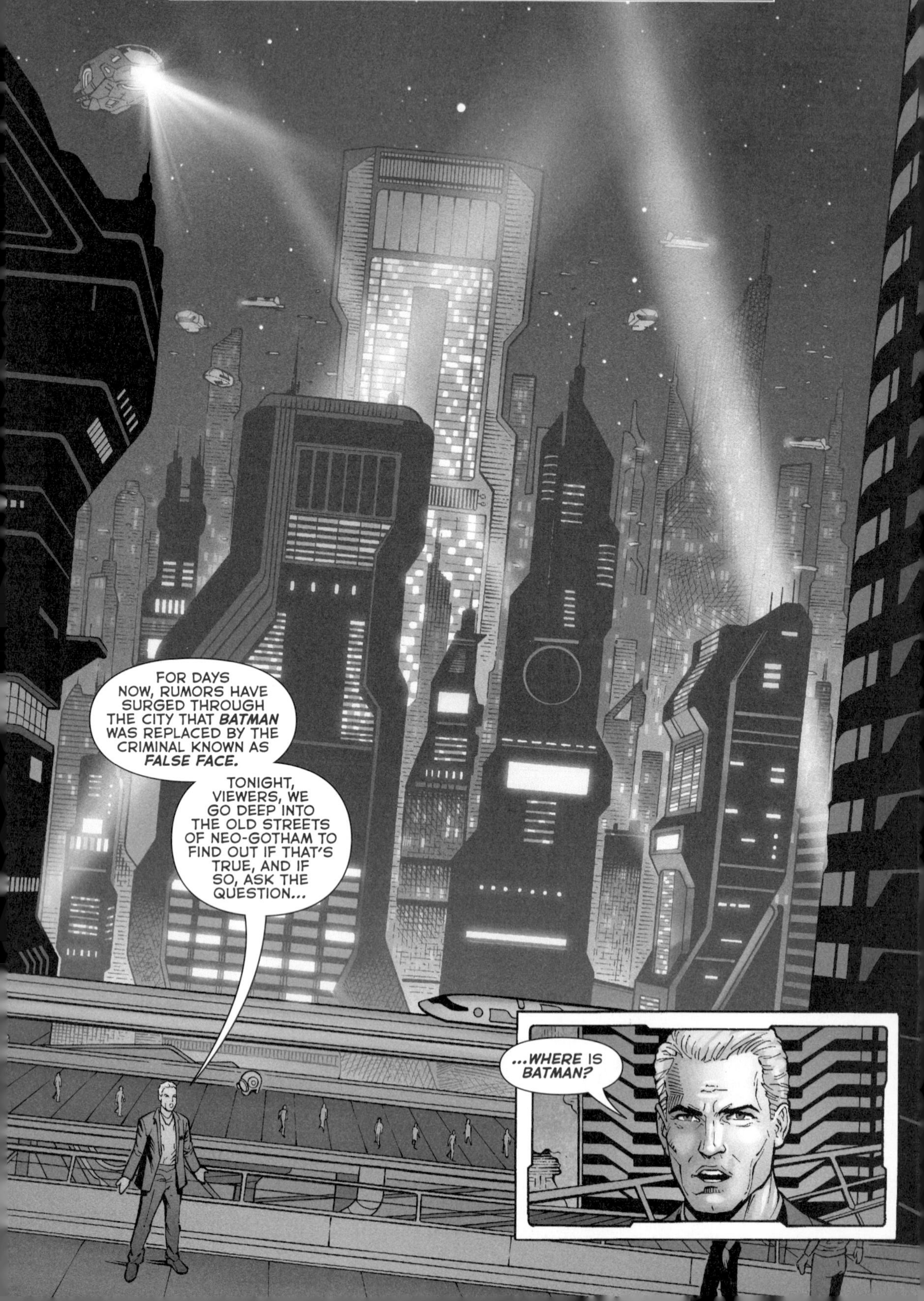
FOR DAYS NOW, RUMORS HAVE SURGED THROUGH THE CITY THAT *BATMAN* WAS REPLACED BY THE CRIMINAL KNOWN AS *FALSE FACE.*
TONIGHT, VIEWERS, WE GO DEEP INTO THE OLD STREETS OF NEO-GOTHAM TO FIND OUT IF THAT'S TRUE, AND IF SO, ASK THE QUESTION...
...*WHERE* IS *BATMAN?*

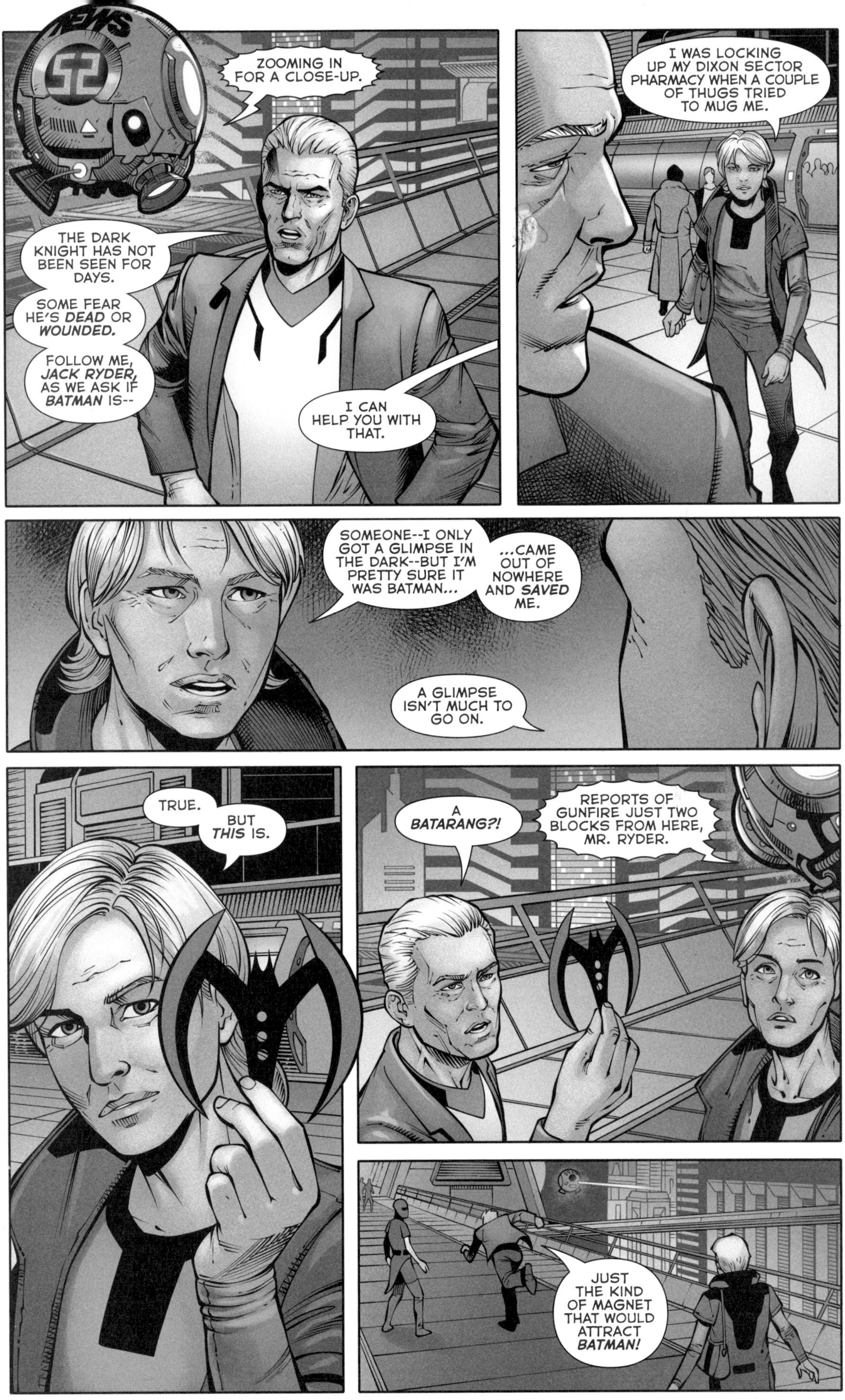
NEWS
52
ZOOMING IN FOR A CLOSE-UP.
THE DARK KNIGHT HAS NOT BEEN SEEN FOR DAYS.
SOME FEAR HE'S DEAD OR WOUNDED.
FOLLOW ME, JACK RYDER, AS WE ASK IF BATMAN IS--
I CAN HELP YOU WITH THAT.
I WAS LOCKING UP MY DIXON SECTOR PHARMACY WHEN A COUPLE OF THUGS TRIED TO MUG ME.
SOMEONE--I ONLY GOT A GLIMPSE IN THE DARK--BUT I'M PRETTY SURE IT WAS BATMAN...
...CAME OUT OF NOWHERE AND SAVED ME.
A GLIMPSE ISN'T MUCH TO GO ON.
TRUE.
BUT THIS IS.
A BATARANG?!
REPORTS OF GUNFIRE JUST TWO BLOCKS FROM HERE, MR. RYDER.
JUST THE KIND OF MAGNET THAT WOULD ATTRACT BATMAN!

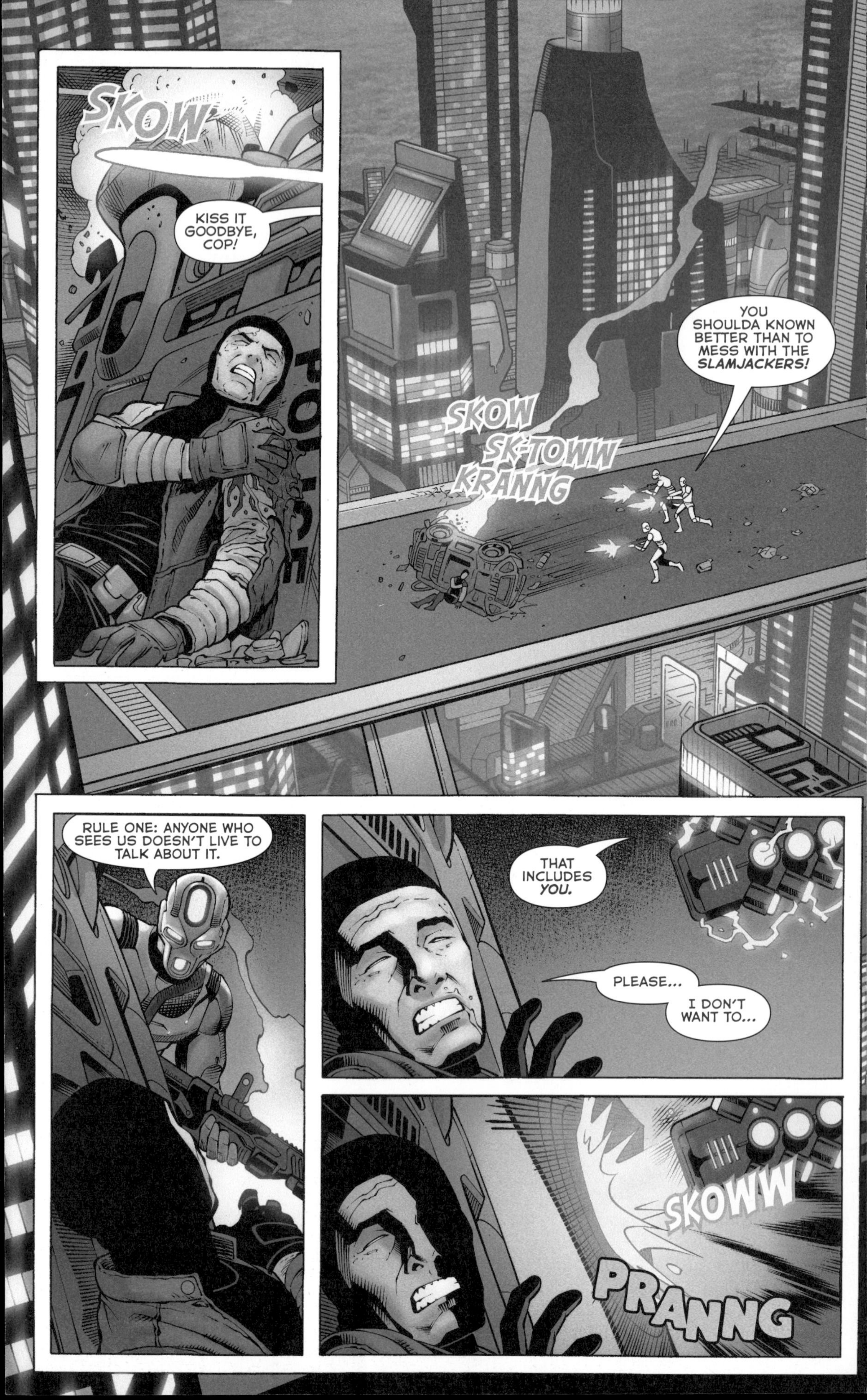
SKOW
KISS IT GOODBYE, COP!
POLICE
SKOW
SK-TOWW
KRANNG
YOU SHOULDA KNOWN BETTER THAN TO MESS WITH THE *SLAMJACKERS!*
RULE ONE: ANYONE WHO SEES US DOESN'T LIVE TO TALK ABOUT IT.
THAT INCLUDES *YOU.*
PLEASE...
I DON'T WANT TO...
SKOWW
PRANNG

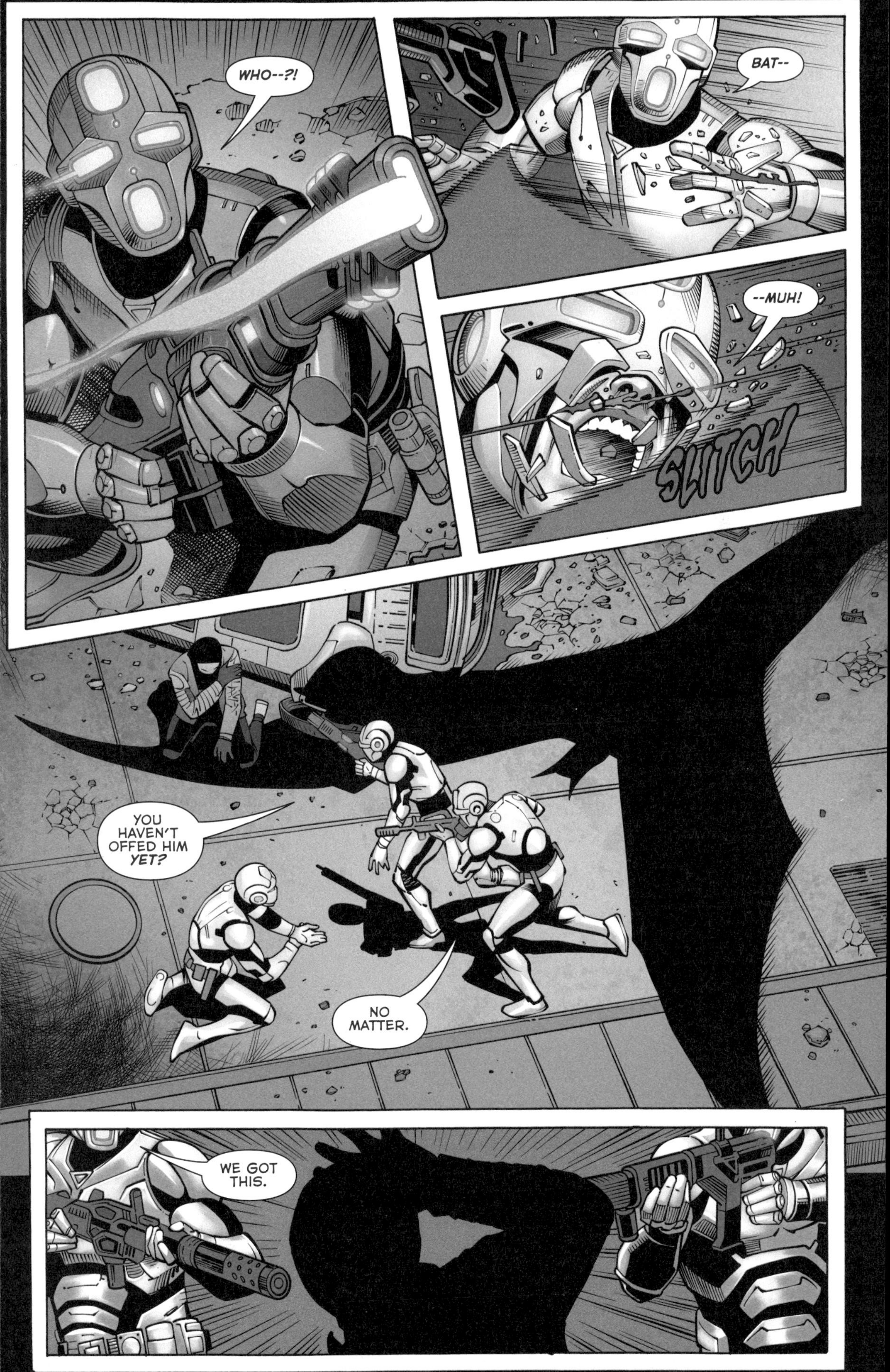
WHO--?!
BAT--
--MUH!
SLITCH
YOU HAVEN'T OFFED HIM *YET?*
NO MATTER.
WE GOT THIS.

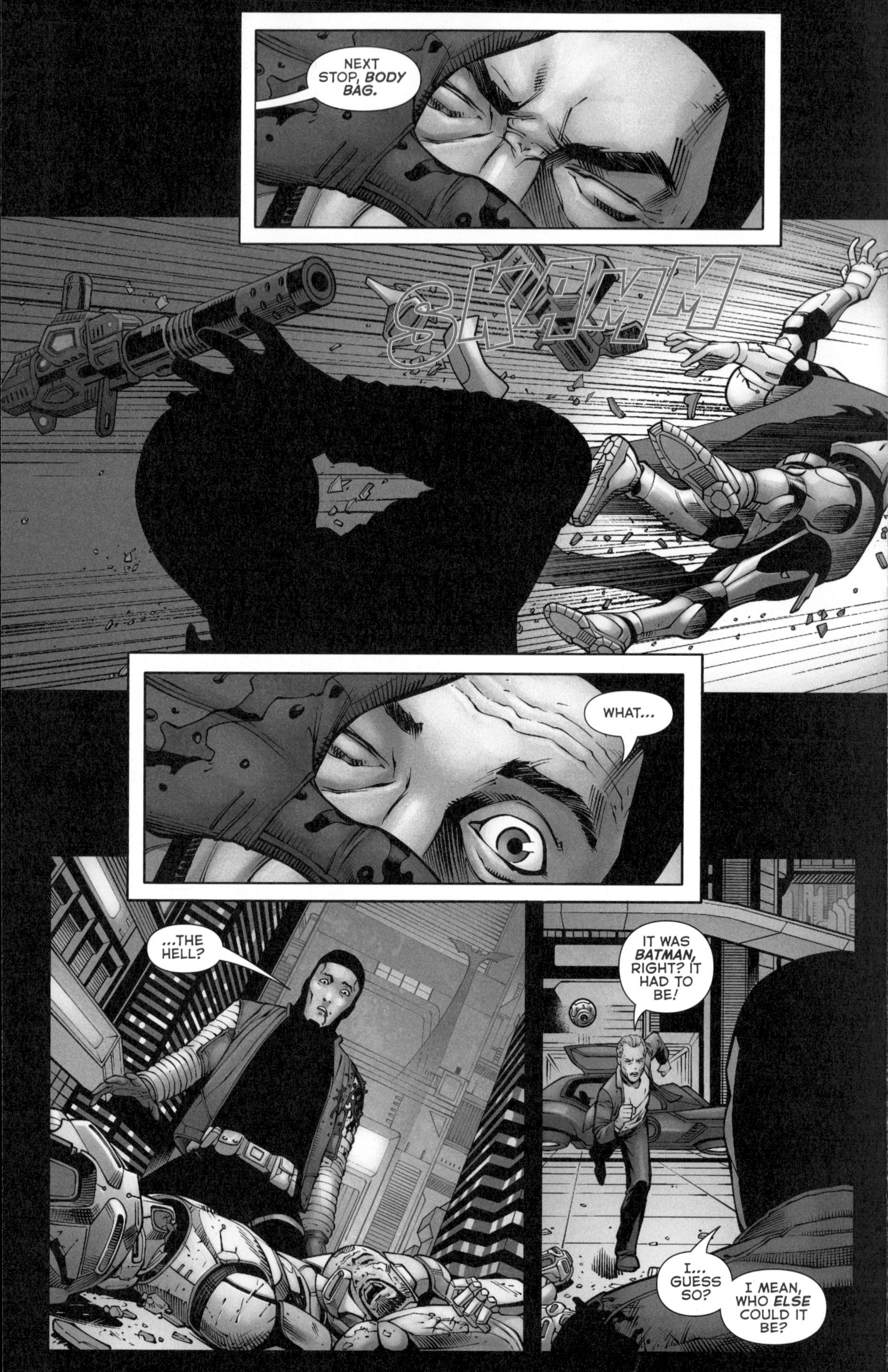
NEXT STOP, BODY BAG.
SKRAMM
WHAT...
...THE HELL?
IT WAS BATMAN, RIGHT? IT HAD TO BE!
I... GUESS SO?
I MEAN, WHO ELSE COULD IT BE?

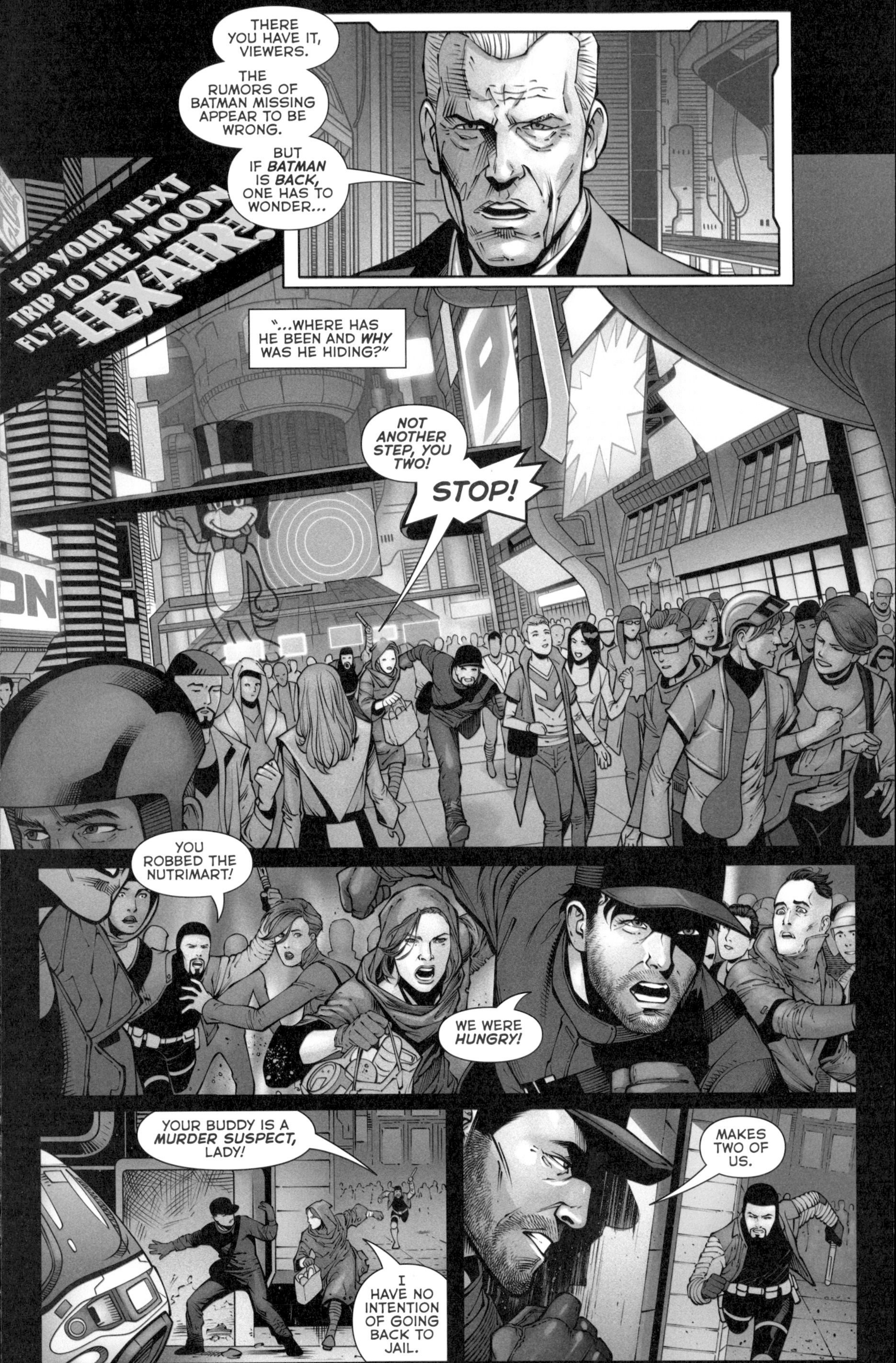

THERE YOU HAVE IT, VIEWERS.
THE RUMORS OF BATMAN MISSING APPEAR TO BE WRONG.
BUT IF *BATMAN* IS *BACK,* ONE HAS TO WONDER...
FOR YOUR NEXT TRIP TO THE MOON FLY LEXAIR!
"...WHERE HAS HE BEEN AND *WHY* WAS HE HIDING?"
NOT ANOTHER STEP, YOU TWO!
STOP!
ON
YOU ROBBED THE NUTRIMART!
WE WERE *HUNGRY!*
YOUR BUDDY IS A *MURDER SUSPECT,* LADY!
I HAVE NO INTENTION OF GOING BACK TO JAIL.
MAKES TWO OF US.

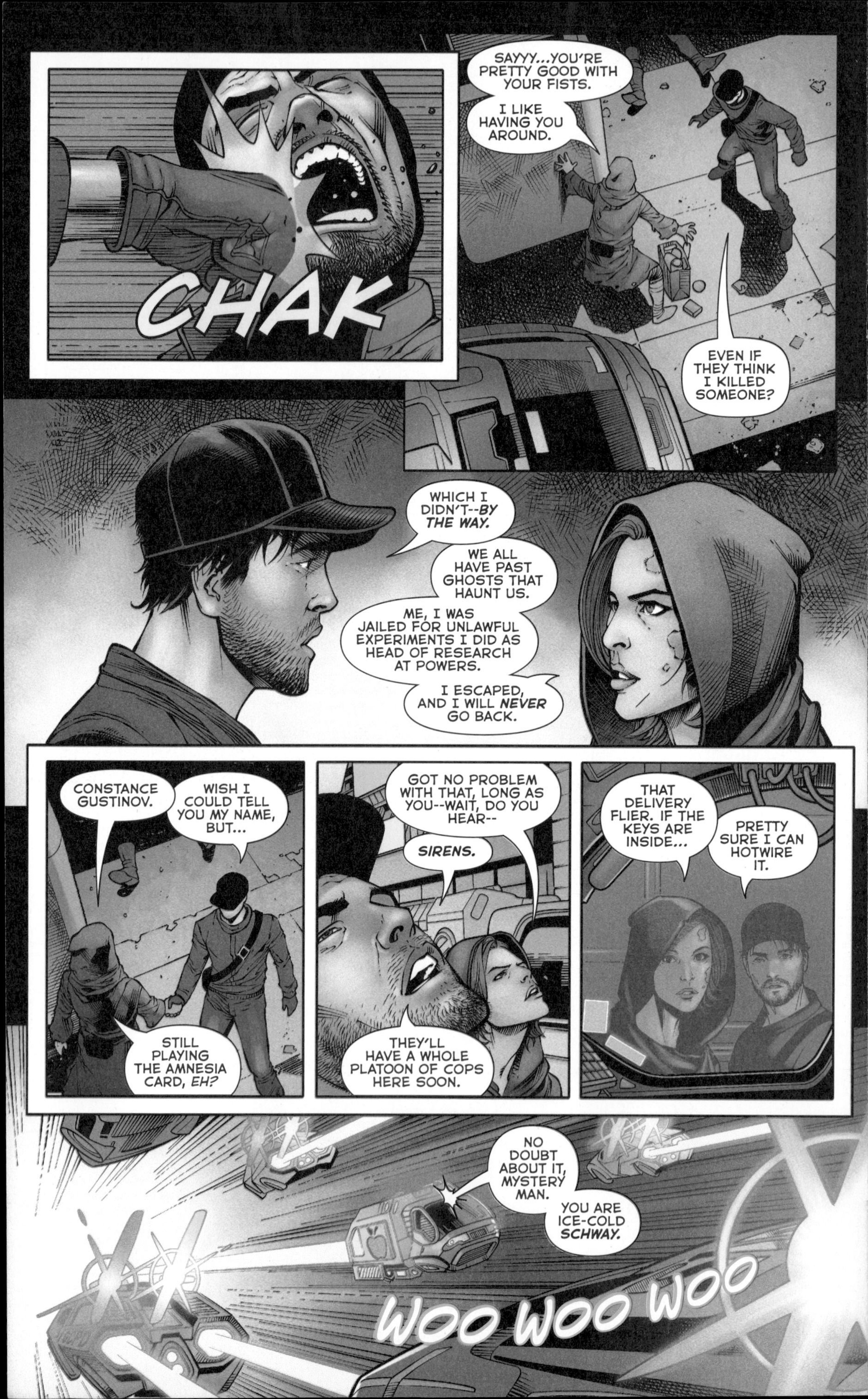
CHAK
SAYYY...YOU'RE PRETTY GOOD WITH YOUR FISTS.
I LIKE HAVING YOU AROUND.
EVEN IF THEY THINK I KILLED SOMEONE?
WHICH I DIDN'T--BY THE WAY.
WE ALL HAVE PAST GHOSTS THAT HAUNT US.
ME, I WAS JAILED FOR UNLAWFUL EXPERIMENTS I DID AS HEAD OF RESEARCH AT POWERS.
I ESCAPED, AND I WILL NEVER GO BACK.
CONSTANCE GUSTINOV.
WISH I COULD TELL YOU MY NAME, BUT...
STILL PLAYING THE AMNESIA CARD, EH?
GOT NO PROBLEM WITH THAT, LONG AS YOU--WAIT, DO YOU HEAR--
SIRENS.
THEY'LL HAVE A WHOLE PLATOON OF COPS HERE SOON.
THAT DELIVERY FLIER. IF THE KEYS ARE INSIDE...
PRETTY SURE I CAN HOTWIRE IT.
NO DOUBT ABOUT IT, MYSTERY MAN.
YOU ARE ICE-COLD SCHWAY.
WOO WOO WOO

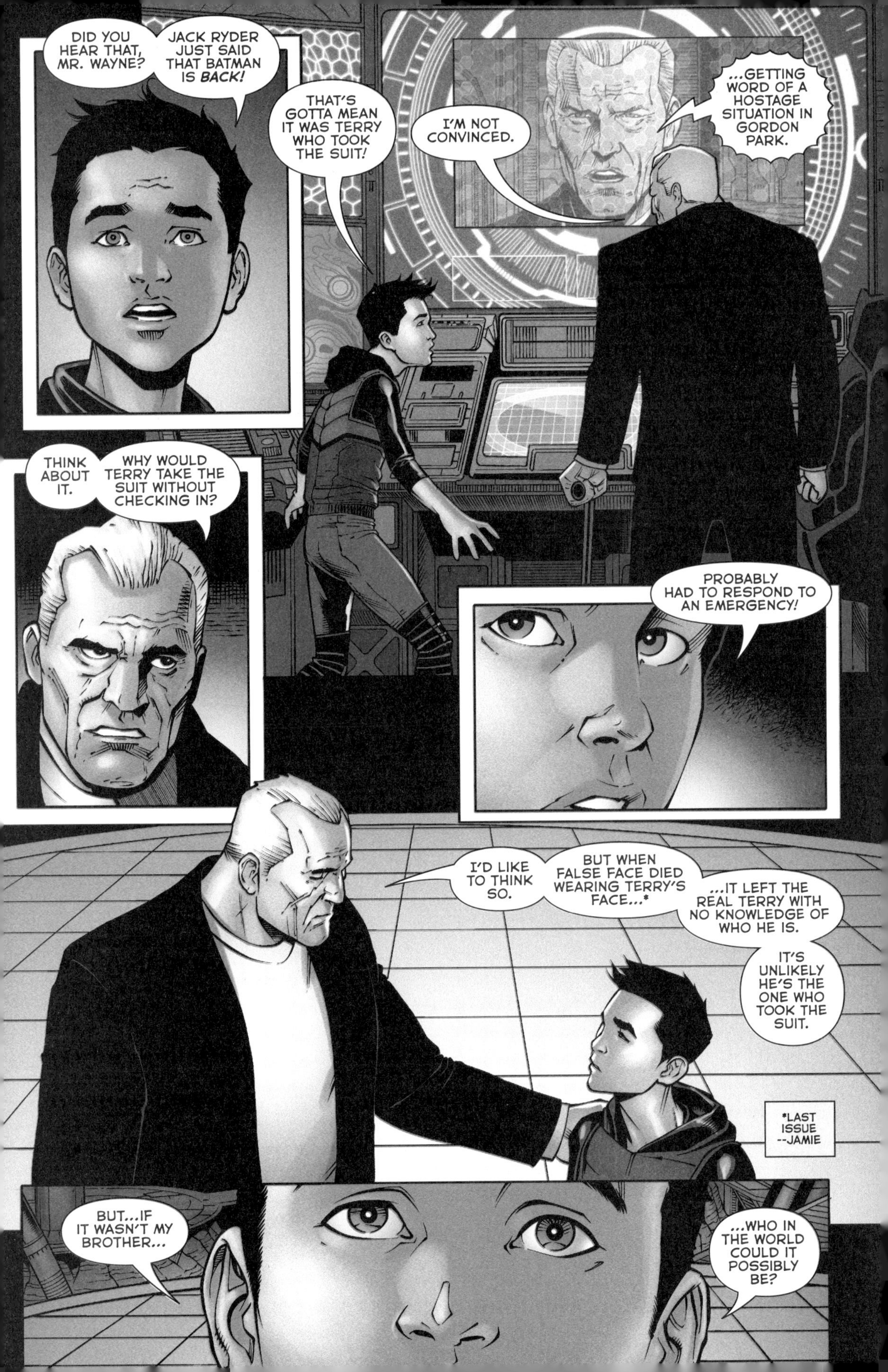
DID YOU HEAR THAT, MR. WAYNE?
JACK RYDER JUST SAID THAT BATMAN IS *BACK!*
THAT'S GOTTA MEAN IT WAS TERRY WHO TOOK THE SUIT!
I'M NOT CONVINCED.
...GETTING WORD OF A HOSTAGE SITUATION IN GORDON PARK.
THINK ABOUT IT.
WHY WOULD TERRY TAKE THE SUIT WITHOUT CHECKING IN?
PROBABLY HAD TO RESPOND TO AN EMERGENCY!
I'D LIKE TO THINK SO.
BUT WHEN FALSE FACE DIED WEARING TERRY'S FACE...*
...IT LEFT THE REAL TERRY WITH NO KNOWLEDGE OF WHO HE IS.
IT'S UNLIKELY HE'S THE ONE WHO TOOK THE SUIT.
*LAST ISSUE --JAMIE
BUT...IF IT WASN'T MY BROTHER...
...WHO IN THE WORLD COULD IT POSSIBLY BE?

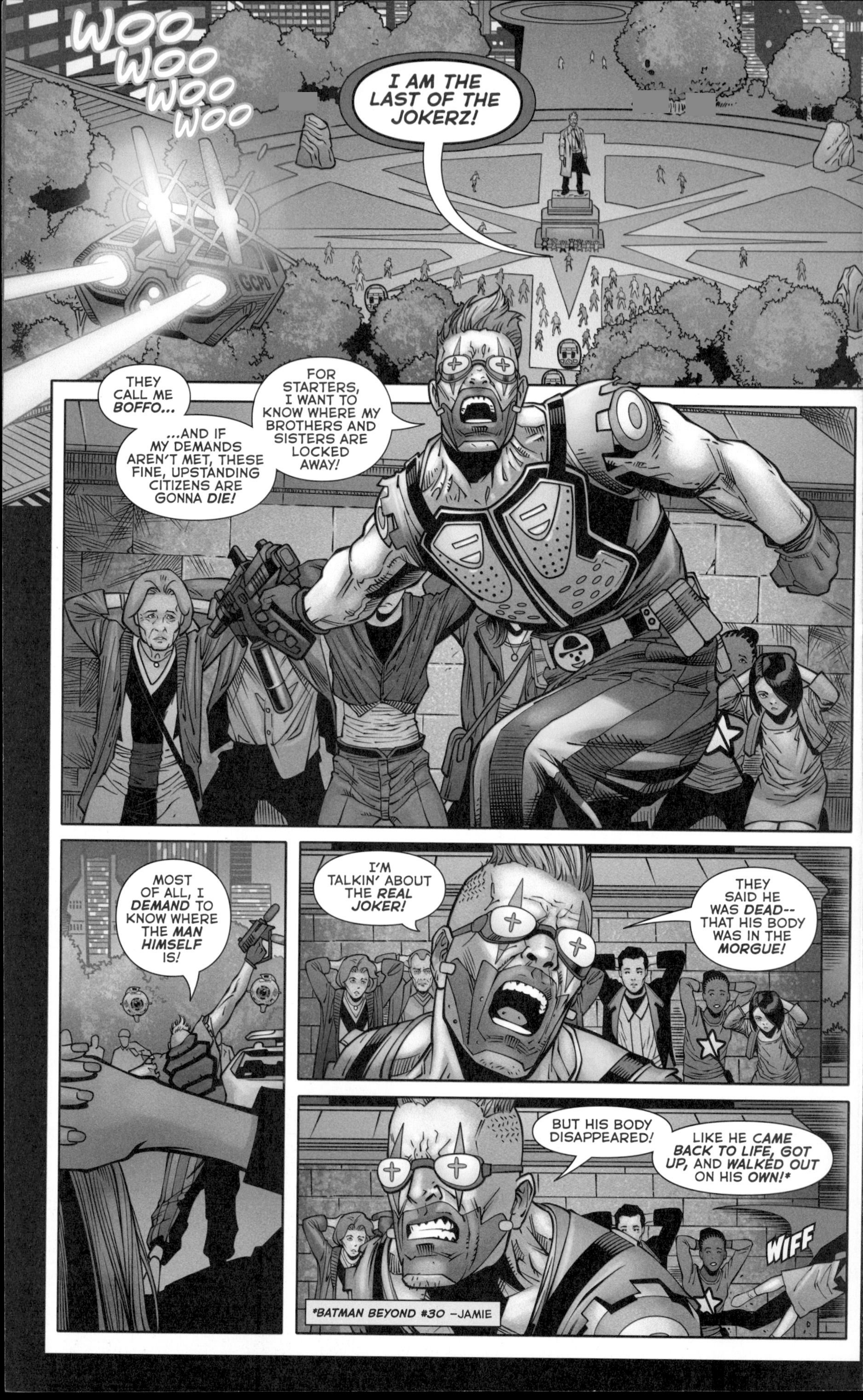
WOO WOO WOO WOO
I AM THE LAST OF THE JOKERZ!
THEY CALL ME BOFFO...
...AND IF MY DEMANDS AREN'T MET, THESE FINE, UPSTANDING CITIZENS ARE GONNA DIE!
FOR STARTERS, I WANT TO KNOW WHERE MY BROTHERS AND SISTERS ARE LOCKED AWAY!
GCPD
MOST OF ALL, I DEMAND TO KNOW WHERE THE MAN HIMSELF IS!
I'M TALKIN' ABOUT THE REAL JOKER!
THEY SAID HE WAS DEAD-- THAT HIS BODY WAS IN THE MORGUE!
BUT HIS BODY DISAPPEARED!
LIKE HE CAME BACK TO LIFE, GOT UP, AND WALKED OUT ON HIS OWN!*
WIFF
*BATMAN BEYOND #30 -JAMIE

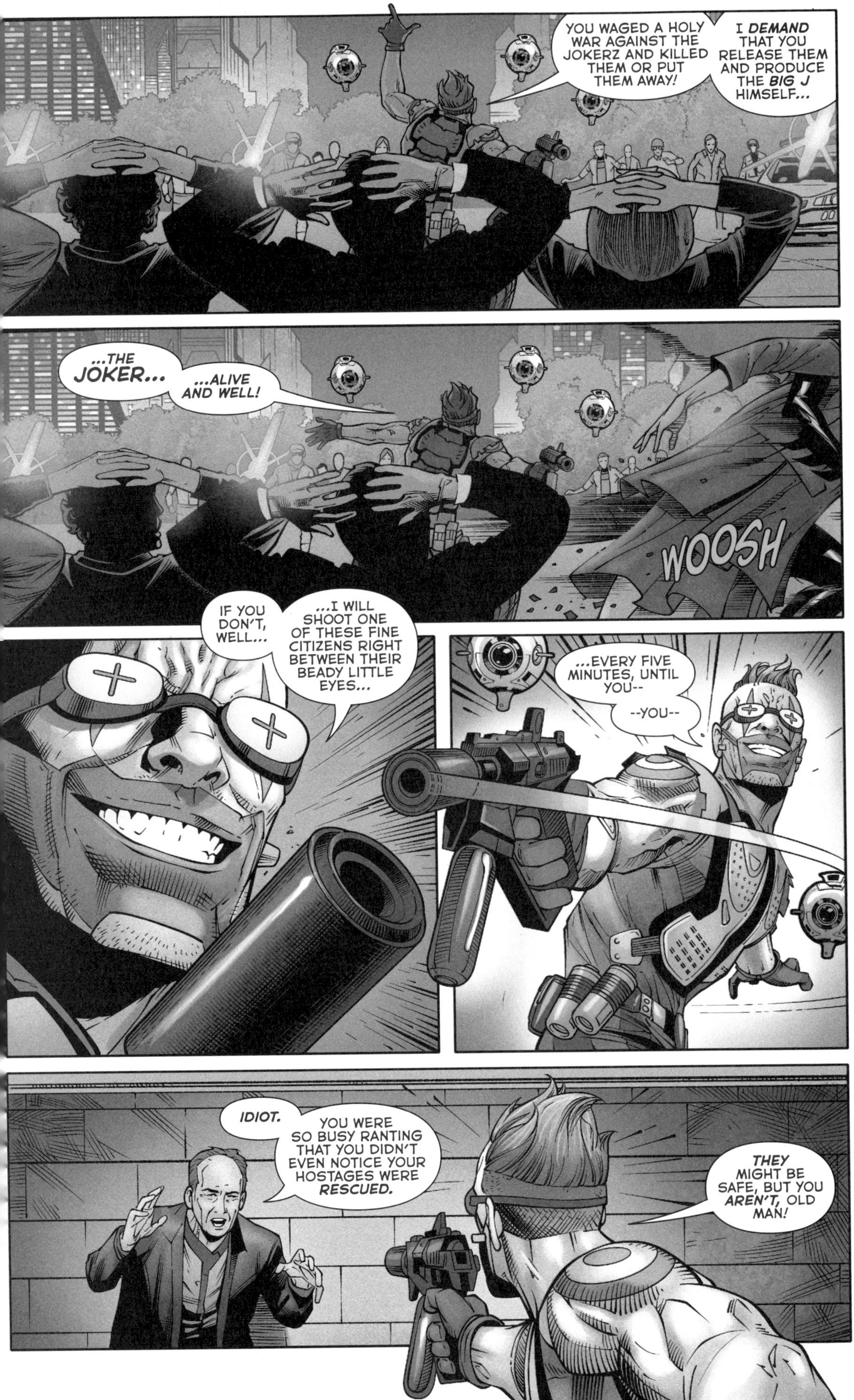
YOU WAGED A HOLY WAR AGAINST THE JOKERZ AND KILLED THEM OR PUT THEM AWAY!
I DEMAND THAT YOU RELEASE THEM AND PRODUCE THE BIG J HIMSELF...
...THE JOKER...
...ALIVE AND WELL!
WOOSH
IF YOU DON'T, WELL...
...I WILL SHOOT ONE OF THESE FINE CITIZENS RIGHT BETWEEN THEIR BEADY LITTLE EYES...
...EVERY FIVE MINUTES, UNTIL YOU--
--YOU--
IDIOT.
YOU WERE SO BUSY RANTING THAT YOU DIDN'T EVEN NOTICE YOUR HOSTAGES WERE RESCUED.
THEY MIGHT BE SAFE, BUT YOU AREN'T, OLD MAN!

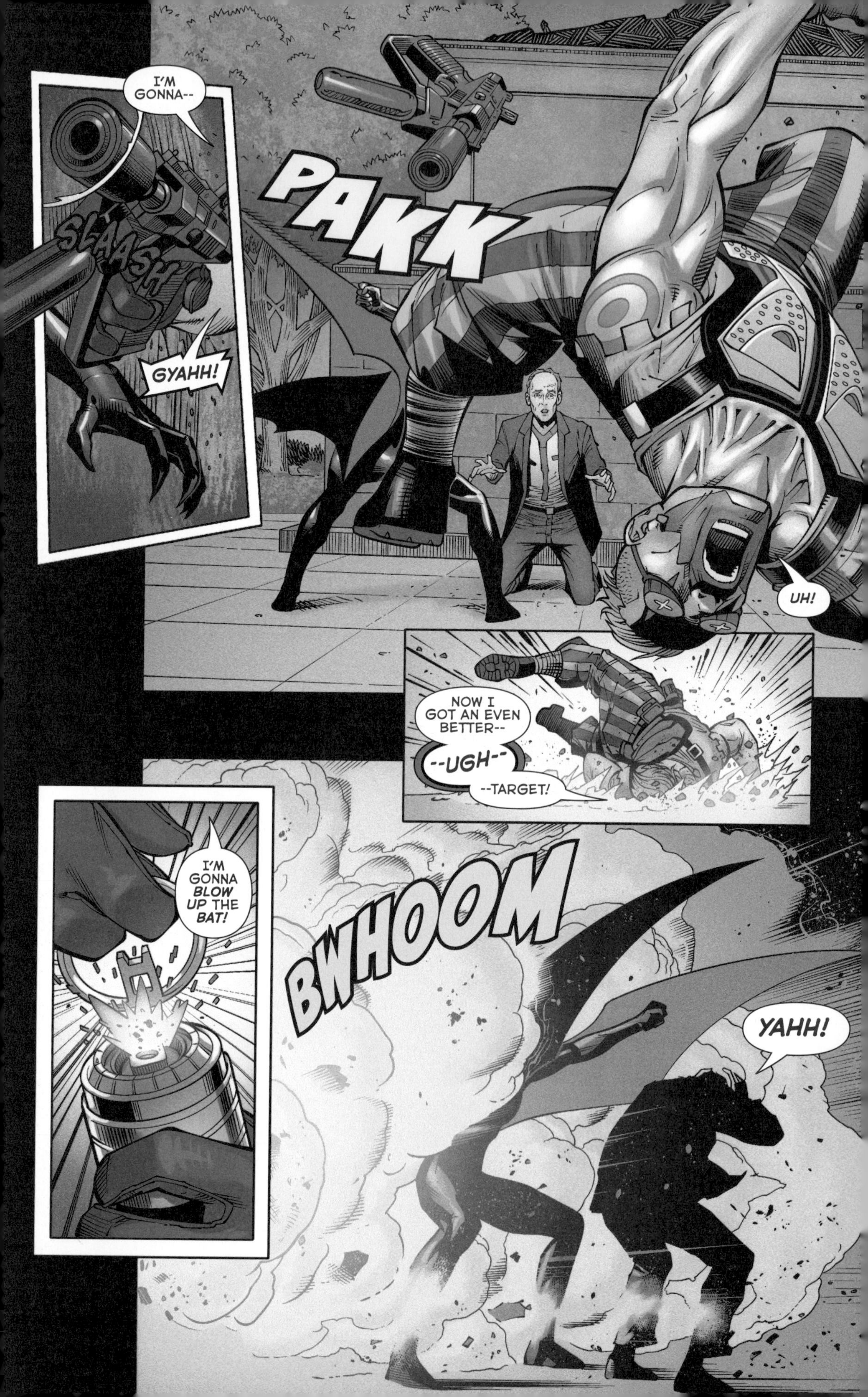
I'M GONNA--
SLAASH
GYAHH!
PAKK
UH!
NOW I GOT AN EVEN BETTER--
--UGH--
--TARGET!
I'M GONNA BLOW UP THE BAT!
BWHOOM
YAHH!

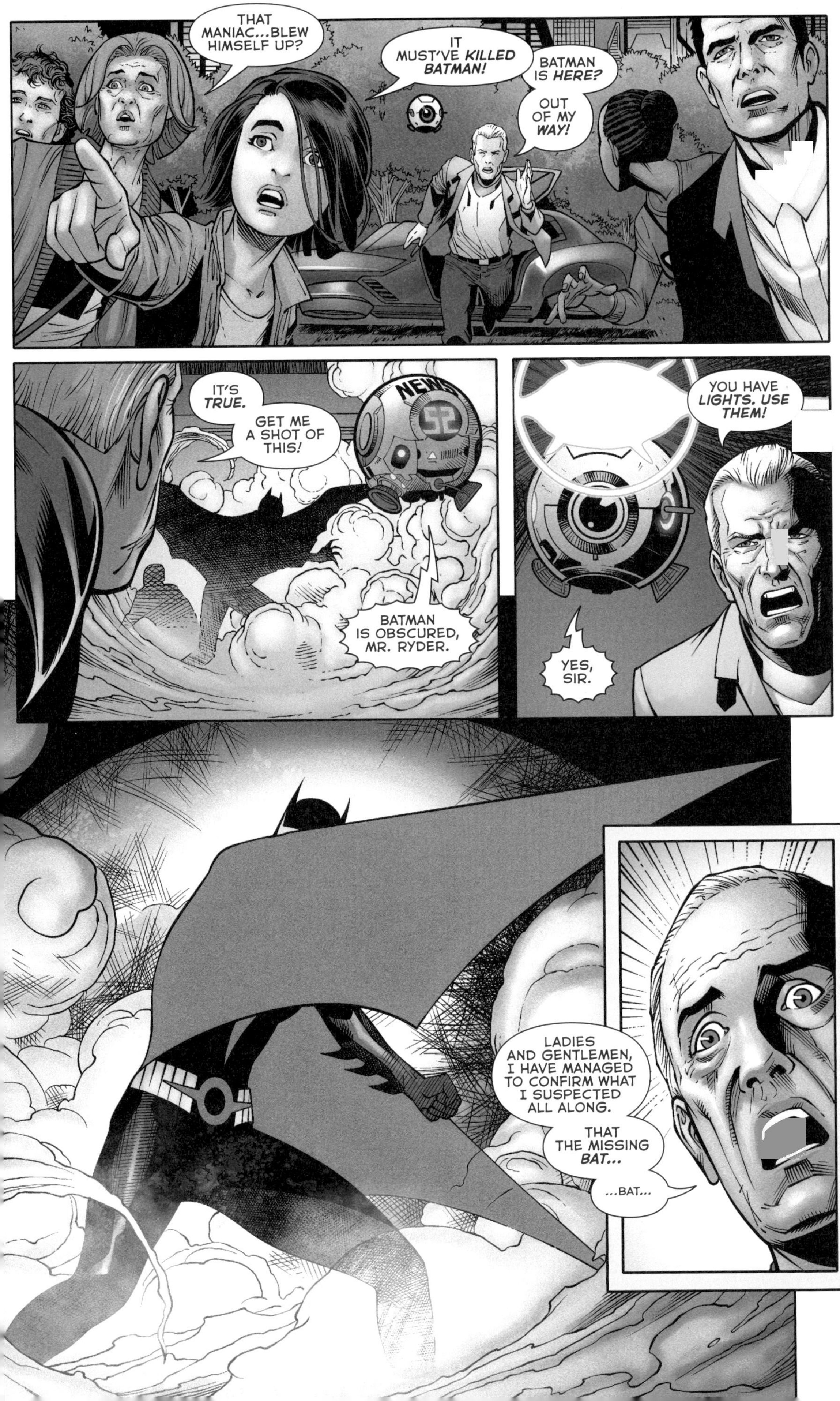
THAT MANIAC...BLEW HIMSELF UP?
IT MUST'VE *KILLED* *BATMAN!*
BATMAN IS *HERE?*
OUT OF MY *WAY!*
IT'S *TRUE.*
GET ME A SHOT OF THIS!
NEWS
52
BATMAN IS OBSCURED, MR. RYDER.
YOU HAVE *LIGHTS.* *USE THEM!*
YES, SIR.
LADIES AND GENTLEMEN, I HAVE MANAGED TO CONFIRM WHAT I SUSPECTED ALL ALONG.
THAT THE MISSING *BAT...*
...BAT...

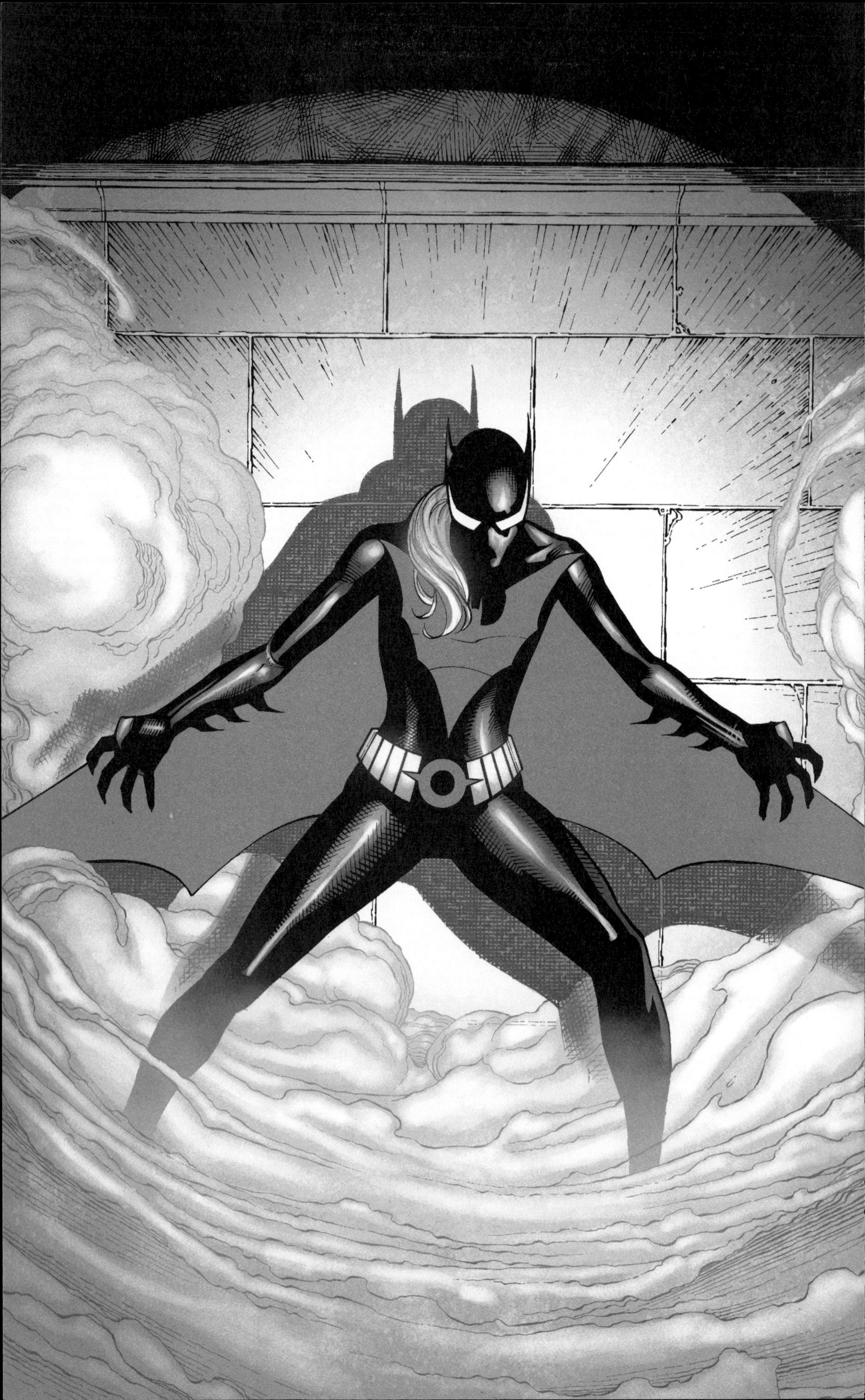

...BAT...

...BATWOMAN?!

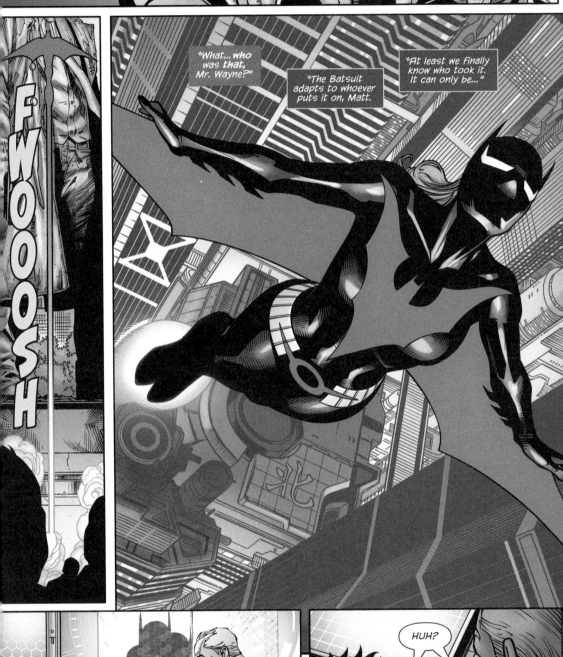

"What... who was *that*, Mr. Wayne?"

"The Batsuit adapts to whoever puts it on, Matt."

"At least we finally know who took it. It can only be..."

FWOOOSH

MELANIE WALKER!

BARBARA GORDON!

HUH?

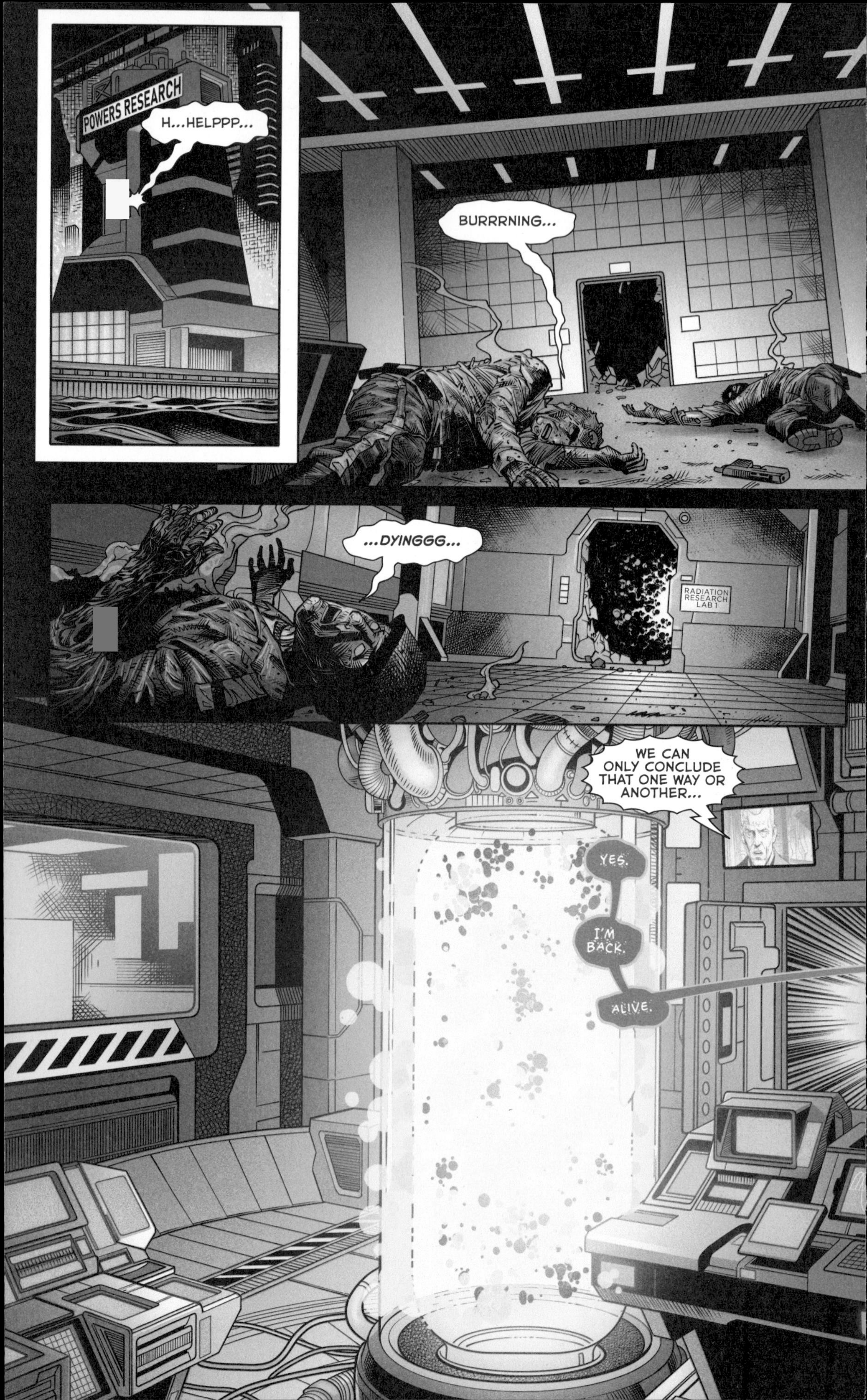
POWERS RESEARCH
H...HELPPP...
BURRRNING...
...DYINGGG...
RADIATION RESEARCH LAB 1
WE CAN ONLY CONCLUDE THAT ONE WAY OR ANOTHER...
YES.
I'M BACK.
ALIVE.

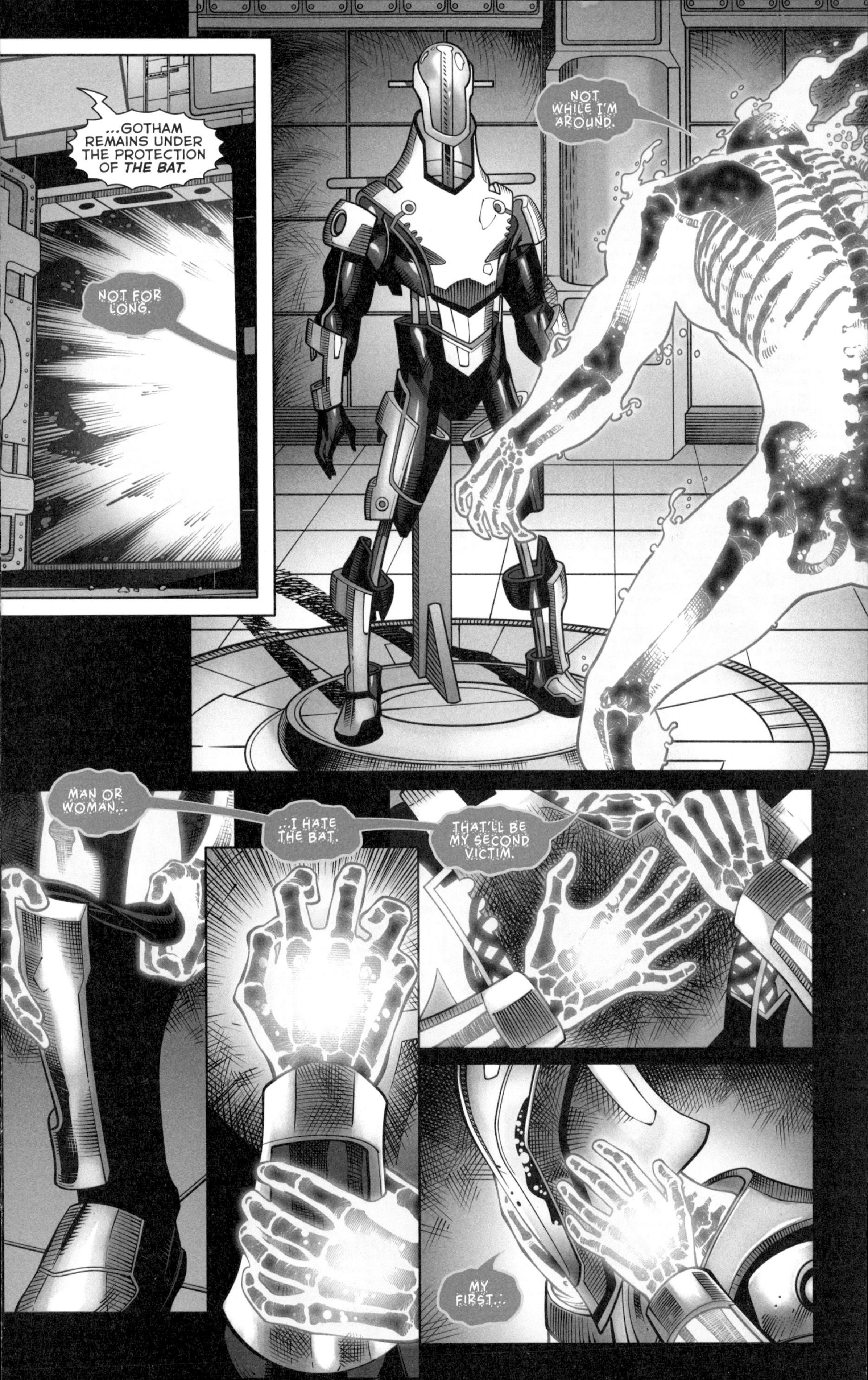
...GOTHAM REMAINS UNDER THE PROTECTION OF THE BAT.
NOT FOR LONG.
NOT WHILE I'M AROUND.
MAN OR WOMAN...
...I HATE THE BAT.
THAT'LL BE MY SECOND VICTIM.
MY FIRST...

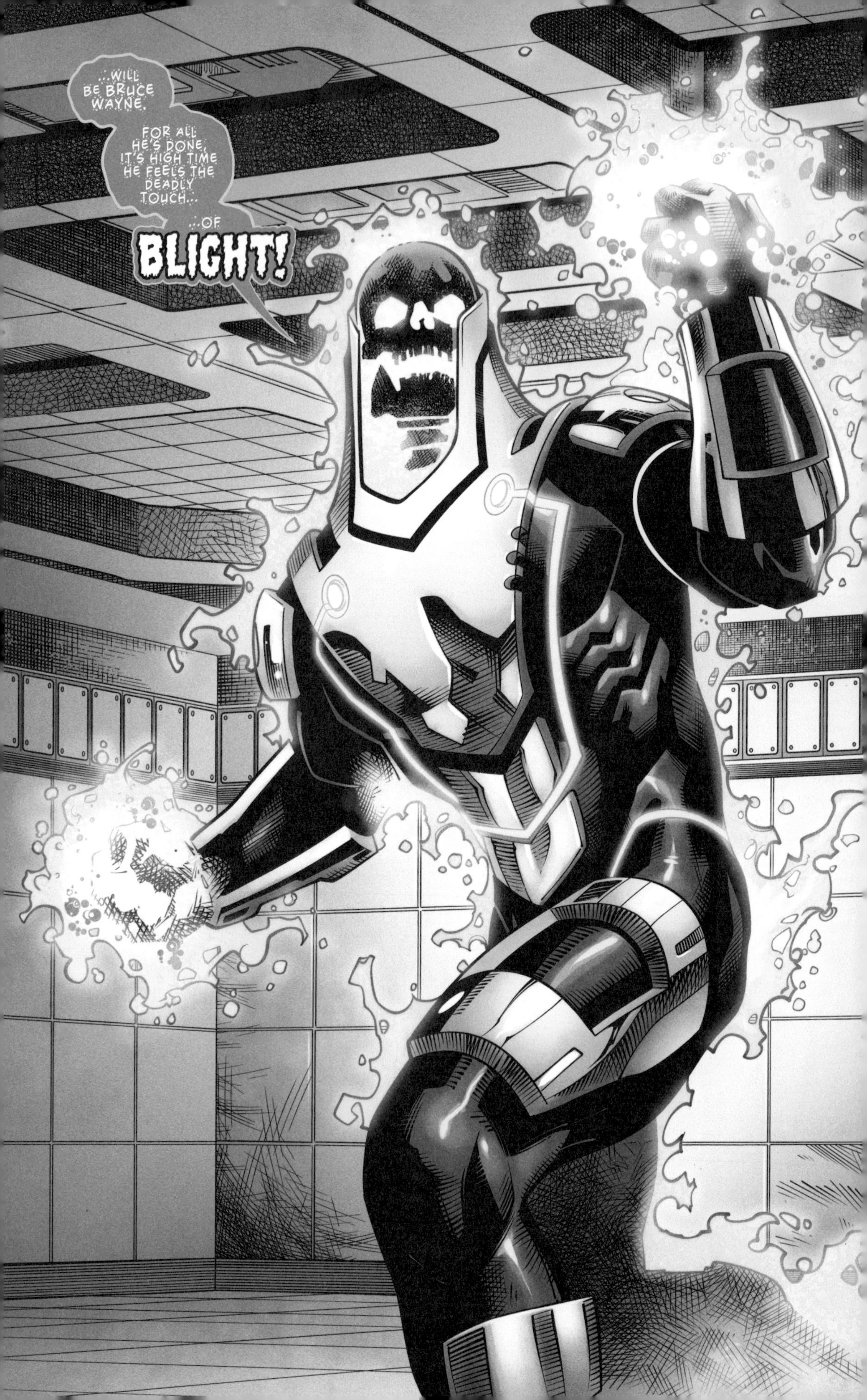
...WILL BE BRUCE WAYNE.
FOR ALL HE'S DONE, IT'S HIGH TIME HE FEELS THE DEADLY TOUCH...
...OF BLIGHT!

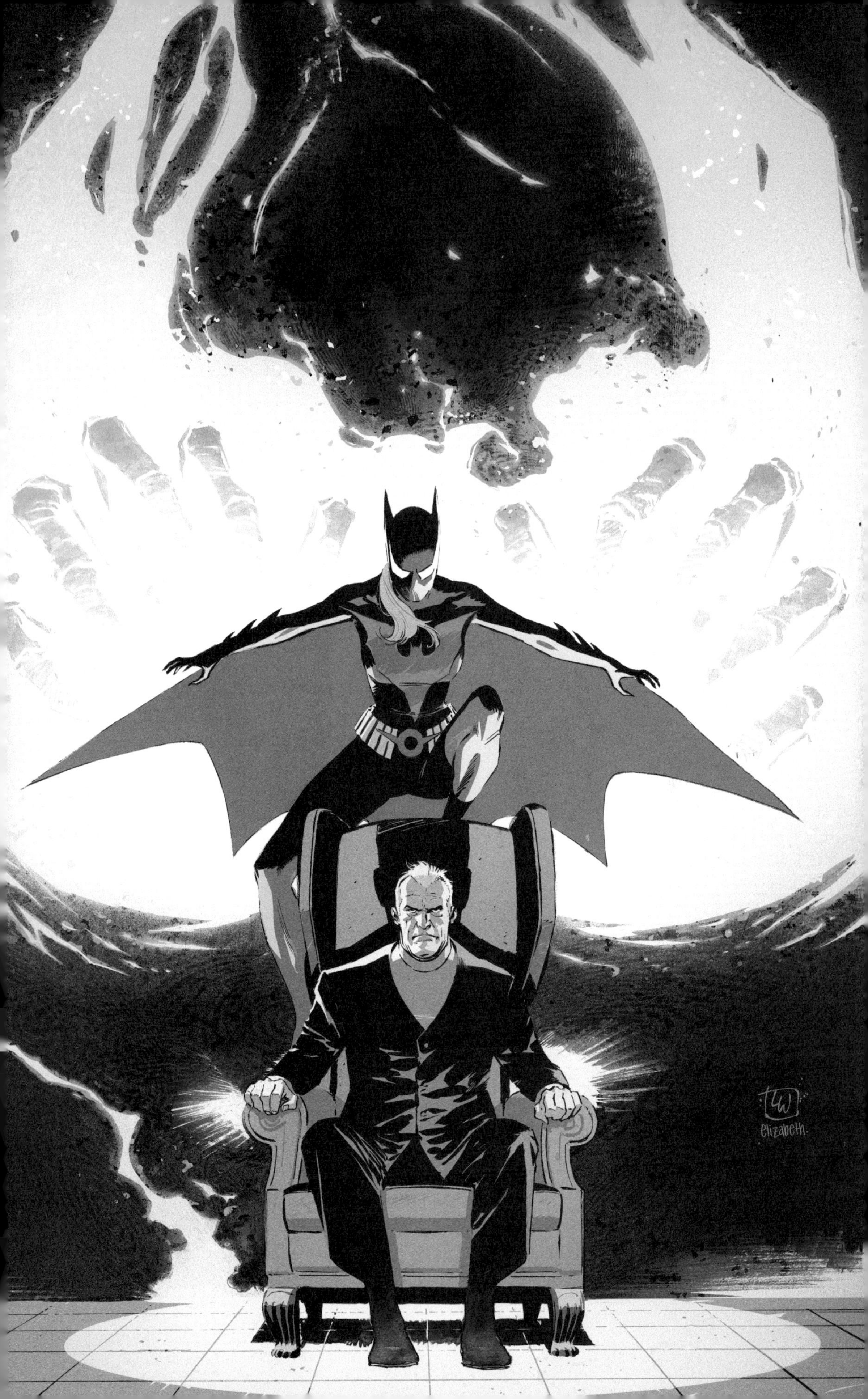
elizabeth.

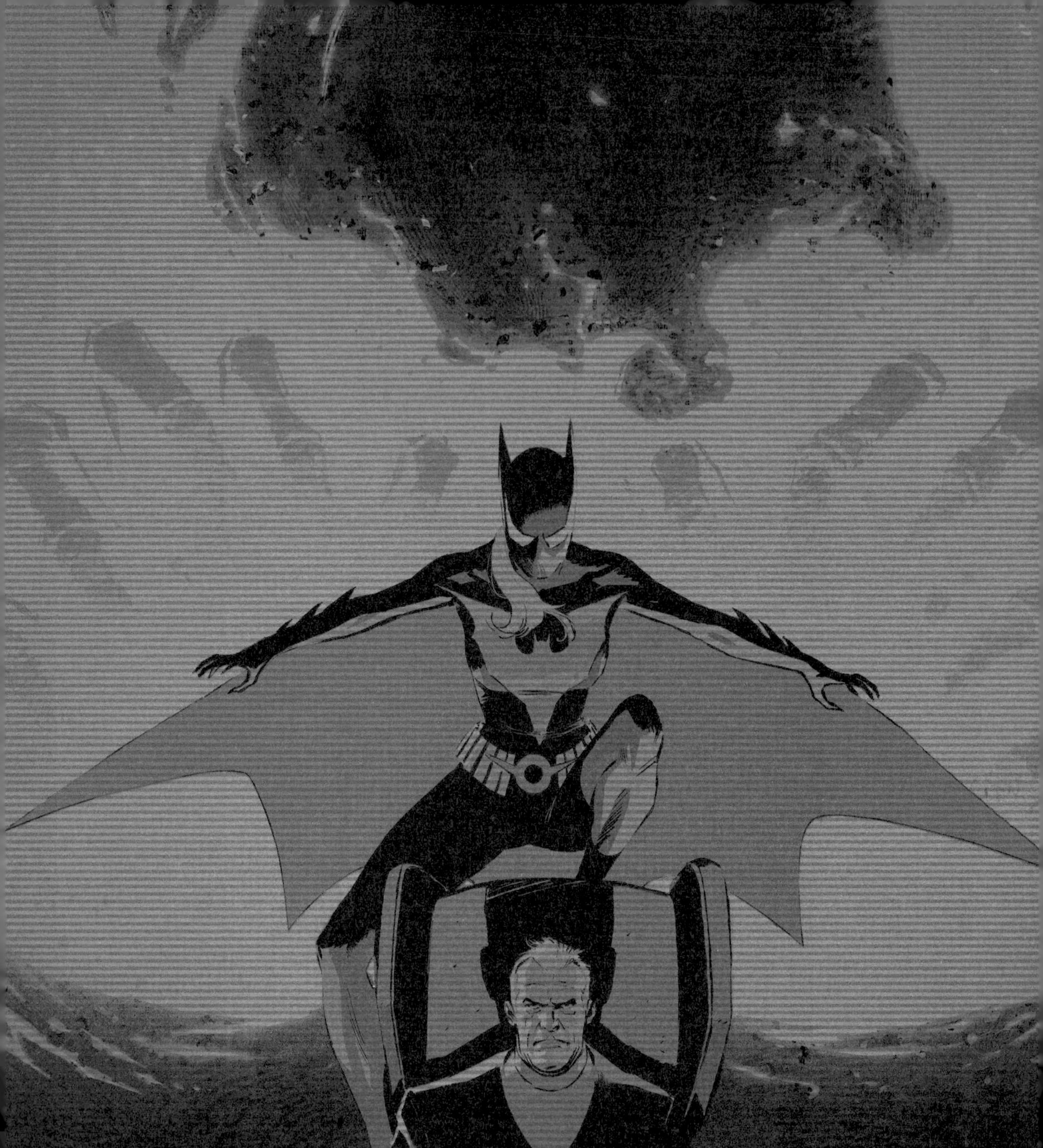

BATMAN

BEYOND

#38

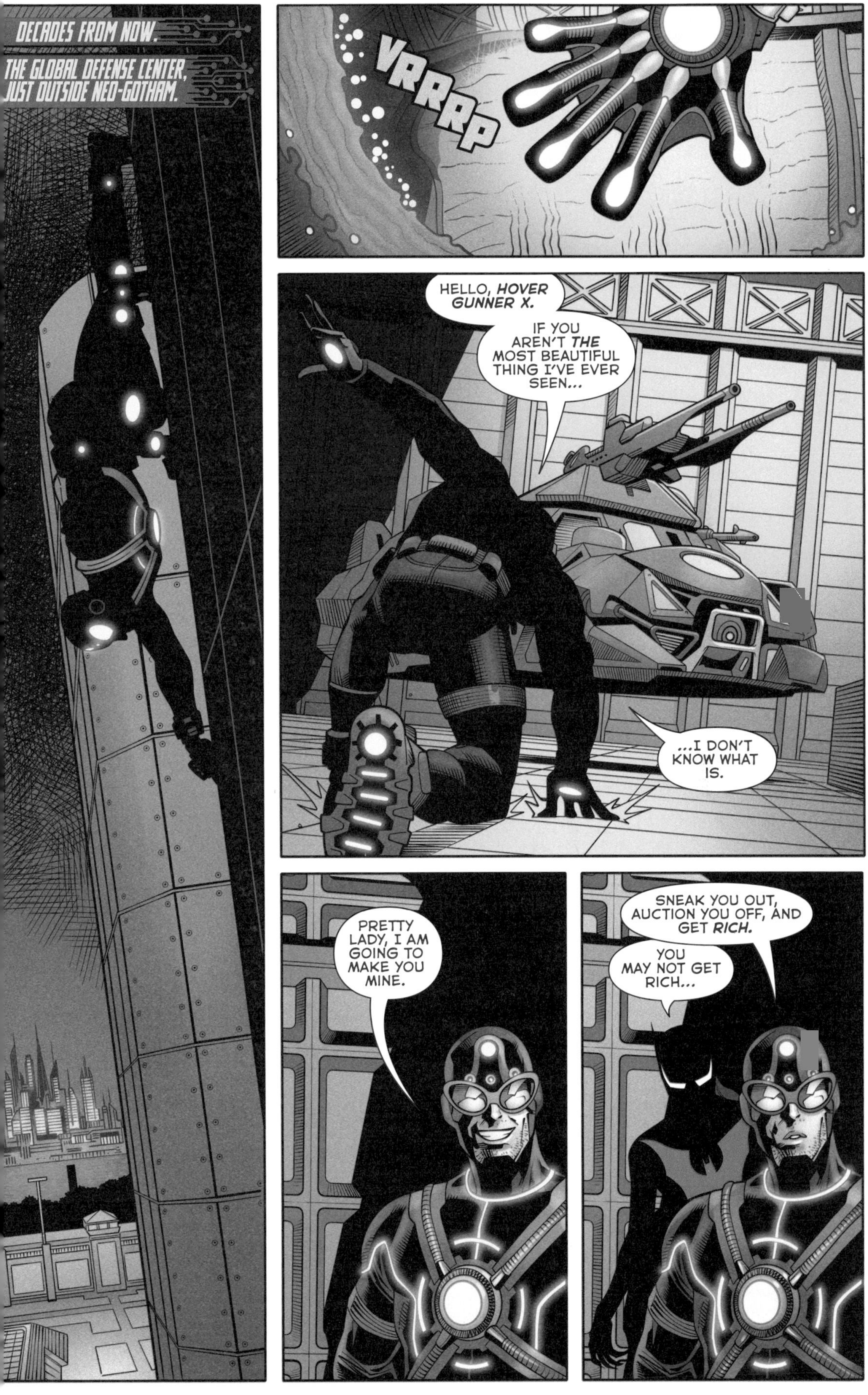
DECADES FROM NOW.
THE GLOBAL DEFENSE CENTER, JUST OUTSIDE NEO-GOTHAM.
VRRRRP
HELLO, HOVER GUNNER X.
IF YOU AREN'T THE MOST BEAUTIFUL THING I'VE EVER SEEN...
...I DON'T KNOW WHAT IS.
PRETTY LADY, I AM GOING TO MAKE YOU MINE.
SNEAK YOU OUT, AUCTION YOU OFF, AND GET RICH.
YOU MAY NOT GET RICH...

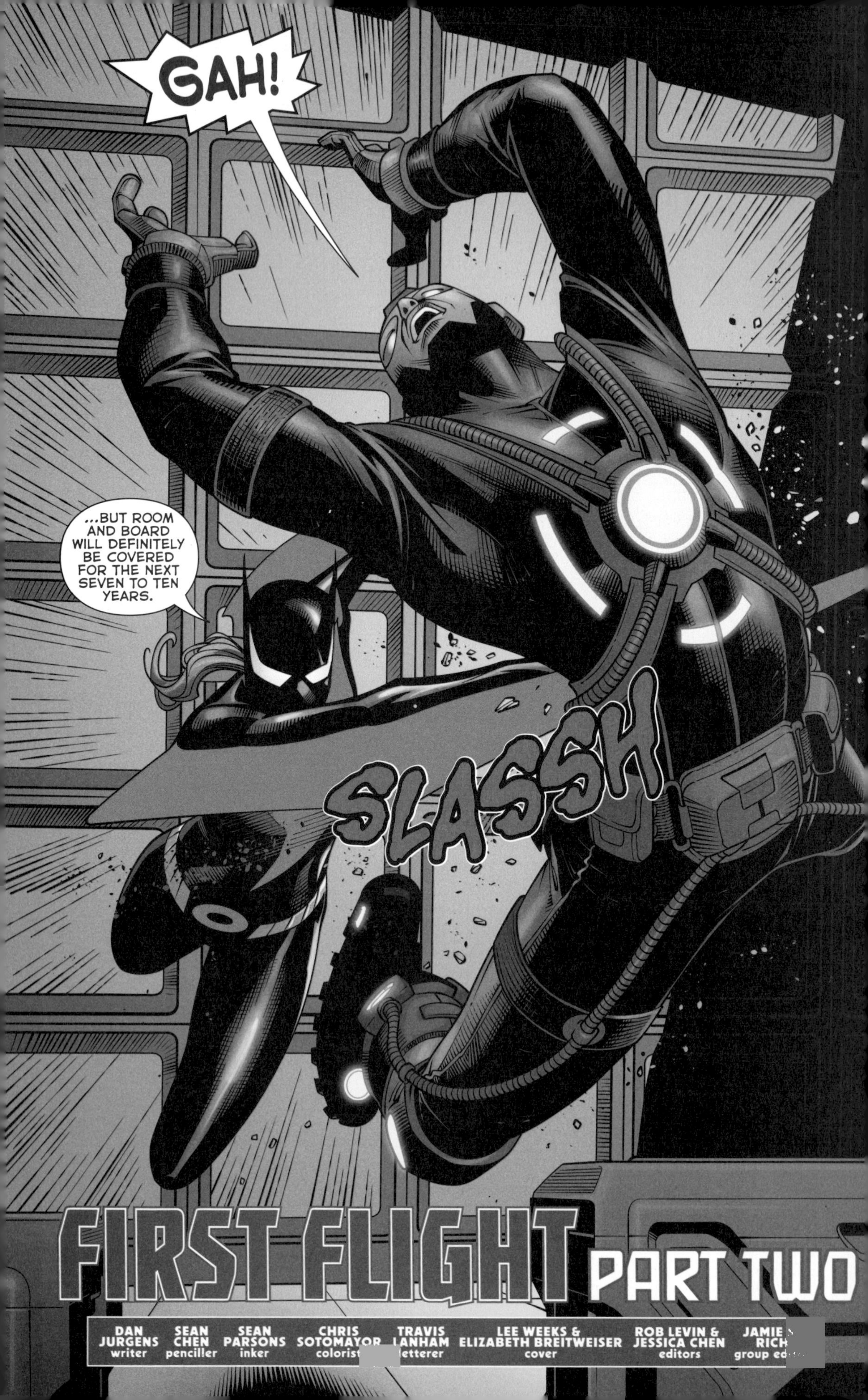
GAH!
...BUT ROOM AND BOARD WILL DEFINITELY BE COVERED FOR THE NEXT SEVEN TO TEN YEARS.
SLASSH
FIRST FLIGHT PART TWO
DAN JURGENS writer
SEAN CHEN penciller
SEAN PARSONS inker
CHRIS SOTOMAYOR colorist
TRAVIS LANHAM letterer
LEE WEEKS & ELIZABETH BREITWEISER cover
ROB LEVIN & JESSICA CHEN editors
JAMIE
group

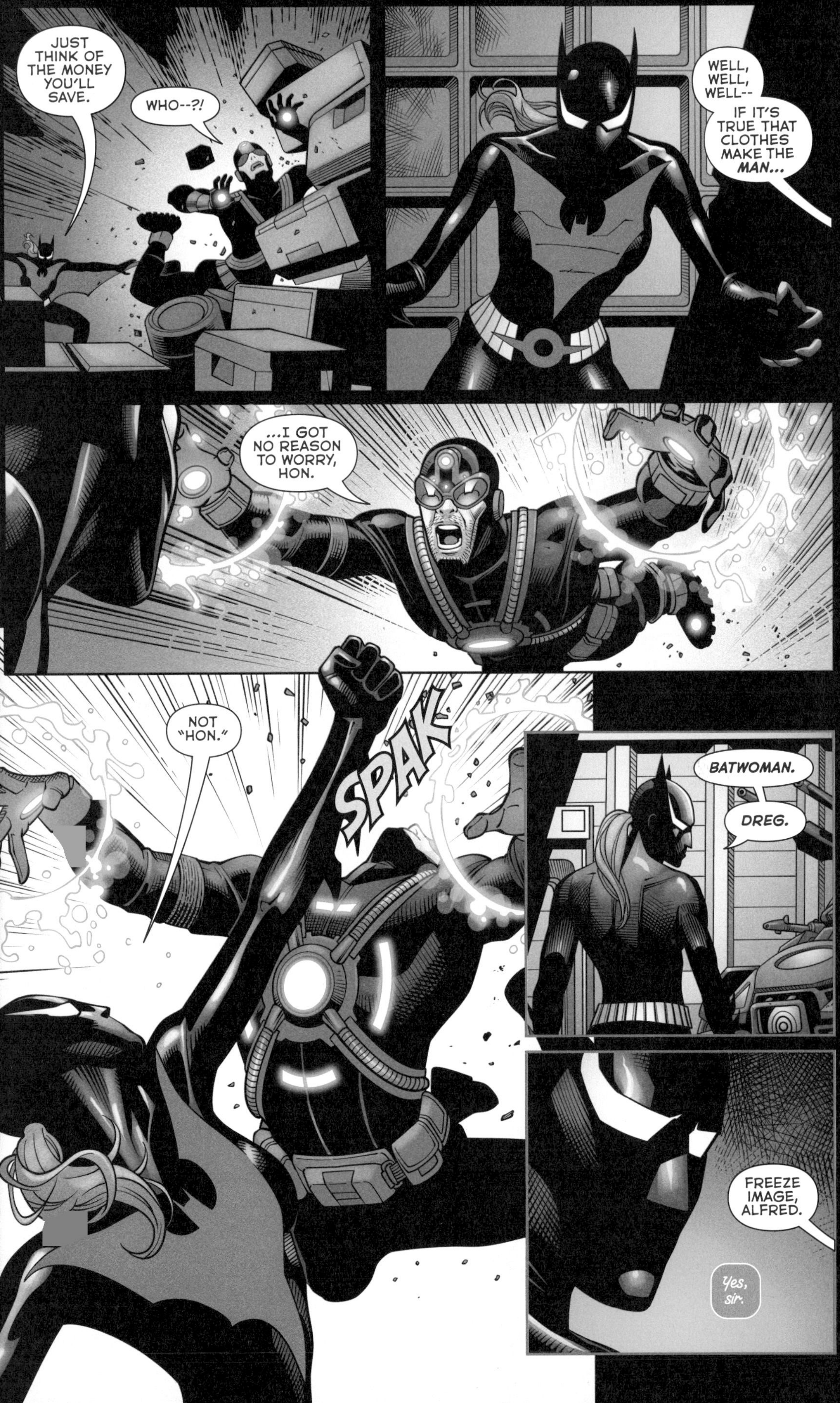
JUST THINK OF THE MONEY YOU'LL SAVE.
WHO--?!
WELL, WELL, WELL--
IF IT'S TRUE THAT CLOTHES MAKE THE *MAN...*
...I GOT NO REASON TO WORRY, HON.
NOT "HON."
SPAK
BATWOMAN.
DREG.
FREEZE IMAGE, ALFRED.
Yes, sir.

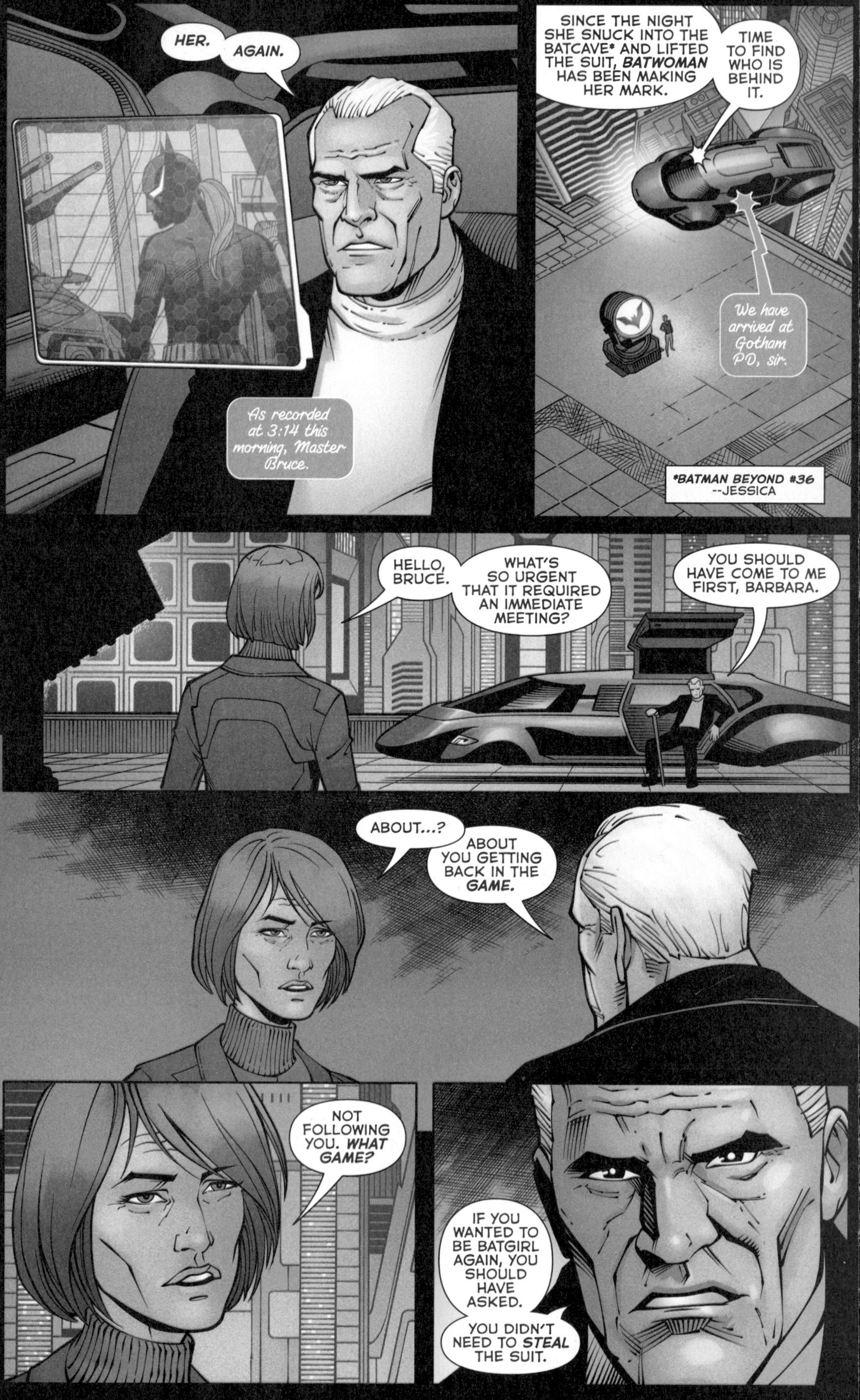
HER.
AGAIN.
As recorded at 3:14 this morning, Master Bruce.
SINCE THE NIGHT SHE SNUCK INTO THE BATCAVE* AND LIFTED THE SUIT, BATWOMAN HAS BEEN MAKING HER MARK.
TIME TO FIND WHO IS BEHIND IT.
We have arrived at Gotham PD, sir.
*BATMAN BEYOND #36 --JESSICA
HELLO, BRUCE.
WHAT'S SO URGENT THAT IT REQUIRED AN IMMEDIATE MEETING?
YOU SHOULD HAVE COME TO ME FIRST, BARBARA.
ABOUT...?
ABOUT YOU GETTING BACK IN THE GAME.
NOT FOLLOWING YOU. WHAT GAME?
IF YOU WANTED TO BE BATGIRL AGAIN, YOU SHOULD HAVE ASKED.
YOU DIDN'T NEED TO STEAL THE SUIT.

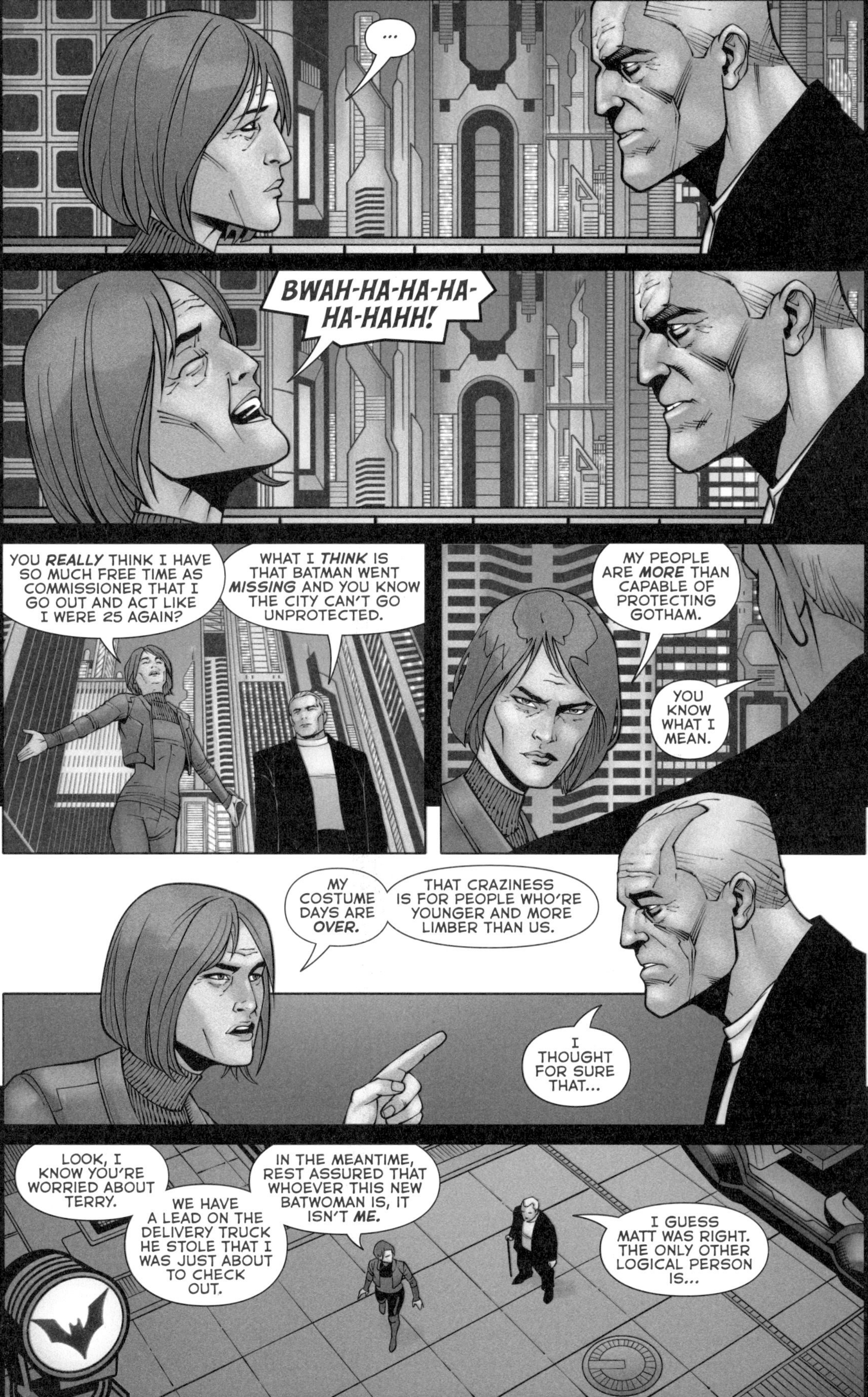
...
BWAH-HA-HA-HA-HA-HAHH!
YOU *REALLY* THINK I HAVE SO MUCH FREE TIME AS COMMISSIONER THAT I GO OUT AND ACT LIKE I WERE 25 AGAIN?
WHAT I *THINK* IS THAT BATMAN WENT *MISSING* AND YOU KNOW THE CITY CAN'T GO UNPROTECTED.
MY PEOPLE ARE *MORE* THAN CAPABLE OF PROTECTING GOTHAM.
YOU KNOW WHAT I MEAN.
MY COSTUME DAYS ARE *OVER.*
THAT CRAZINESS IS FOR PEOPLE WHO'RE YOUNGER AND MORE LIMBER THAN US.
I THOUGHT FOR SURE THAT...
LOOK, I KNOW YOU'RE WORRIED ABOUT TERRY.
WE HAVE A LEAD ON THE DELIVERY TRUCK HE STOLE THAT I WAS JUST ABOUT TO CHECK OUT.
IN THE MEANTIME, REST ASSURED THAT WHOEVER THIS NEW BATWOMAN IS, IT ISN'T *ME.*
I GUESS MATT WAS RIGHT. THE ONLY OTHER LOGICAL PERSON IS...

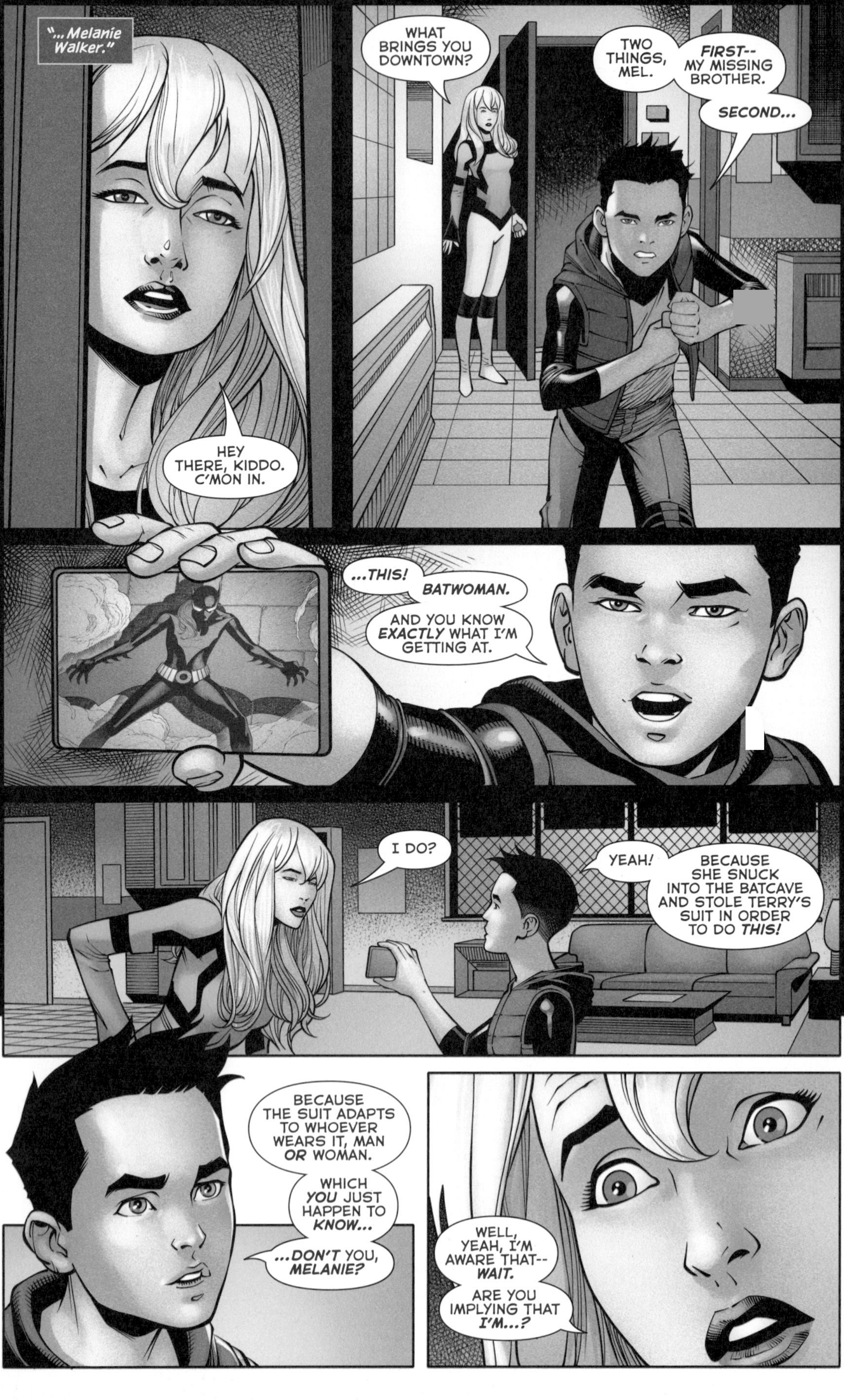

"...Melanie Walker."
HEY THERE, KIDDO. C'MON IN.
WHAT BRINGS YOU DOWNTOWN?
TWO THINGS, MEL.
FIRST-- MY MISSING BROTHER.
SECOND...
...THIS!
BATWOMAN.
AND YOU KNOW EXACTLY WHAT I'M GETTING AT.
I DO?
YEAH!
BECAUSE SHE SNUCK INTO THE BATCAVE AND STOLE TERRY'S SUIT IN ORDER TO DO THIS!
BECAUSE THE SUIT ADAPTS TO WHOEVER WEARS IT, MAN OR WOMAN.
WHICH YOU JUST HAPPEN TO KNOW...
...DON'T YOU, MELANIE?
WELL, YEAH, I'M AWARE THAT-- WAIT.
ARE YOU IMPLYING THAT I'M...?

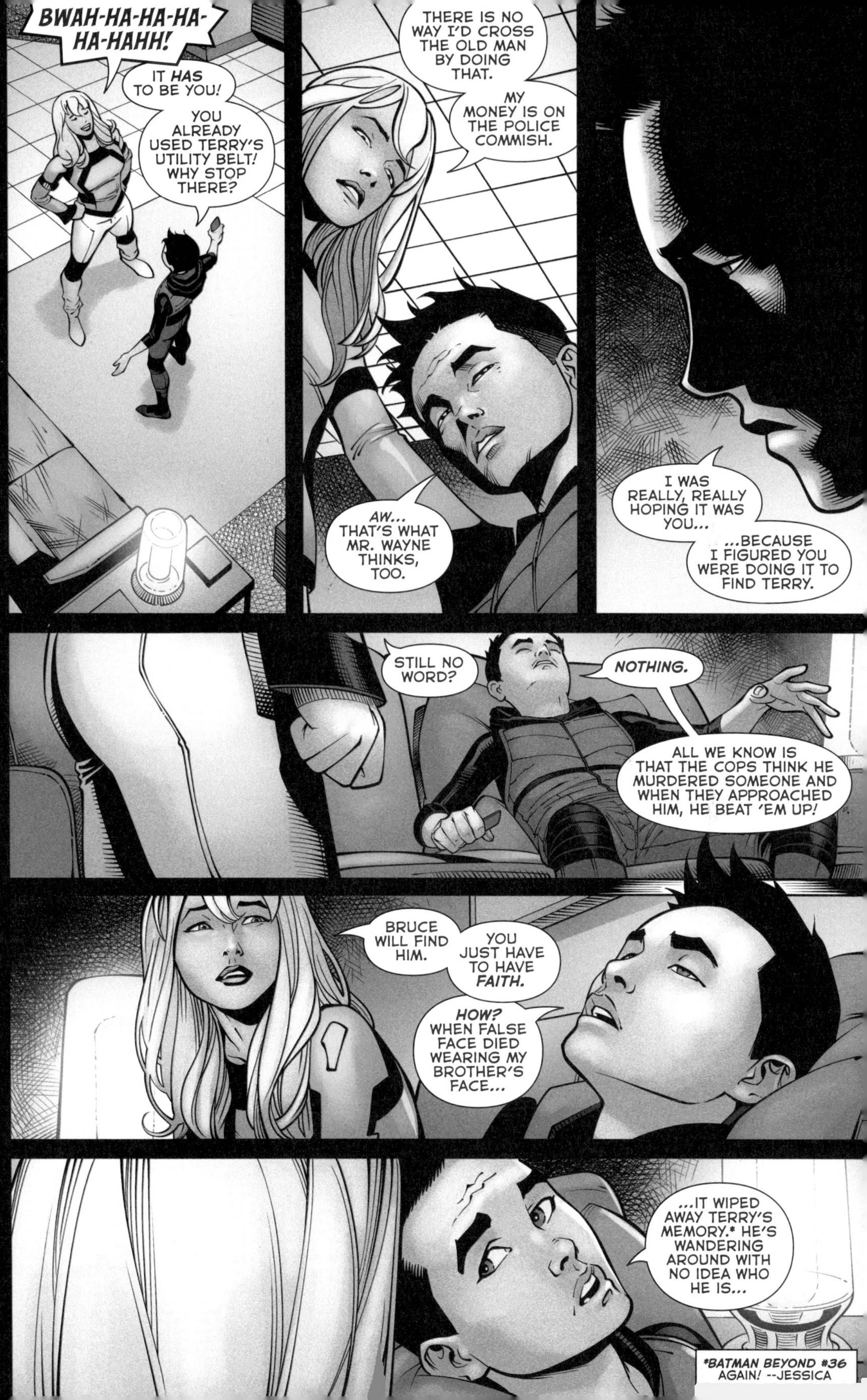
BWAH-HA-HA-HA-HA-HAHH!
IT HAS TO BE YOU!
YOU ALREADY USED TERRY'S UTILITY BELT! WHY STOP THERE?
THERE IS NO WAY I'D CROSS THE OLD MAN BY DOING THAT.
MY MONEY IS ON THE POLICE COMMISH.
AW... THAT'S WHAT MR. WAYNE THINKS, TOO.
I WAS REALLY, REALLY HOPING IT WAS YOU...
...BECAUSE I FIGURED YOU WERE DOING IT TO FIND TERRY.
STILL NO WORD?
NOTHING.
ALL WE KNOW IS THAT THE COPS THINK HE MURDERED SOMEONE AND WHEN THEY APPROACHED HIM, HE BEAT 'EM UP!
BRUCE WILL FIND HIM.
YOU JUST HAVE TO HAVE FAITH.
HOW? WHEN FALSE FACE DIED WEARING MY BROTHER'S FACE...
...IT WIPED AWAY TERRY'S MEMORY.* HE'S WANDERING AROUND WITH NO IDEA WHO HE IS...
*BATMAN BEYOND #36 AGAIN! --JESSICA

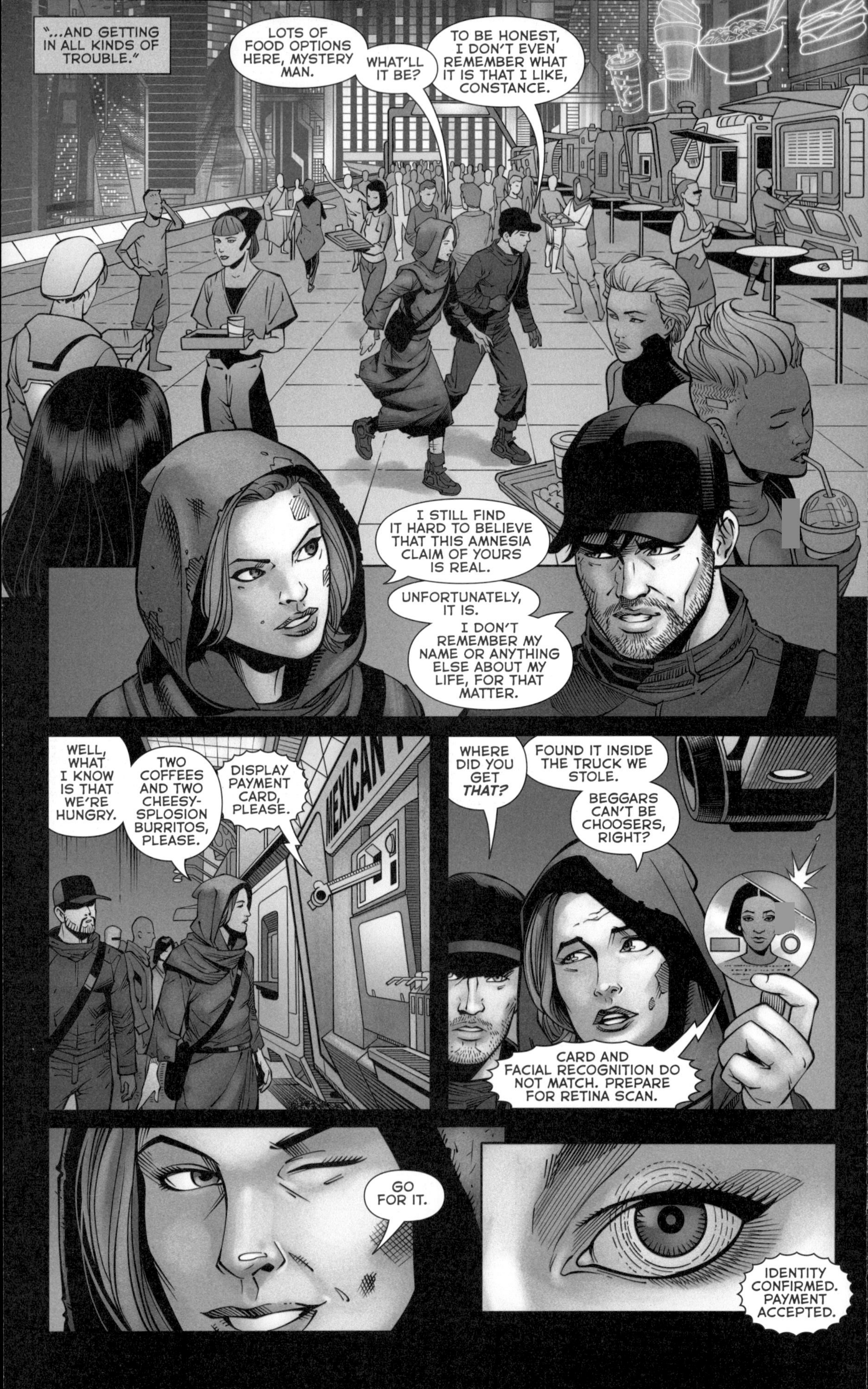
"...AND GETTING IN ALL KINDS OF TROUBLE."
LOTS OF FOOD OPTIONS HERE, MYSTERY MAN.
WHAT'LL IT BE?
TO BE HONEST, I DON'T EVEN REMEMBER WHAT IT IS THAT I LIKE, CONSTANCE.
I STILL FIND IT HARD TO BELIEVE THAT THIS AMNESIA CLAIM OF YOURS IS REAL.
UNFORTUNATELY, IT IS.
I DON'T REMEMBER MY NAME OR ANYTHING ELSE ABOUT MY LIFE, FOR THAT MATTER.
WELL, WHAT I KNOW IS THAT WE'RE HUNGRY.
TWO COFFEES AND TWO CHEESY-SPLOSION BURRITOS, PLEASE.
DISPLAY PAYMENT CARD, PLEASE.
MEXICAN
WHERE DID YOU GET *THAT?*
FOUND IT INSIDE THE TRUCK WE STOLE.
BEGGARS CAN'T BE CHOOSERS, RIGHT?
CARD AND FACIAL RECOGNITION DO NOT MATCH. PREPARE FOR RETINA SCAN.
GO FOR IT.
IDENTITY CONFIRMED. PAYMENT ACCEPTED.

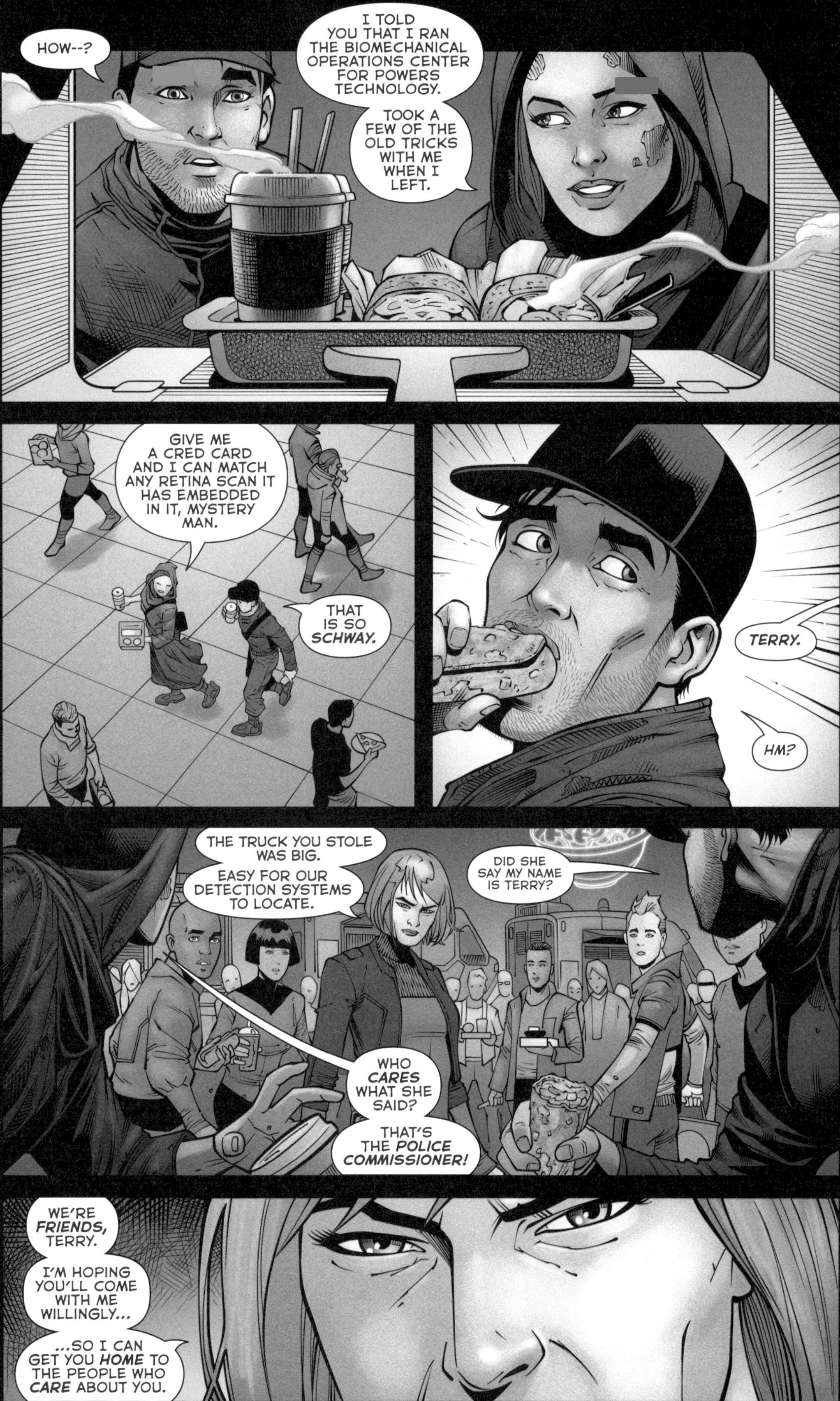
HOW--?
I TOLD YOU THAT I RAN THE BIOMECHANICAL OPERATIONS CENTER FOR POWERS TECHNOLOGY.
TOOK A FEW OF THE OLD TRICKS WITH ME WHEN I LEFT.
GIVE ME A CRED CARD AND I CAN MATCH ANY RETINA SCAN IT HAS EMBEDDED IN IT, MYSTERY MAN.
THAT IS SO *SCHWAY.*
TERRY.
HM?
THE TRUCK YOU STOLE WAS BIG.
EASY FOR OUR DETECTION SYSTEMS TO LOCATE.
DID SHE SAY MY NAME IS TERRY?
WHO *CARES* WHAT SHE SAID?
THAT'S THE *POLICE COMMISSIONER!*
WE'RE *FRIENDS,* TERRY.
I'M HOPING YOU'LL COME WITH ME WILLINGLY...
...SO I CAN GET YOU *HOME* TO THE PEOPLE WHO *CARE* ABOUT YOU.

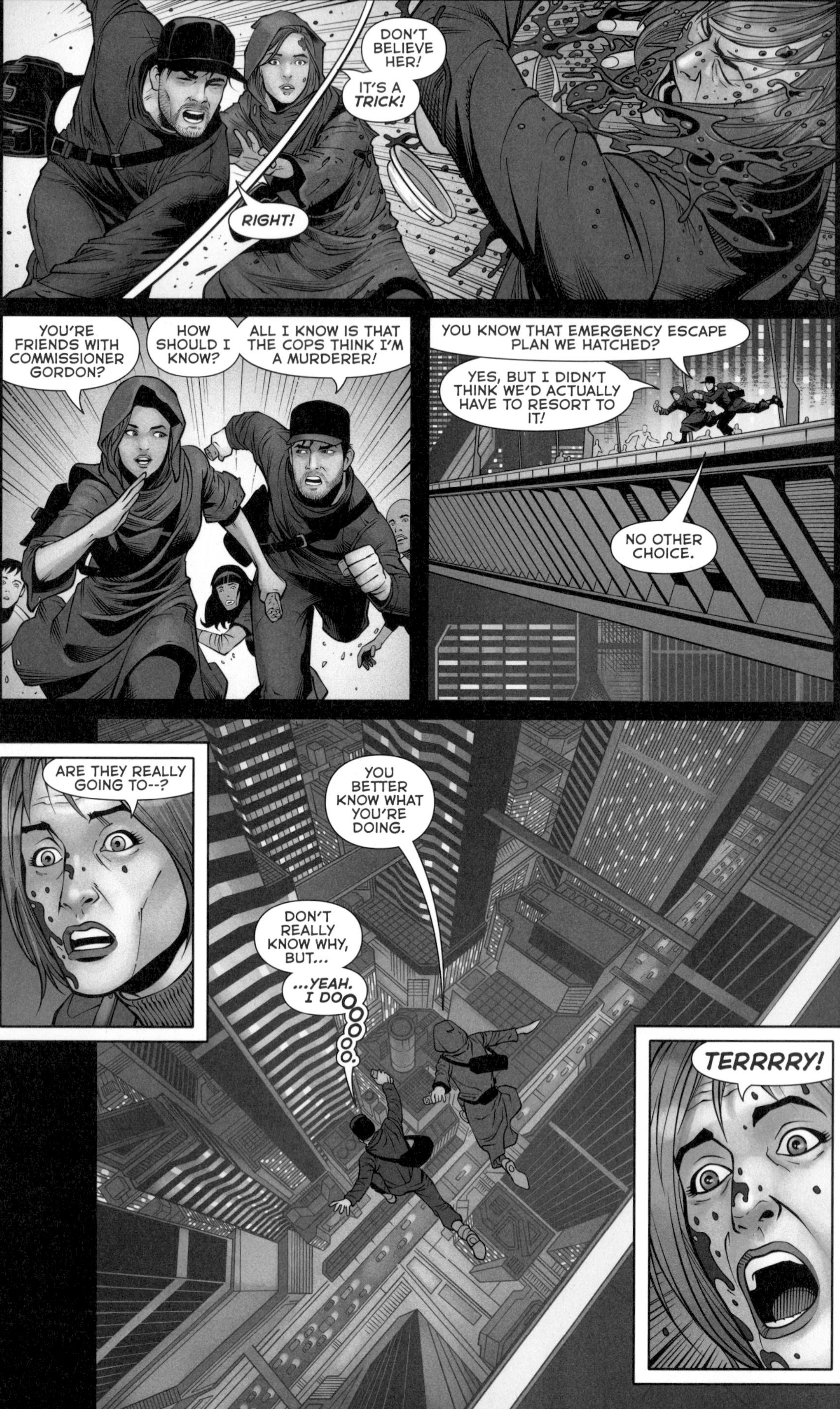
DON'T BELIEVE HER!
IT'S A TRICK!
RIGHT!
YOU'RE FRIENDS WITH COMMISSIONER GORDON?
HOW SHOULD I KNOW?
ALL I KNOW IS THAT THE COPS THINK I'M A MURDERER!
YOU KNOW THAT EMERGENCY ESCAPE PLAN WE HATCHED?
YES, BUT I DIDN'T THINK WE'D ACTUALLY HAVE TO RESORT TO IT!
NO OTHER CHOICE.
ARE THEY REALLY GOING TO--?
YOU BETTER KNOW WHAT YOU'RE DOING.
DON'T REALLY KNOW WHY, BUT...
...YEAH. I DOOOOOO.
TERRRRY!

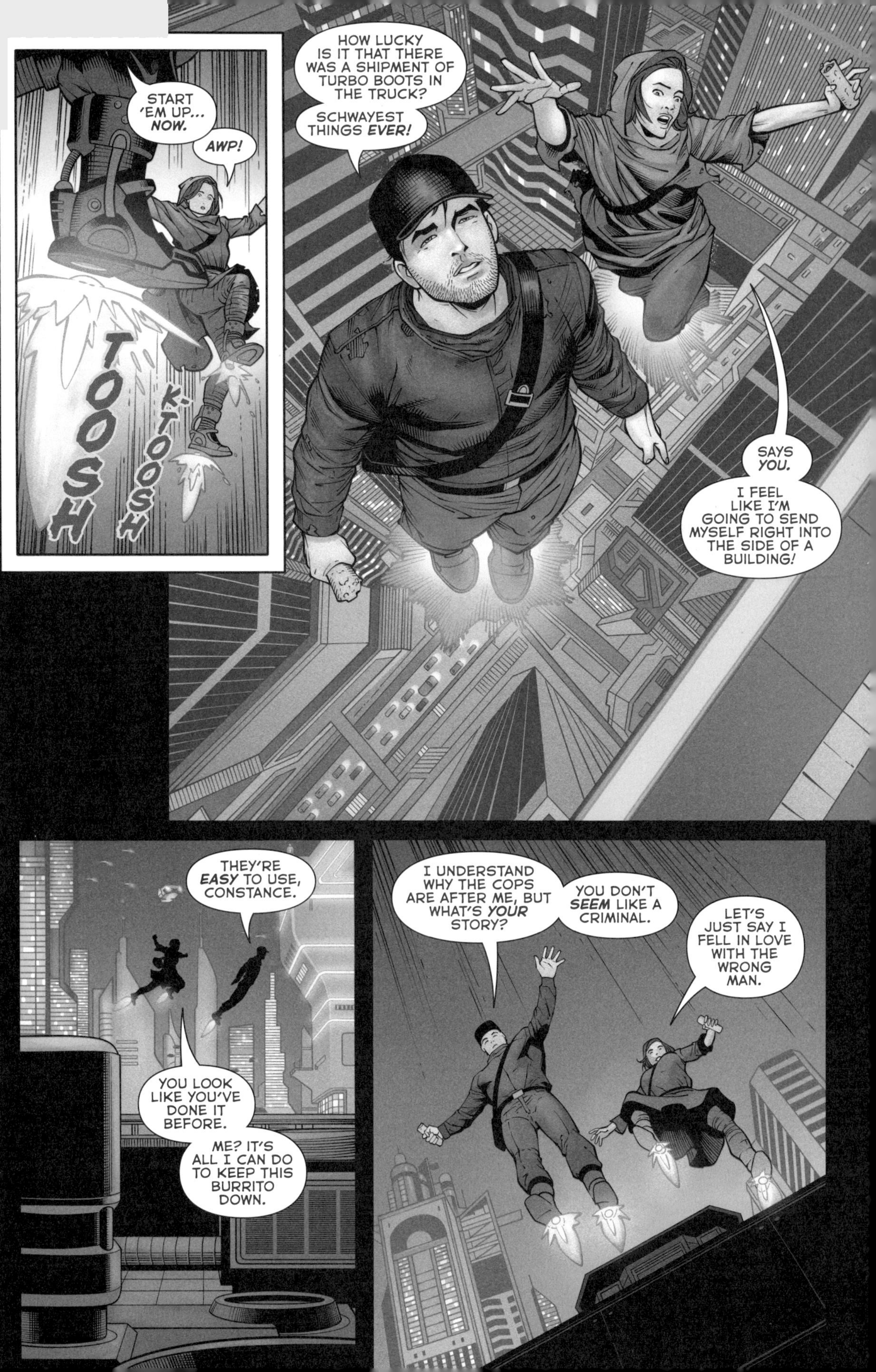

START 'EM UP... NOW.
AWP!
TOOSH
K-TOOSH
HOW LUCKY IS IT THAT THERE WAS A SHIPMENT OF TURBO BOOTS IN THE TRUCK?
SCHWAYEST THINGS EVER!
SAYS YOU.
I FEEL LIKE I'M GOING TO SEND MYSELF RIGHT INTO THE SIDE OF A BUILDING!
THEY'RE EASY TO USE, CONSTANCE.
YOU LOOK LIKE YOU'VE DONE IT BEFORE.
ME? IT'S ALL I CAN DO TO KEEP THIS BURRITO DOWN.
I UNDERSTAND WHY THE COPS ARE AFTER ME, BUT WHAT'S YOUR STORY?
YOU DON'T SEEM LIKE A CRIMINAL.
LET'S JUST SAY I FELL IN LOVE WITH THE WRONG MAN.

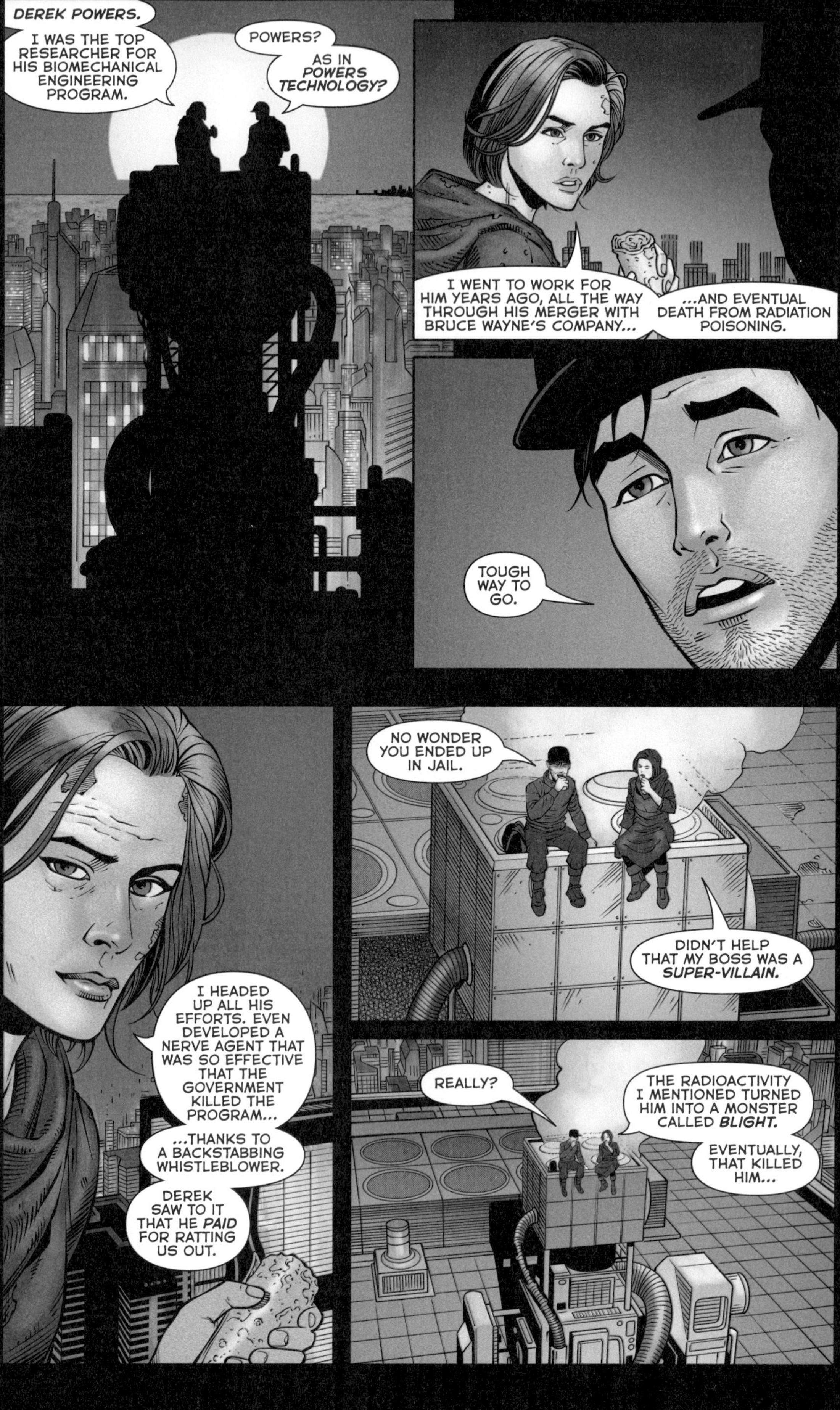
DEREK POWERS.
I WAS THE TOP RESEARCHER FOR HIS BIOMECHANICAL ENGINEERING PROGRAM.
POWERS?
AS IN *POWERS TECHNOLOGY?*
I WENT TO WORK FOR HIM YEARS AGO, ALL THE WAY THROUGH HIS MERGER WITH BRUCE WAYNE'S COMPANY...
...AND EVENTUAL DEATH FROM RADIATION POISONING.
TOUGH WAY TO GO.
I HEADED UP ALL HIS EFFORTS. EVEN DEVELOPED A NERVE AGENT THAT WAS SO EFFECTIVE THAT THE GOVERNMENT KILLED THE PROGRAM...
...THANKS TO A BACKSTABBING WHISTLEBLOWER.
DEREK SAW TO IT THAT HE *PAID* FOR RATTING US OUT.
NO WONDER YOU ENDED UP IN JAIL.
DIDN'T HELP THAT MY BOSS WAS A *SUPER-VILLAIN.*
REALLY?
THE RADIOACTIVITY I MENTIONED TURNED HIM INTO A MONSTER CALLED *BLIGHT.*
EVENTUALLY, THAT KILLED HIM...

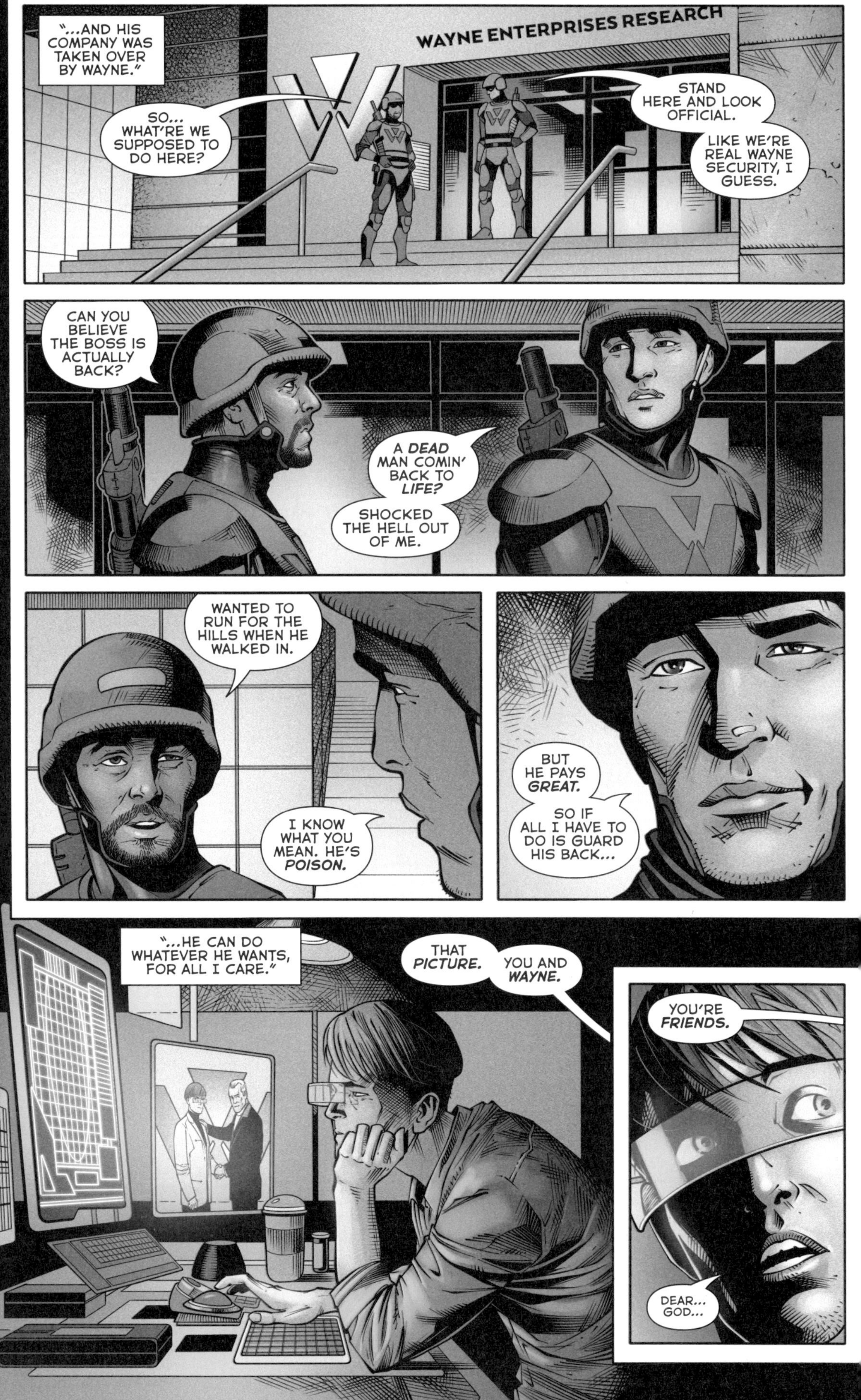

"...AND HIS COMPANY WAS TAKEN OVER BY WAYNE."
WAYNE ENTERPRISES RESEARCH
SO... WHAT'RE WE SUPPOSED TO DO HERE?
STAND HERE AND LOOK OFFICIAL.
LIKE WE'RE REAL WAYNE SECURITY, I GUESS.
CAN YOU BELIEVE THE BOSS IS ACTUALLY BACK?
A *DEAD* MAN COMIN' BACK TO *LIFE?*
SHOCKED THE HELL OUT OF ME.
WANTED TO RUN FOR THE HILLS WHEN HE WALKED IN.
I KNOW WHAT YOU MEAN. HE'S *POISON.*
BUT HE PAYS *GREAT.*
SO IF ALL I HAVE TO DO IS GUARD HIS BACK...
"...HE CAN DO WHATEVER HE WANTS, FOR ALL I CARE."
THAT *PICTURE.*
YOU AND *WAYNE.*
YOU'RE *FRIENDS.*
DEAR... GOD...

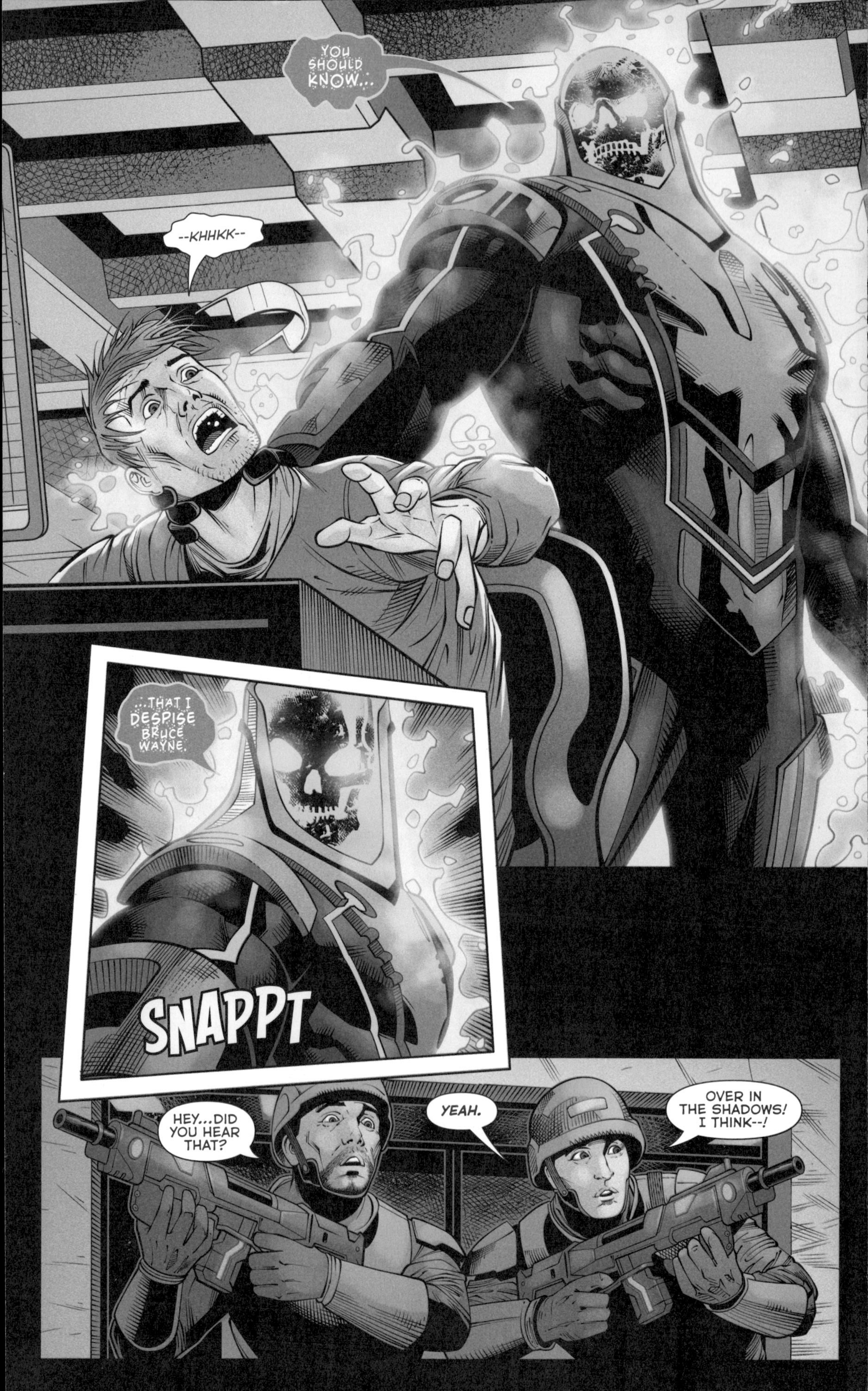
YOU SHOULD KNOW...
--KHHKK--
...THAT I DESPISE BRUCE WAYNE.
SNAPPT
HEY...DID YOU HEAR THAT?
YEAH.
OVER IN THE SHADOWS! I THINK--!

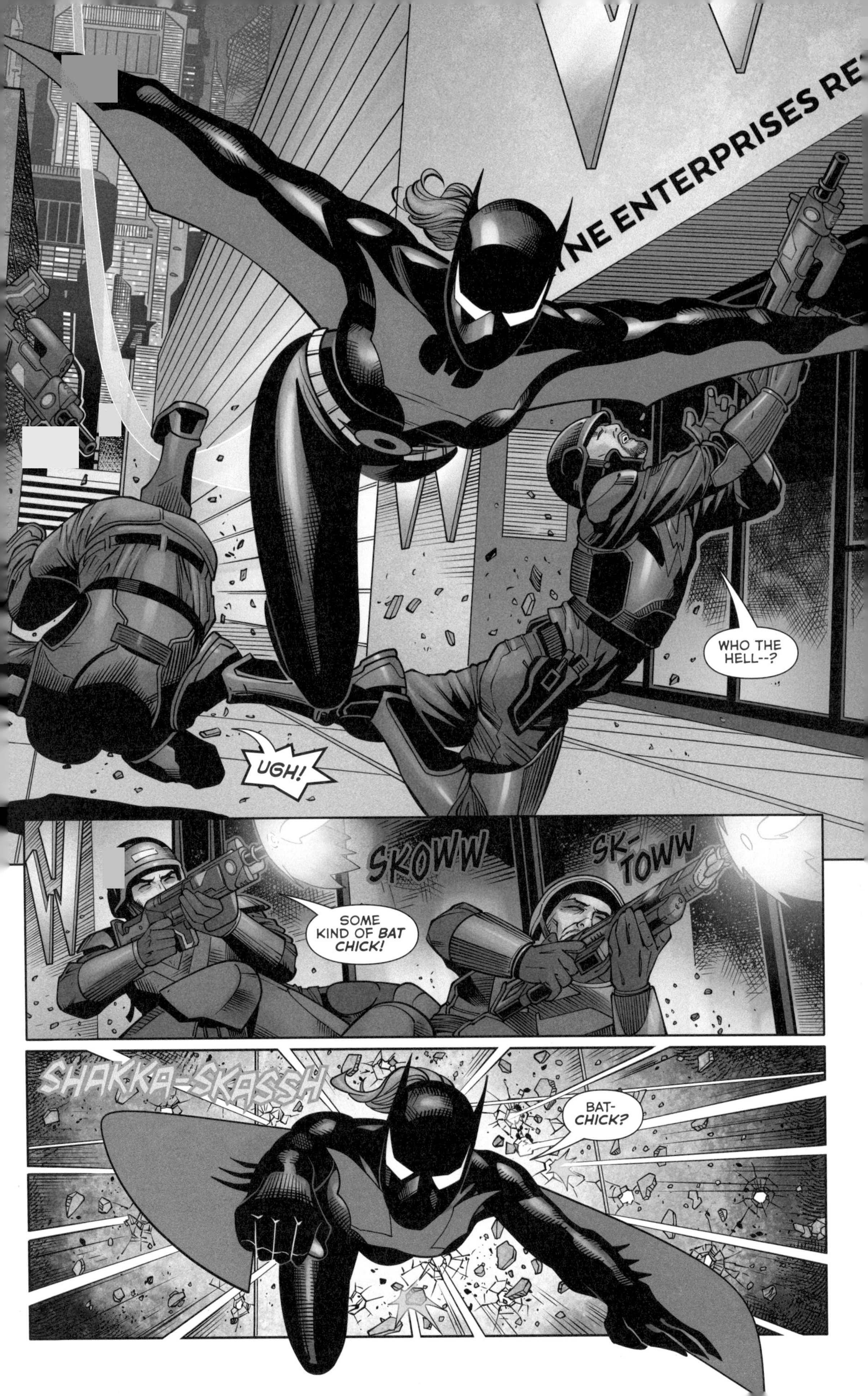
NE ENTERPRISES RE
WHO THE HELL--?
UGH!
SKOWW
SK-TOWW
SOME KIND OF *BAT CHICK!*
SHAKKA-SKASSH
BAT-CHICK?

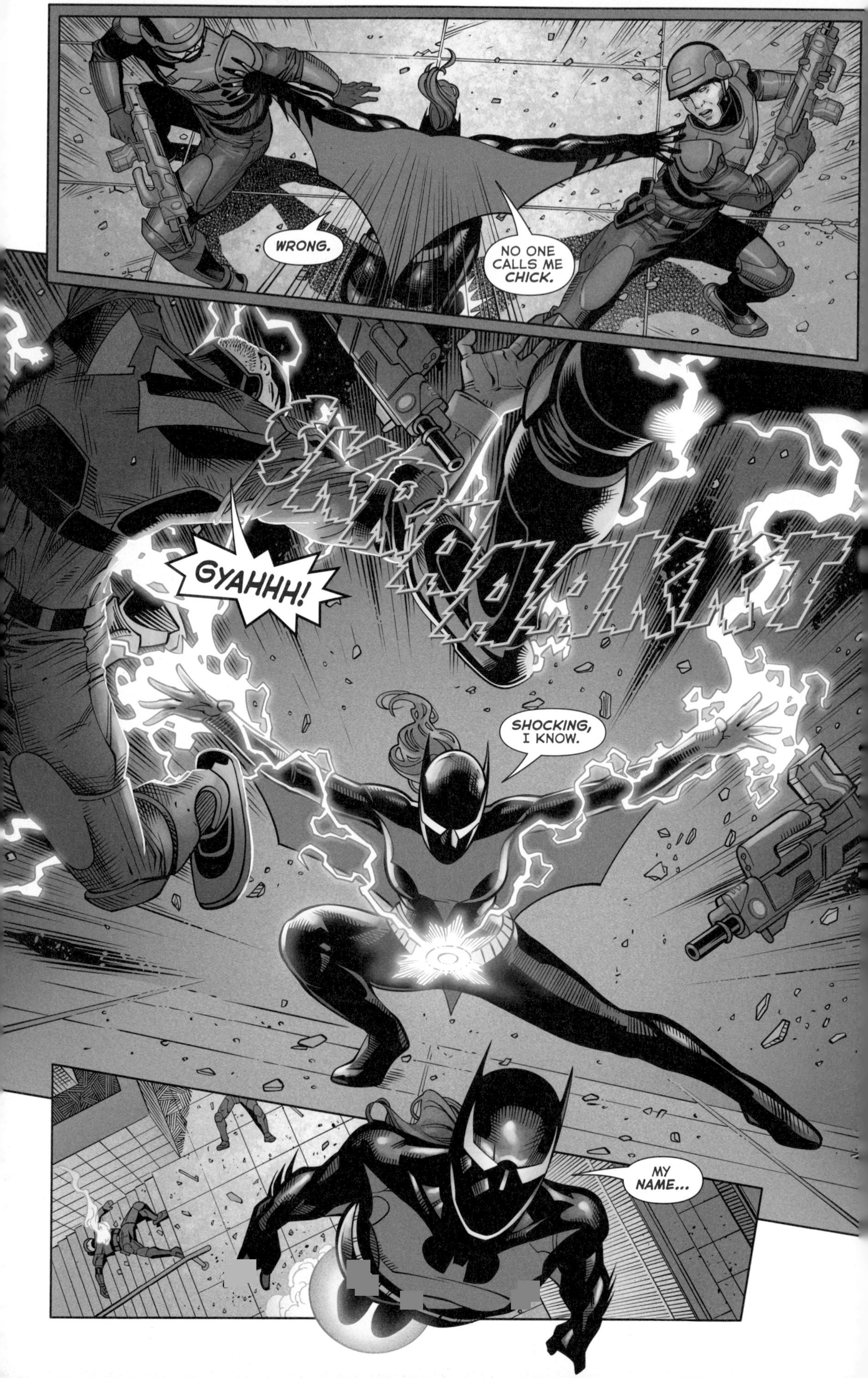
WRONG.
NO ONE CALLS ME CHICK.
GYAHHH!
SHOCKING, I KNOW.
MY NAME...

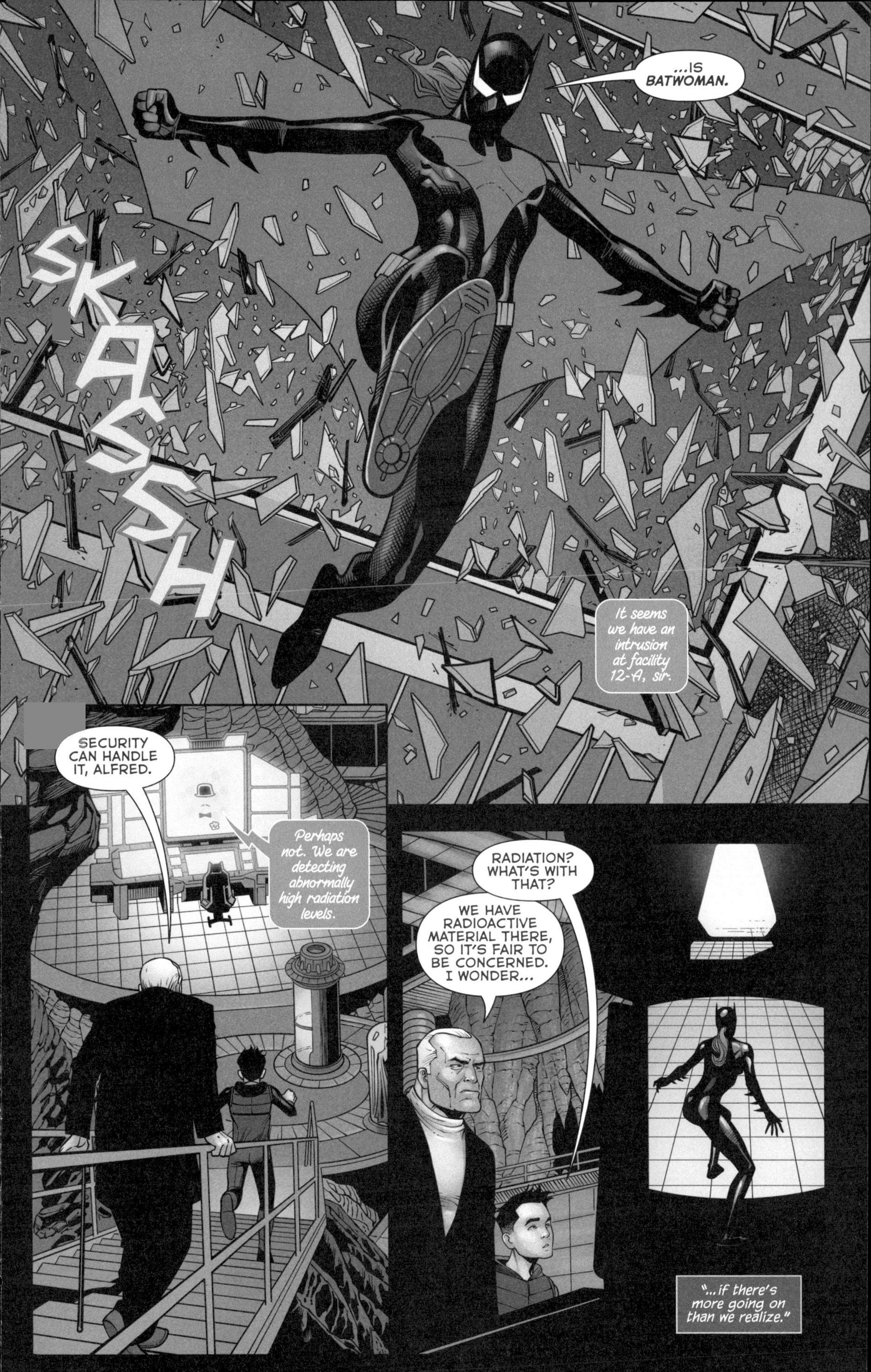
...IS BATWOMAN.
SKASSH
It seems we have an intrusion at facility 12-A, sir.
SECURITY CAN HANDLE IT, ALFRED.
Perhaps not. We are detecting abnormally high radiation levels.
RADIATION? WHAT'S WITH THAT?
WE HAVE RADIOACTIVE MATERIAL THERE, SO IT'S FAIR TO BE CONCERNED. I WONDER...
"...if there's more going on than we realize."

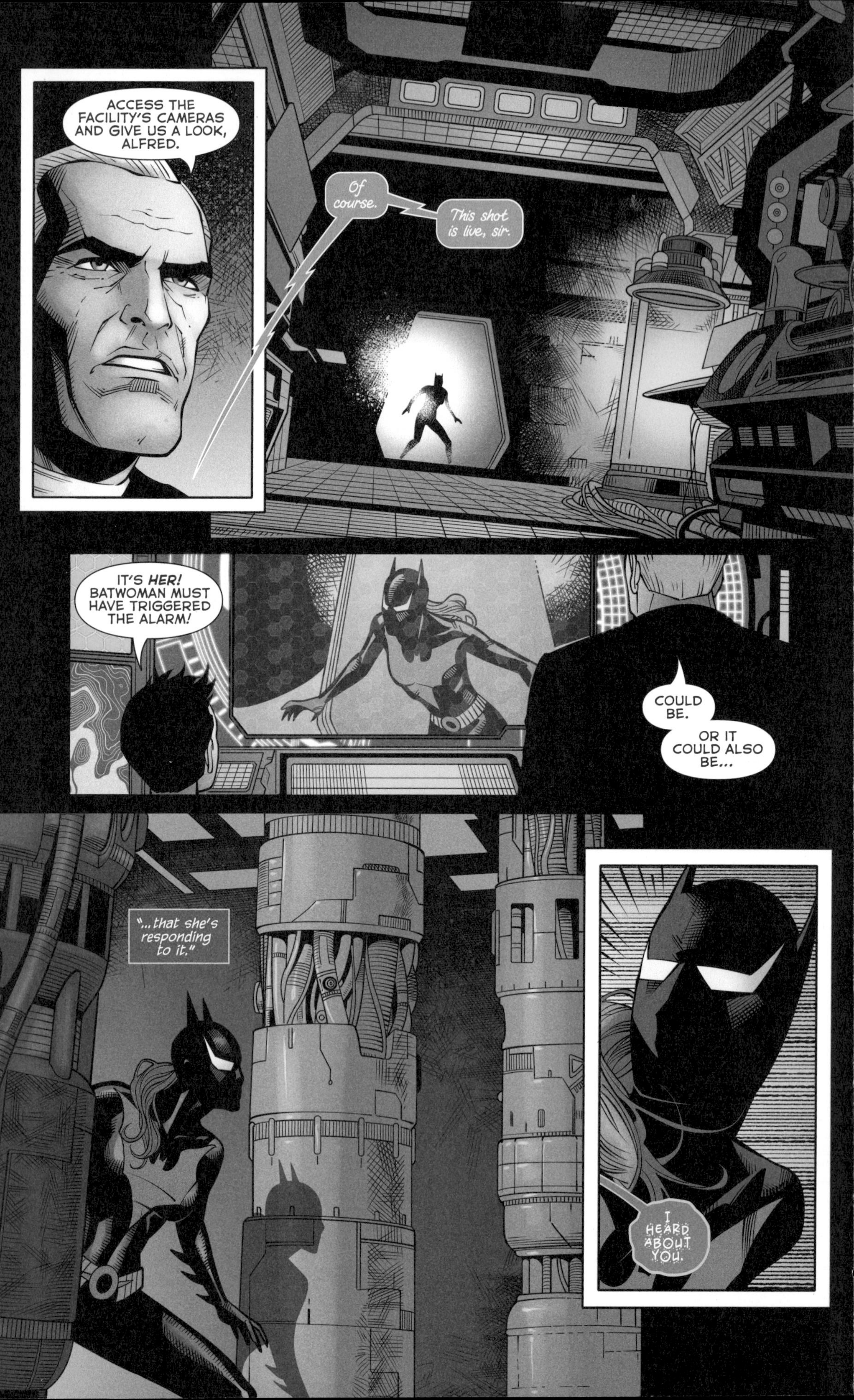
ACCESS THE FACILITY'S CAMERAS AND GIVE US A LOOK, ALFRED.
Of course.
This shot is live, sir.
IT'S HER! BATWOMAN MUST HAVE TRIGGERED THE ALARM!
COULD BE.
OR IT COULD ALSO BE...
"...that she's responding to it."
I HEARD ABOUT YOU.

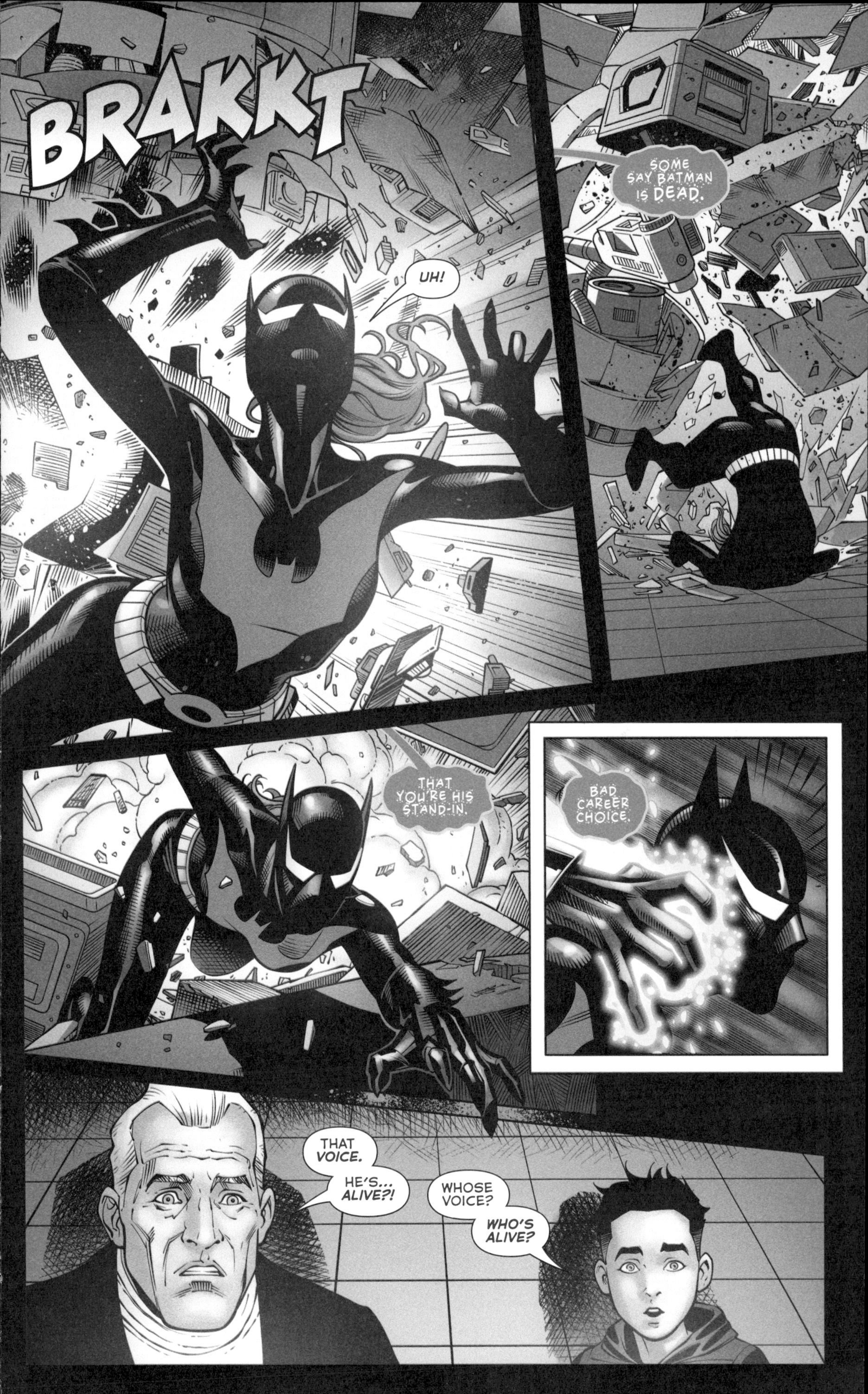
BRAKKT
UH!
SOME SAY BATMAN IS DEAD.
THAT YOU'RE HIS STAND-IN.
BAD CAREER CHOICE.
THAT VOICE.
HE'S... ALIVE?!
WHOSE VOICE?
WHO'S ALIVE?

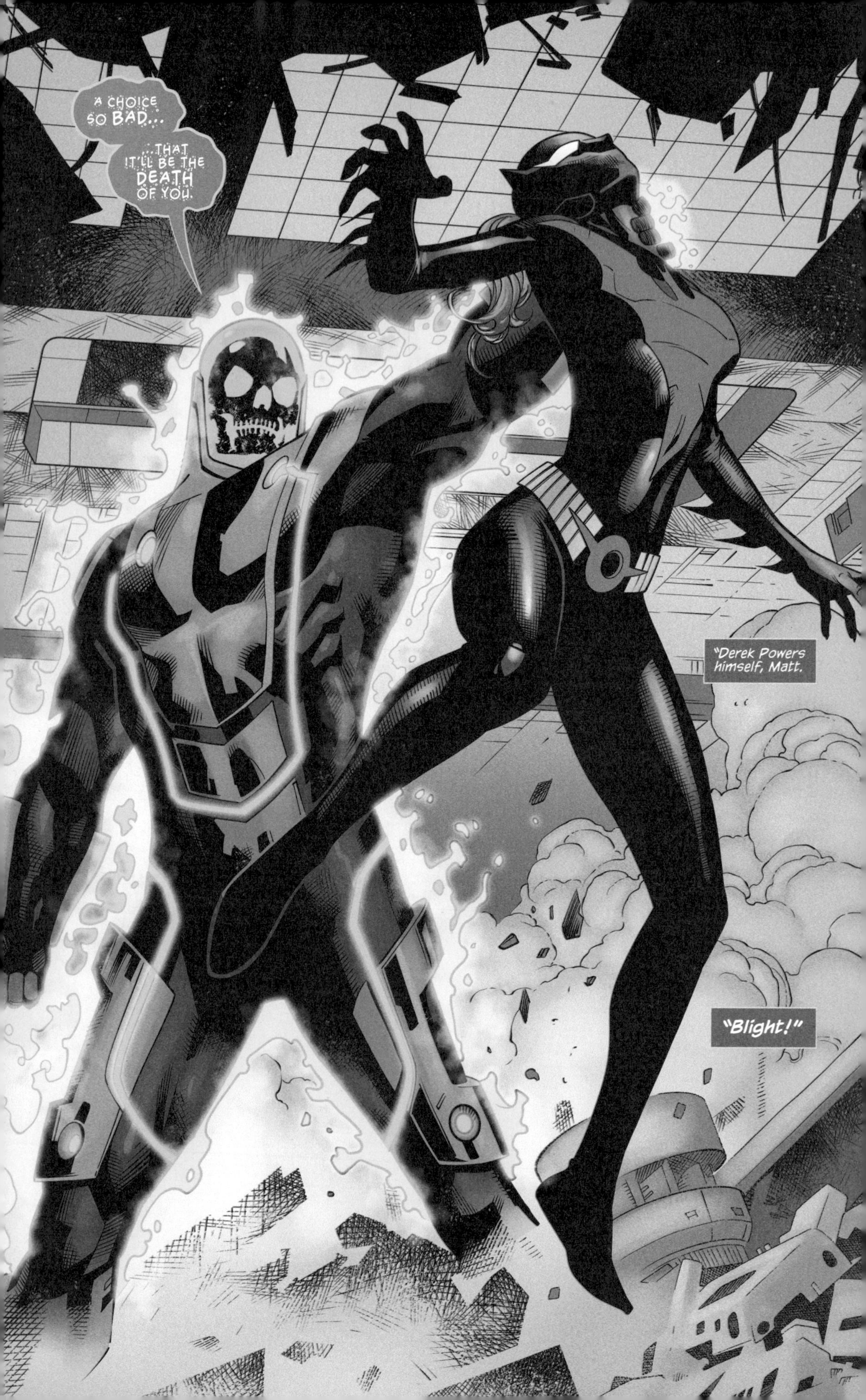
A CHOICE SO BAD...
...THAT IT'LL BE THE DEATH OF YOU.
"Derek Powers himself, Matt.
"Blight!"

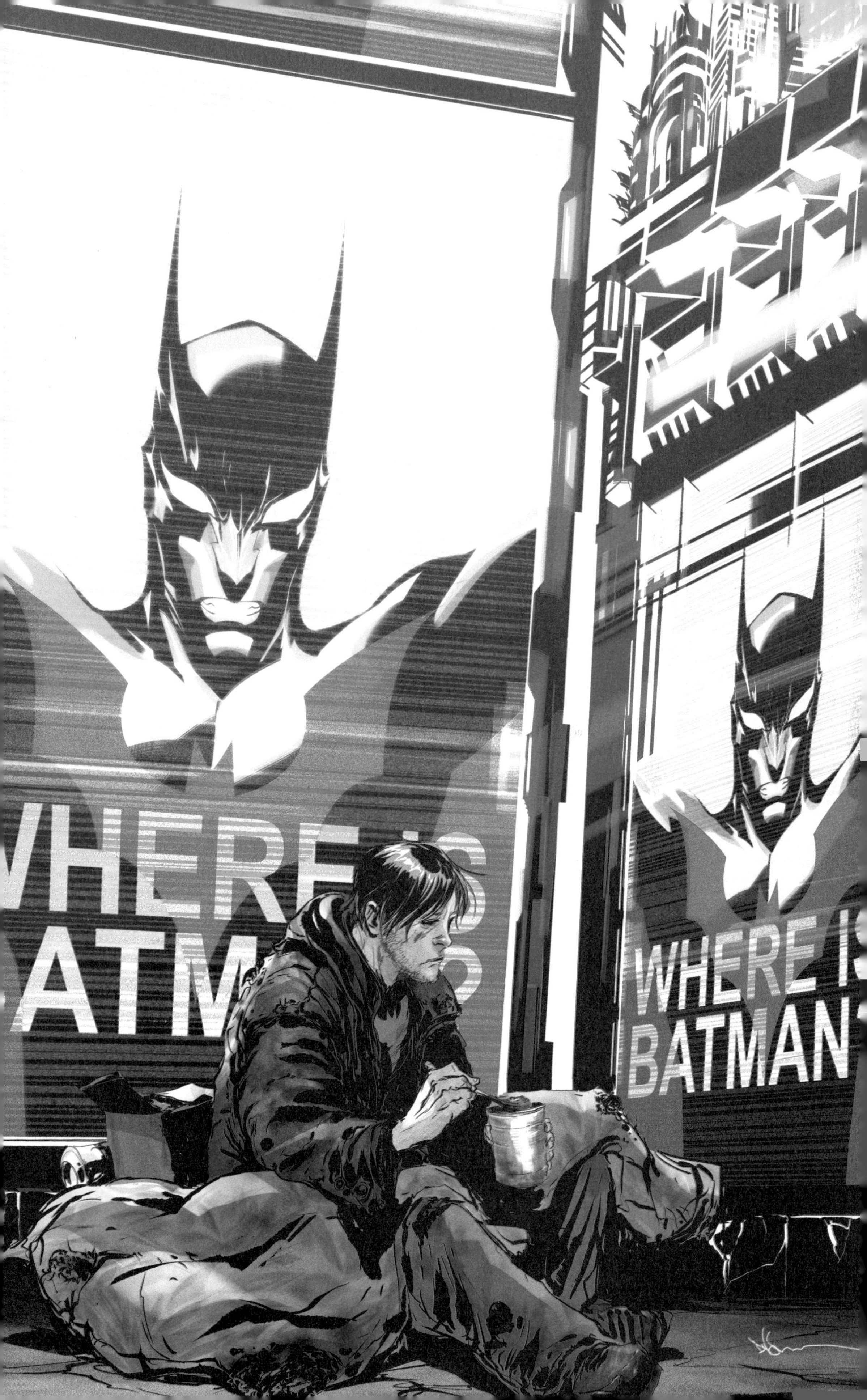
WHERE IS
BATMAN

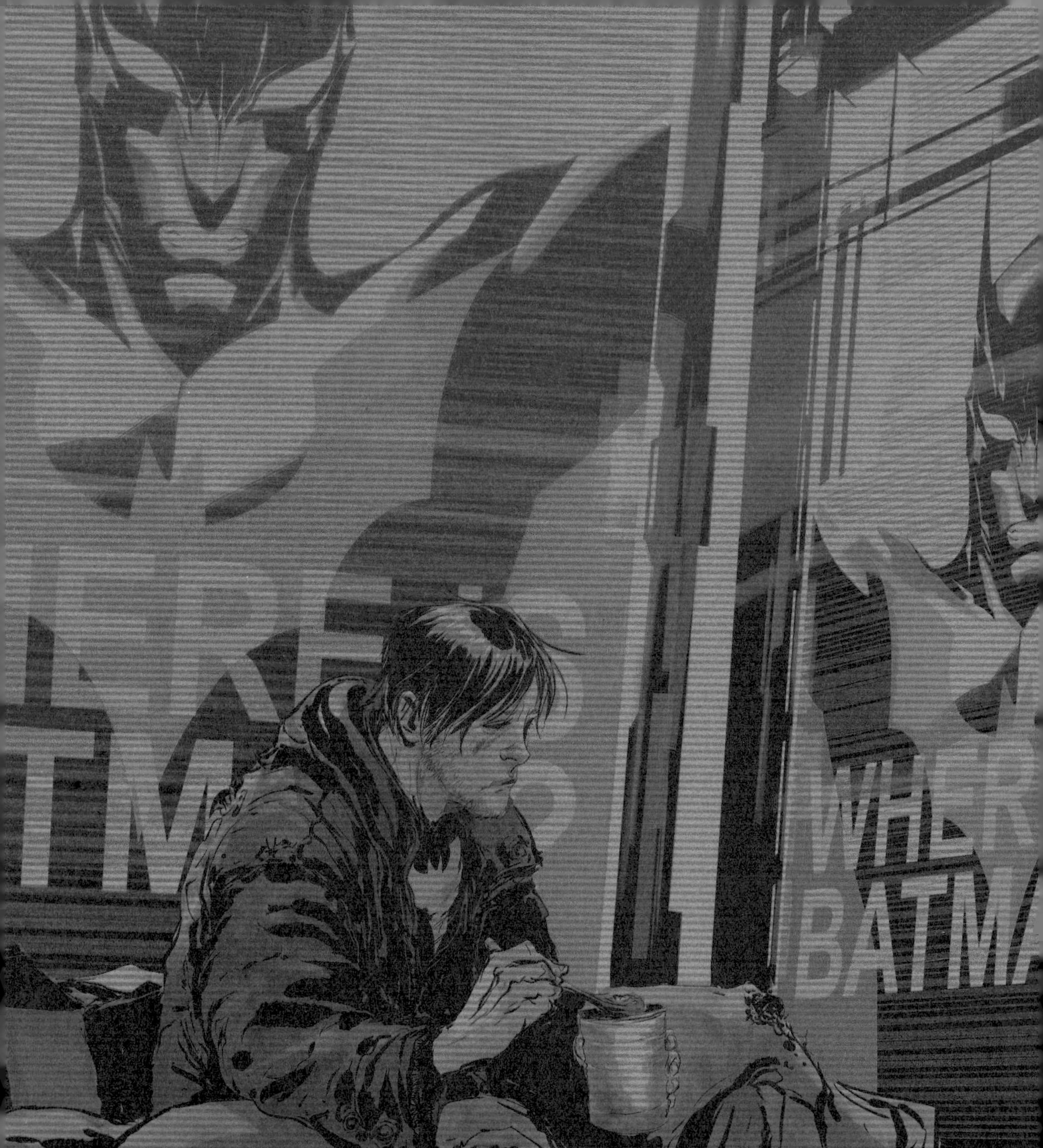

BATMAN
BEYOND
#39

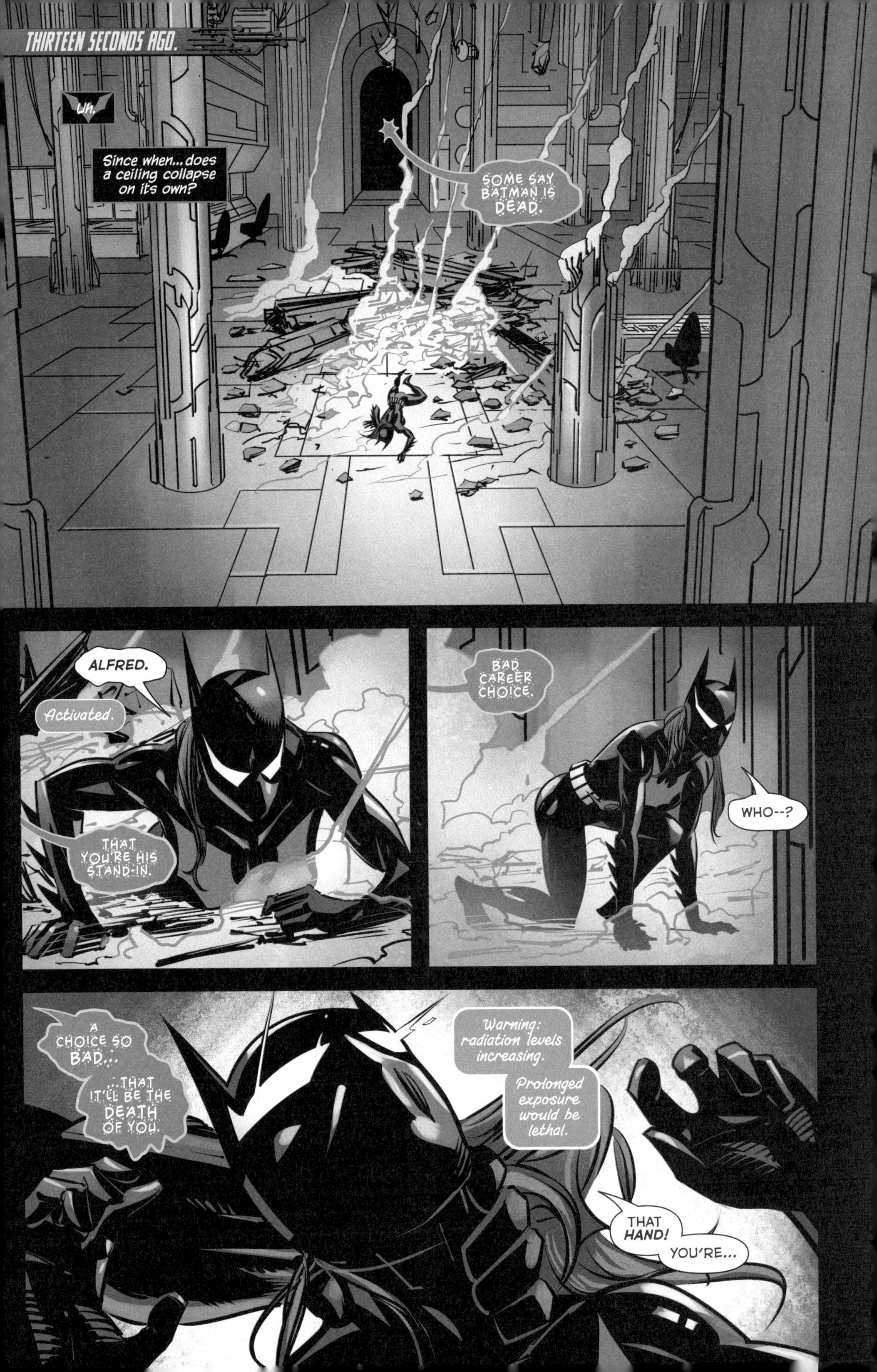
THIRTEEN SECONDS AGO.
Uh.
Since when...does a ceiling collapse on its own?
SOME SAY BATMAN IS DEAD.
ALFRED.
Activated.
THAT YOU'RE HIS STAND-IN.
BAD CAREER CHOICE.
WHO--?
A CHOICE SO BAD...
...THAT IT'LL BE THE DEATH OF YOU.
Warning: radiation levels increasing.
Prolonged exposure would be lethal.
THAT HAND!
YOU'RE...

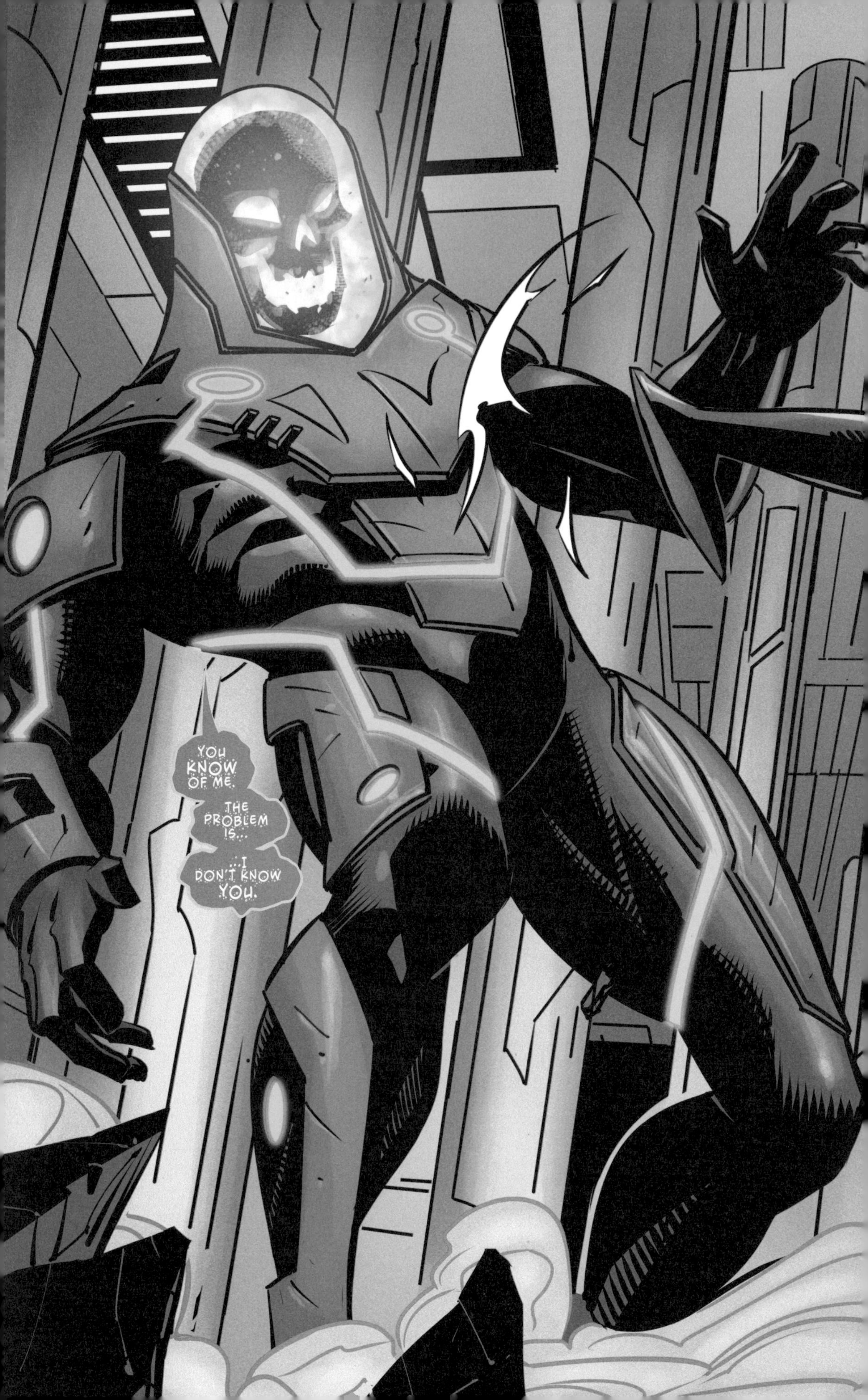
YOU KNOW OF ME.
THE PROBLEM IS...
...I DON'T KNOW YOU.

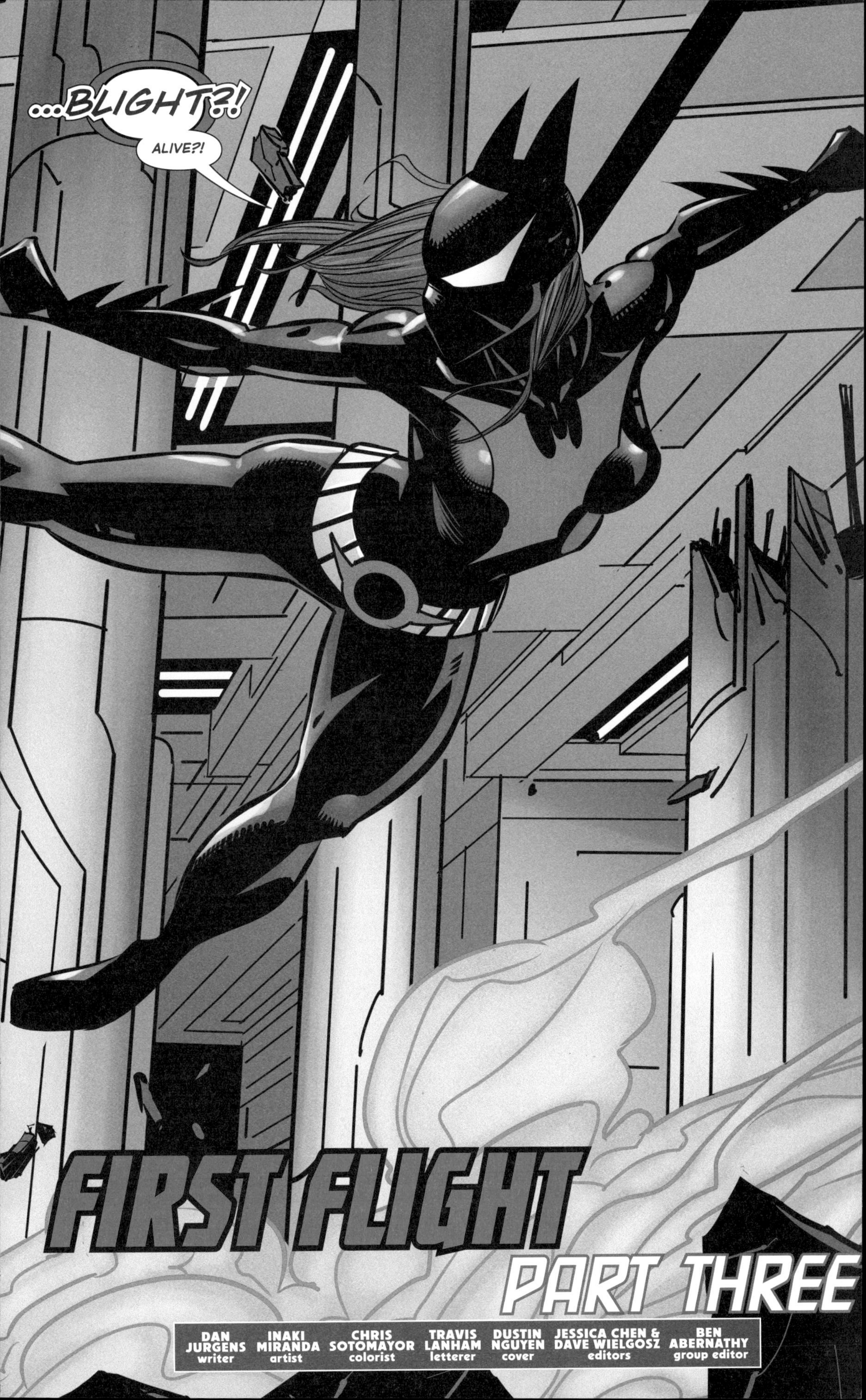
...BLIGHT?!
ALIVE?!
FIRST FLIGHT
PART THREE
DAN JURGENS writer
INAKI MIRANDA artist
CHRIS SOTOMAYOR colorist
TRAVIS LANHAM letterer
DUSTIN NGUYEN cover
JESSICA CHEN & DAVE WIELGOSZ editors
BEN ABERNATHY group editor

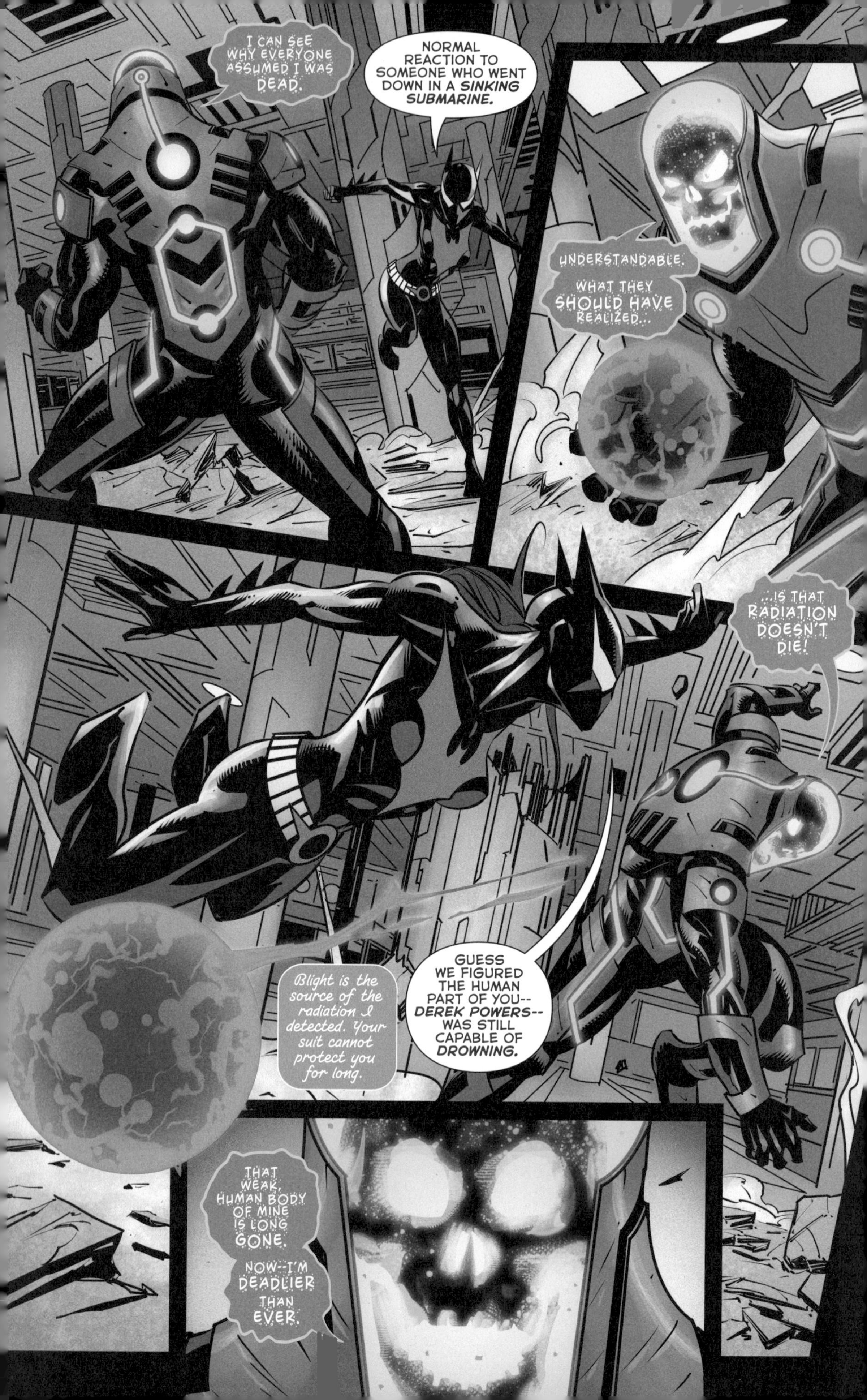
I CAN SEE WHY EVERYONE ASSUMED I WAS DEAD.
NORMAL REACTION TO SOMEONE WHO WENT DOWN IN A *SINKING SUBMARINE.*
UNDERSTANDABLE.
WHAT THEY SHOULD HAVE REALIZED...
...IS THAT RADIATION DOESN'T DIE!
Blight is the source of the radiation I detected. Your suit cannot protect you for long.
GUESS WE FIGURED THE HUMAN PART OF YOU-- *DEREK POWERS*-- WAS STILL CAPABLE OF *DROWNING.*
THAT WEAK, HUMAN BODY OF MINE IS LONG GONE.
NOW--I'M DEADLIER THAN EVER.

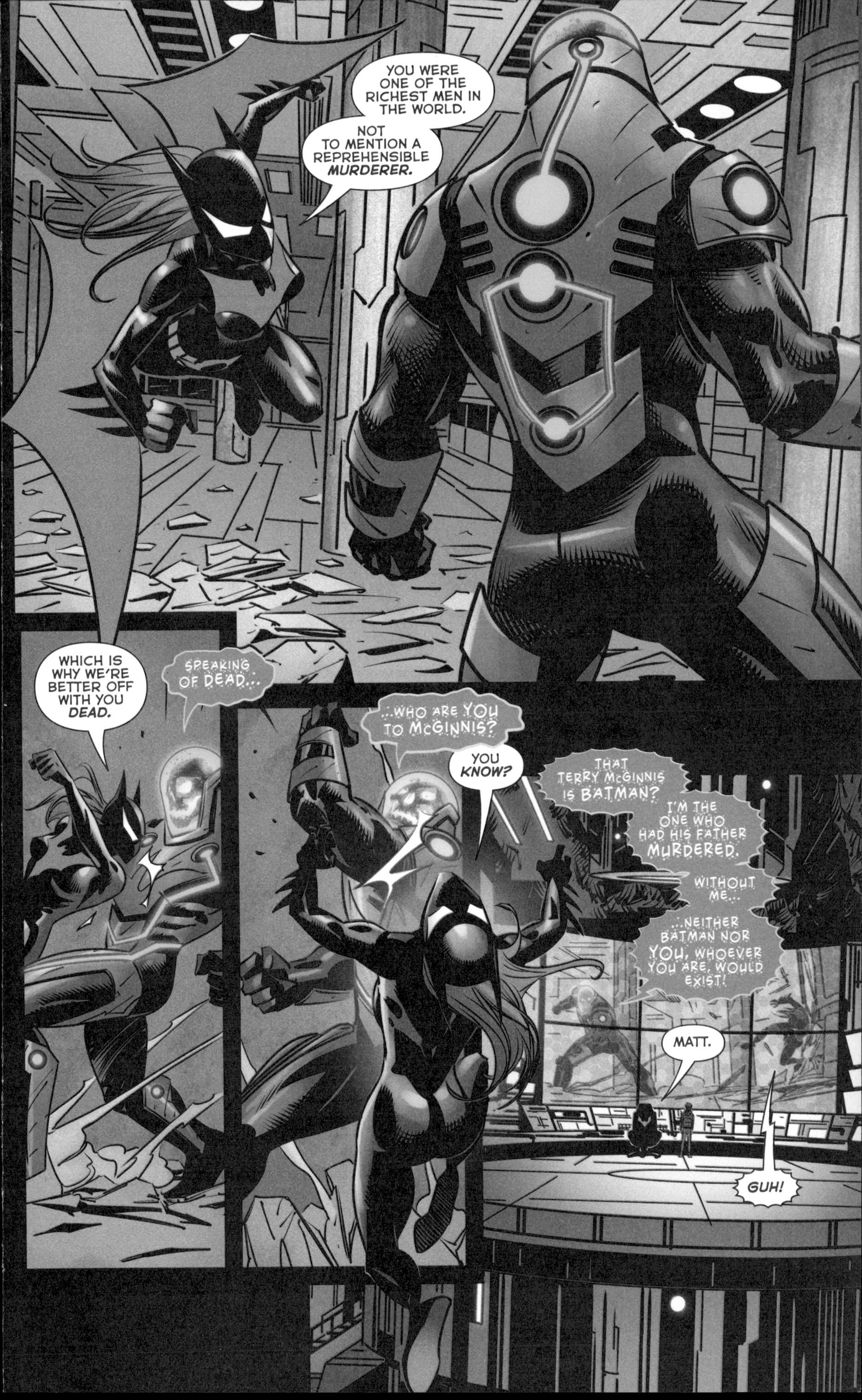
YOU WERE ONE OF THE RICHEST MEN IN THE WORLD.
NOT TO MENTION A REPREHENSIBLE *MURDERER.*
WHICH IS WHY WE'RE BETTER OFF WITH YOU *DEAD.*
SPEAKING OF DEAD...
...WHO ARE YOU TO McGINNIS?
YOU *KNOW?*
THAT TERRY McGINNIS IS BATMAN?
I'M THE ONE WHO HAD HIS FATHER MURDERED.
WITHOUT ME...
...NEITHER BATMAN NOR YOU, WHOEVER YOU ARE, WOULD EXIST!
MATT.
GUH!

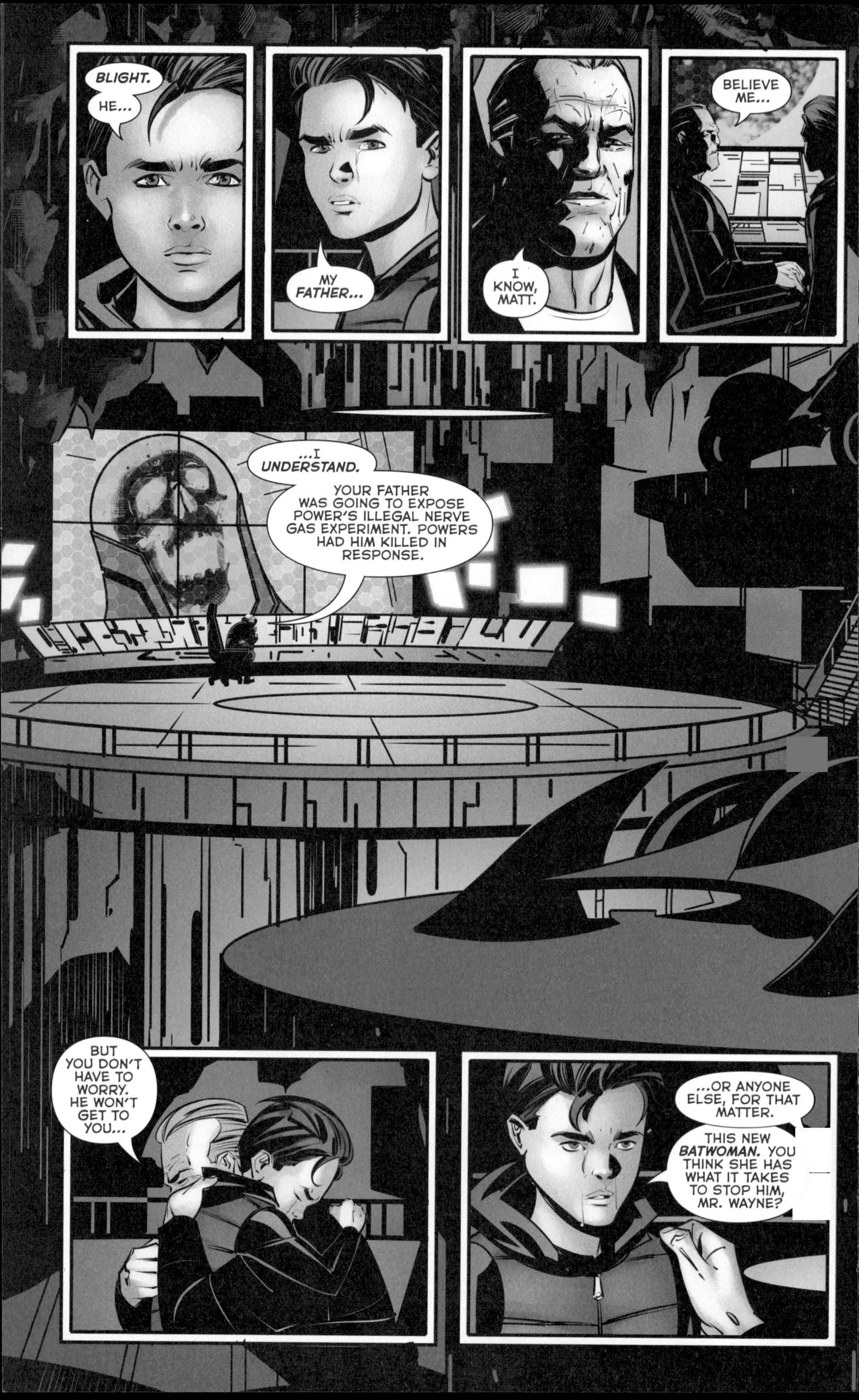
BLIGHT.
HE...
MY FATHER...
I KNOW, MATT.
BELIEVE ME...
...I UNDERSTAND.
YOUR FATHER WAS GOING TO EXPOSE POWER'S ILLEGAL NERVE GAS EXPERIMENT. POWERS HAD HIM KILLED IN RESPONSE.
BUT YOU DON'T HAVE TO WORRY. HE WON'T GET TO YOU...
...OR ANYONE ELSE, FOR THAT MATTER.
THIS NEW BATWOMAN. YOU THINK SHE HAS WHAT IT TAKES TO STOP HIM, MR. WAYNE?

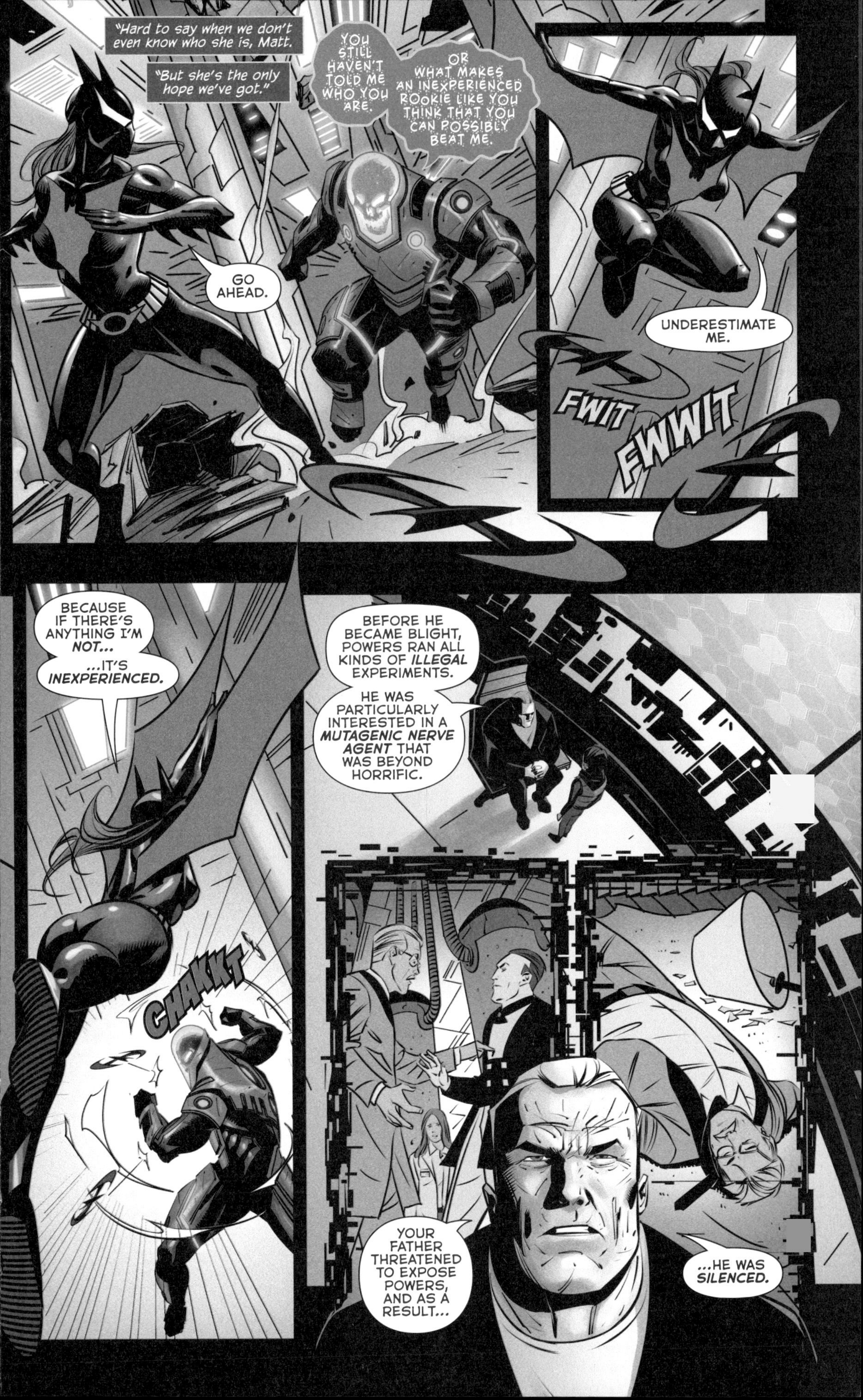
"Hard to say when we don't even know who she is, Matt.
"But she's the only hope we've got."
YOU STILL HAVEN'T TOLD ME WHO YOU ARE.
OR WHAT MAKES AN INEXPERIENCED ROOKIE LIKE YOU THINK THAT YOU CAN POSSIBLY BEAT ME.
GO AHEAD.
UNDERESTIMATE ME.
FWIT
FWWIT
BECAUSE IF THERE'S ANYTHING I'M NOT...
...IT'S INEXPERIENCED.
CHAKKT
BEFORE HE BECAME BLIGHT, POWERS RAN ALL KINDS OF ILLEGAL EXPERIMENTS.
HE WAS PARTICULARLY INTERESTED IN A MUTAGENIC NERVE AGENT THAT WAS BEYOND HORRIFIC.
YOUR FATHER THREATENED TO EXPOSE POWERS, AND AS A RESULT...
...HE WAS SILENCED.

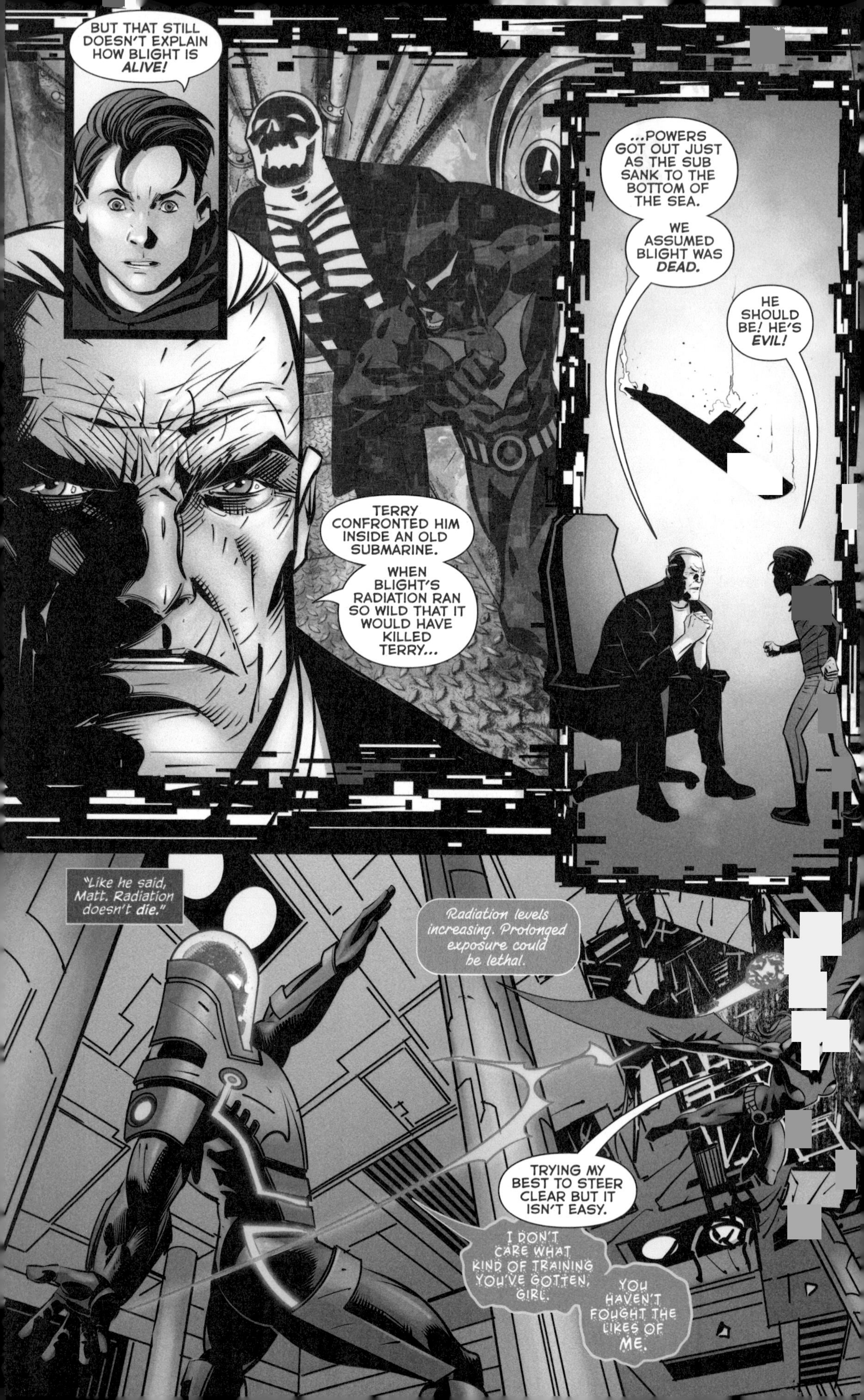
BUT THAT STILL DOESN'T EXPLAIN HOW BLIGHT IS ALIVE!
TERRY CONFRONTED HIM INSIDE AN OLD SUBMARINE.
WHEN BLIGHT'S RADIATION RAN SO WILD THAT IT WOULD HAVE KILLED TERRY...
...POWERS GOT OUT JUST AS THE SUB SANK TO THE BOTTOM OF THE SEA.
WE ASSUMED BLIGHT WAS DEAD.
HE SHOULD BE! HE'S EVIL!
"Like he said, Matt. Radiation doesn't die."
Radiation levels increasing. Prolonged exposure could be lethal.
TRYING MY BEST TO STEER CLEAR BUT IT ISN'T EASY.
I DON'T CARE WHAT KIND OF TRAINING YOU'VE GOTTEN, GIRL.
YOU HAVEN'T FOUGHT THE LIKES OF ME.

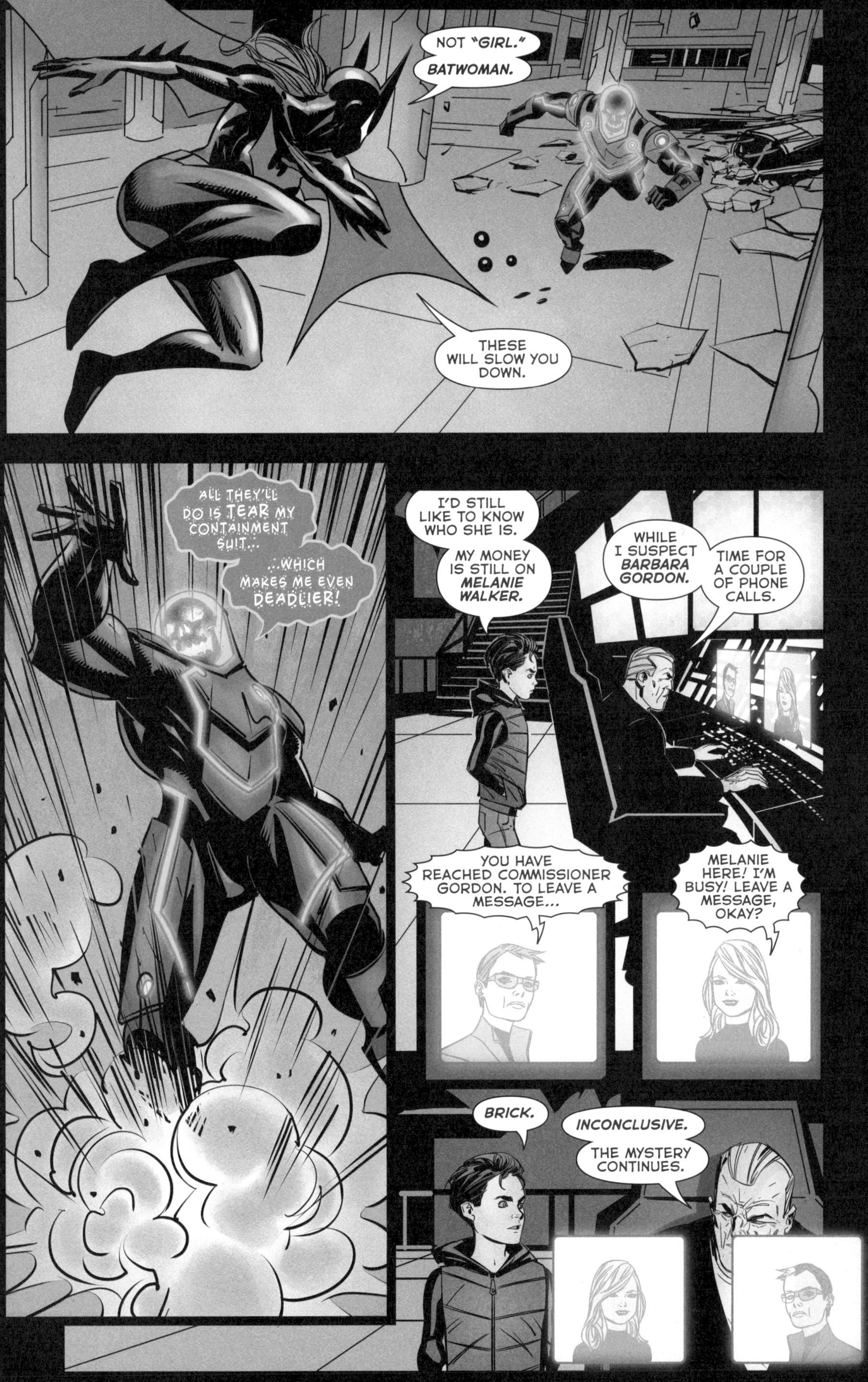
NOT "GIRL." BATWOMAN.
THESE WILL SLOW YOU DOWN.
ALL THEY'LL DO IS TEAR MY CONTAINMENT SUIT...
...WHICH MAKES ME EVEN DEADLIER!
I'D STILL LIKE TO KNOW WHO SHE IS.
MY MONEY IS STILL ON MELANIE WALKER.
WHILE I SUSPECT BARBARA GORDON.
TIME FOR A COUPLE OF PHONE CALLS.
YOU HAVE REACHED COMMISSIONER GORDON. TO LEAVE A MESSAGE...
MELANIE HERE! I'M BUSY! LEAVE A MESSAGE, OKAY?
BRICK.
INCONCLUSIVE.
THE MYSTERY CONTINUES.

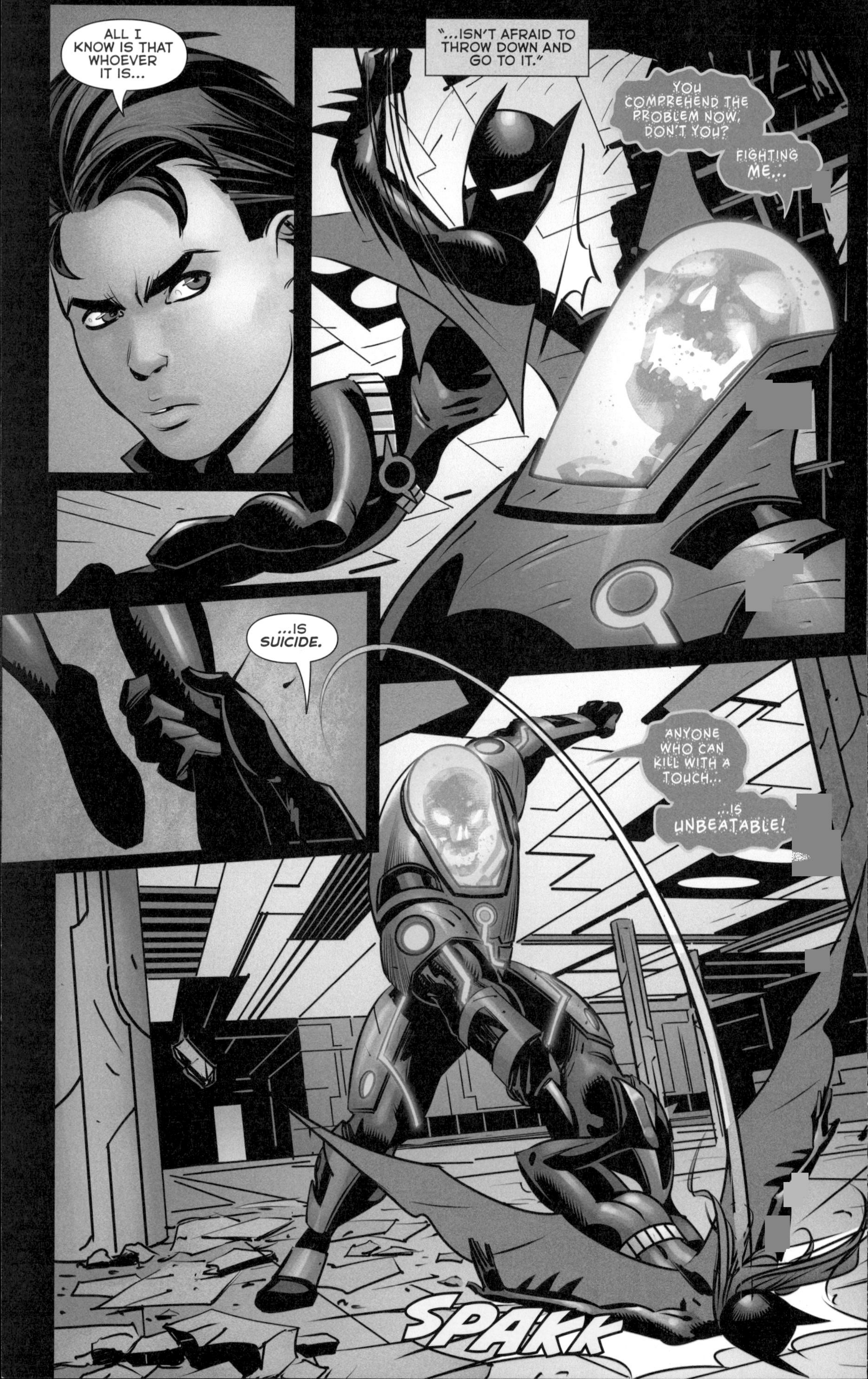
ALL I KNOW IS THAT WHOEVER IT IS...
"...ISN'T AFRAID TO THROW DOWN AND GO TO IT."
YOU COMPREHEND THE PROBLEM NOW, DON'T YOU?
FIGHTING ME...
...IS SUICIDE.
ANYONE WHO CAN KILL WITH A TOUCH...
...IS UNBEATABLE!
SPAKK

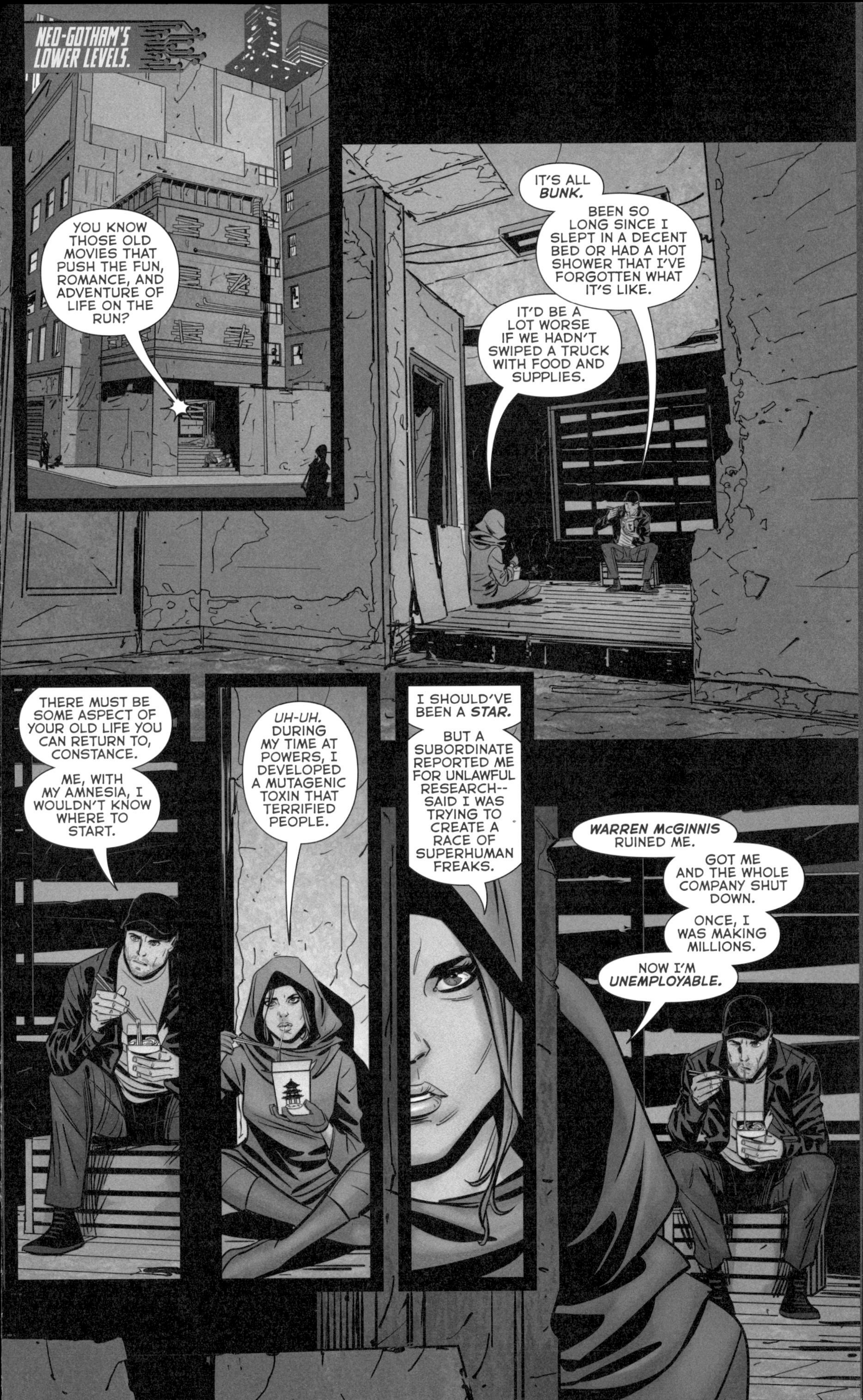
NEO-GOTHAM'S LOWER LEVELS.
YOU KNOW THOSE OLD MOVIES THAT PUSH THE FUN, ROMANCE, AND ADVENTURE OF LIFE ON THE RUN?
IT'S ALL BUNK.
BEEN SO LONG SINCE I SLEPT IN A DECENT BED OR HAD A HOT SHOWER THAT I'VE FORGOTTEN WHAT IT'S LIKE.
IT'D BE A LOT WORSE IF WE HADN'T SWIPED A TRUCK WITH FOOD AND SUPPLIES.
THERE MUST BE SOME ASPECT OF YOUR OLD LIFE YOU CAN RETURN TO, CONSTANCE.
ME, WITH MY AMNESIA, I WOULDN'T KNOW WHERE TO START.
UH-UH. DURING MY TIME AT POWERS, I DEVELOPED A MUTAGENIC TOXIN THAT TERRIFIED PEOPLE.
I SHOULD'VE BEEN A STAR.
BUT A SUBORDINATE REPORTED ME FOR UNLAWFUL RESEARCH--SAID I WAS TRYING TO CREATE A RACE OF SUPERHUMAN FREAKS.
WARREN McGINNIS RUINED ME.
GOT ME AND THE WHOLE COMPANY SHUT DOWN.
ONCE, I WAS MAKING MILLIONS.
NOW I'M UNEMPLOYABLE.

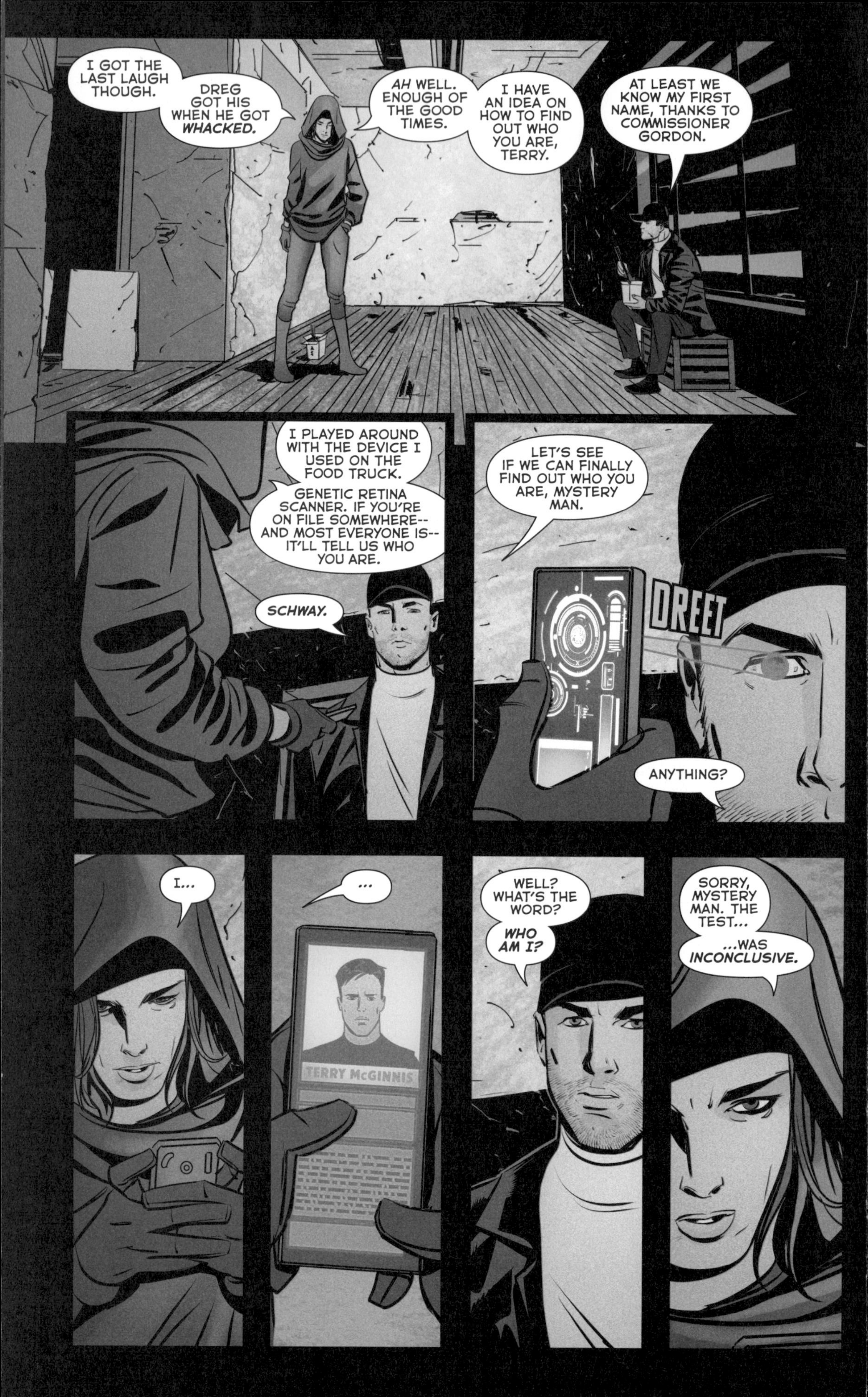
I GOT THE LAST LAUGH THOUGH.
DREG GOT HIS WHEN HE GOT *WHACKED.*
AH WELL. ENOUGH OF THE GOOD TIMES.
I HAVE AN IDEA ON HOW TO FIND OUT WHO YOU ARE, TERRY.
AT LEAST WE KNOW MY FIRST NAME, THANKS TO COMMISSIONER GORDON.
I PLAYED AROUND WITH THE DEVICE I USED ON THE FOOD TRUCK.
GENETIC RETINA SCANNER. IF YOU'RE ON FILE SOMEWHERE--AND MOST EVERYONE IS--IT'LL TELL US WHO YOU ARE.
SCHWAY.
LET'S SEE IF WE CAN FINALLY FIND OUT WHO YOU ARE, MYSTERY MAN.
DREET
ANYTHING?
I...
...
TERRY McGINNIS
WELL? WHAT'S THE WORD?
WHO AM I?
SORRY, MYSTERY MAN. THE TEST...
...WAS *INCONCLUSIVE.*

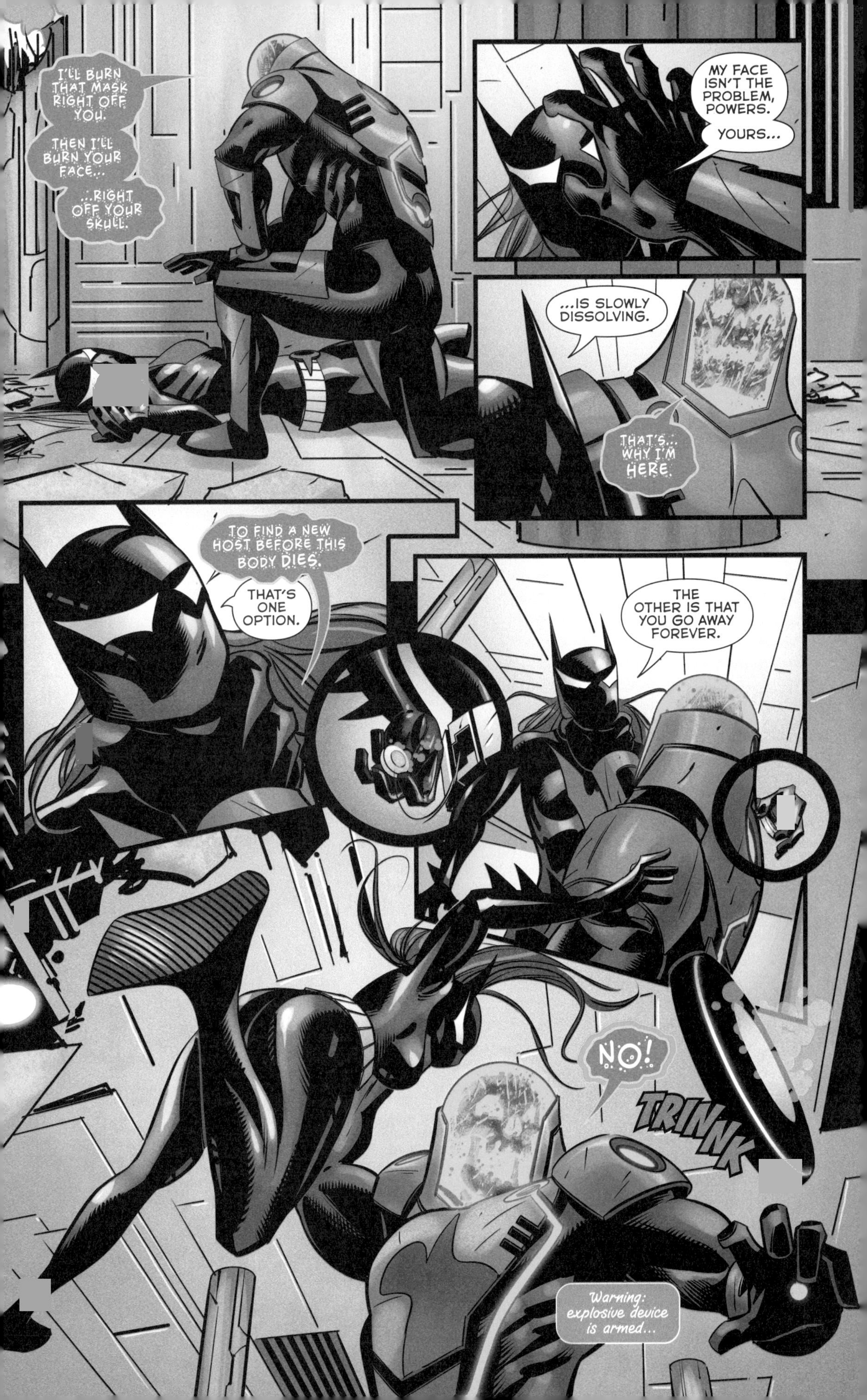
I'LL BURN THAT MASK RIGHT OFF YOU.
THEN I'LL BURN YOUR FACE...
...RIGHT OFF YOUR SKULL.
MY FACE ISN'T THE PROBLEM, POWERS.
YOURS...
...IS SLOWLY DISSOLVING.
THAT'S... WHY I'M HERE.
TO FIND A NEW HOST BEFORE THIS BODY DIES.
THAT'S ONE OPTION.
THE OTHER IS THAT YOU GO AWAY FOREVER.
NO!
TRINNK
Warning: explosive device is armed...

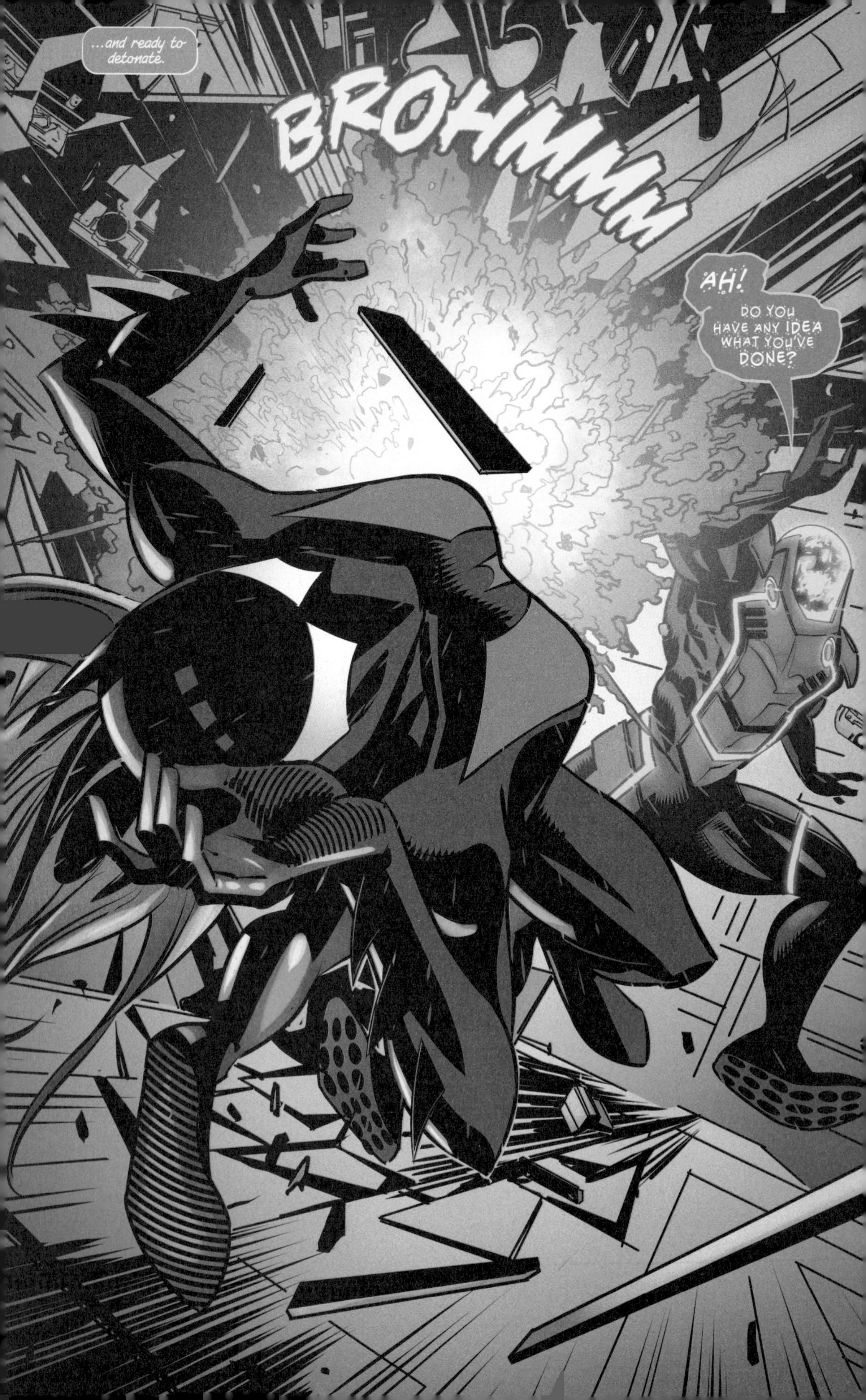
...and ready to detonate.
BROHMMM
AH!
DO YOU HAVE ANY IDEA WHAT YOU'VE DONE?

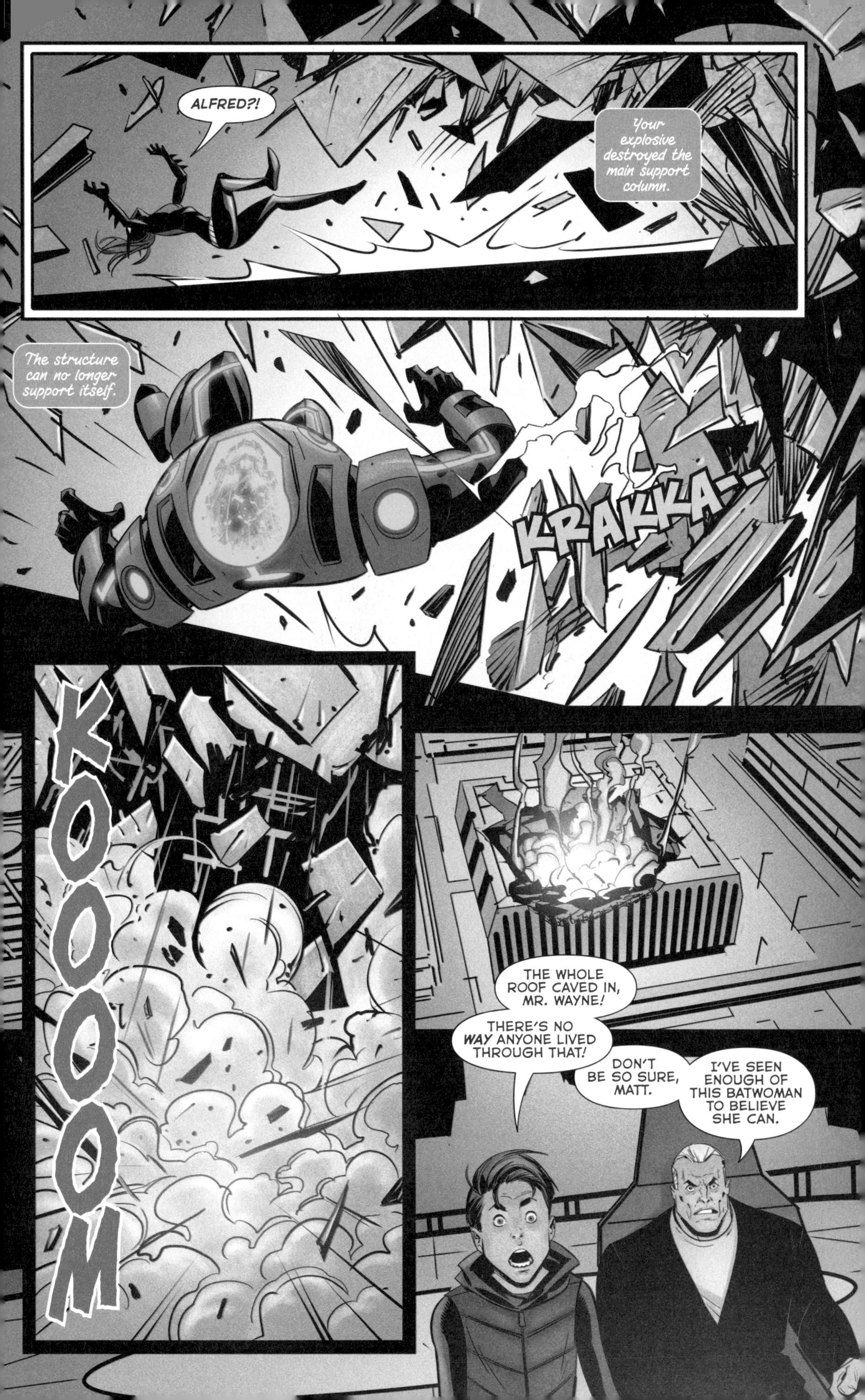
ALFRED?!
Your explosive destroyed the main support column.
The structure can no longer support itself.
KRAKKA--
KOOOOOM
THE WHOLE ROOF CAVED IN, MR. WAYNE!
THERE'S NO *WAY* ANYONE LIVED THROUGH THAT!
DON'T BE SO SURE, MATT.
I'VE SEEN ENOUGH OF THIS BATWOMAN TO BELIEVE SHE CAN.

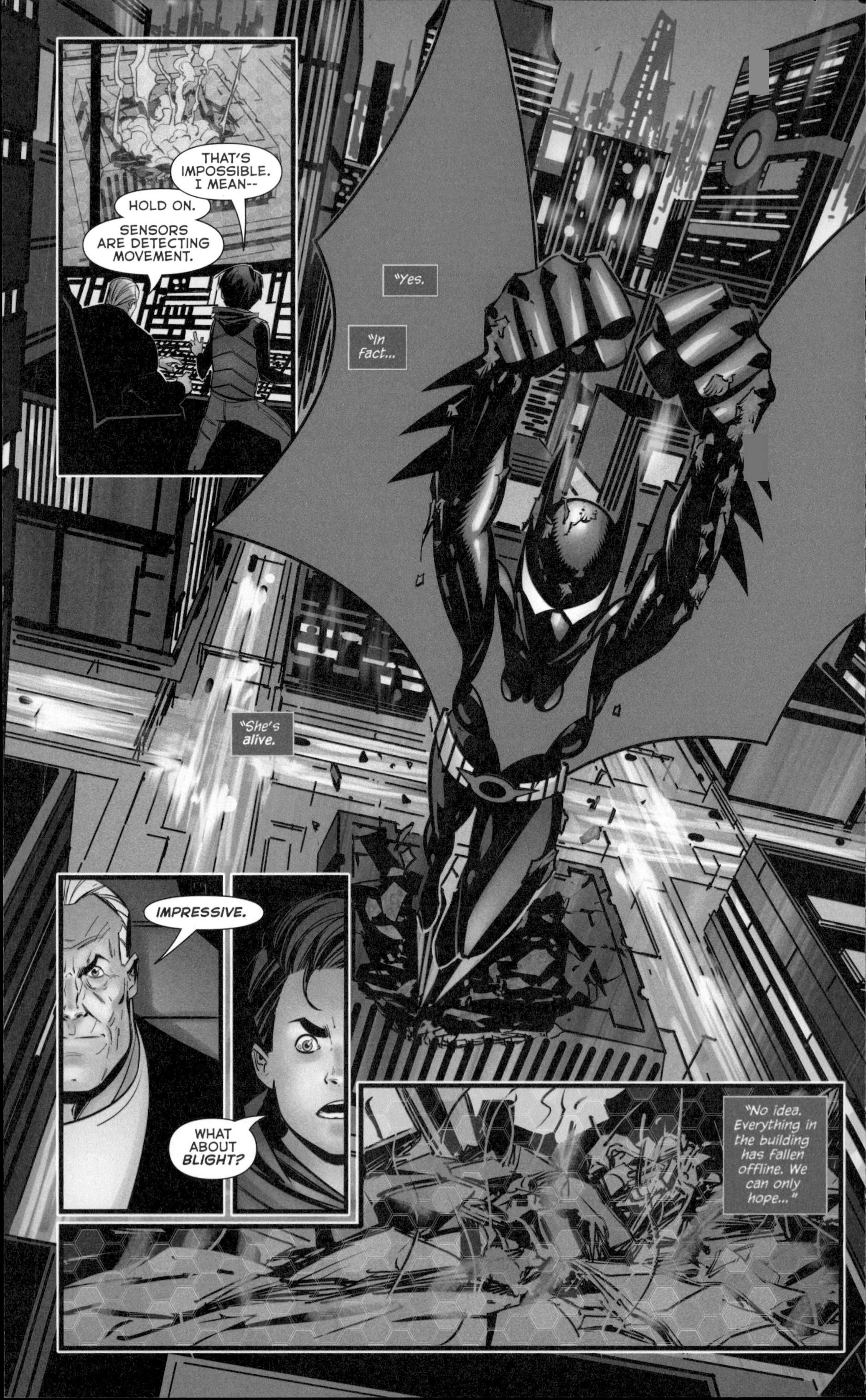
THAT'S IMPOSSIBLE. I MEAN--
HOLD ON.
SENSORS ARE DETECTING MOVEMENT.
"Yes.
"In fact...
"She's alive.
IMPRESSIVE.
WHAT ABOUT BLIGHT?
"No idea. Everything in the building has fallen offline. We can only hope..."

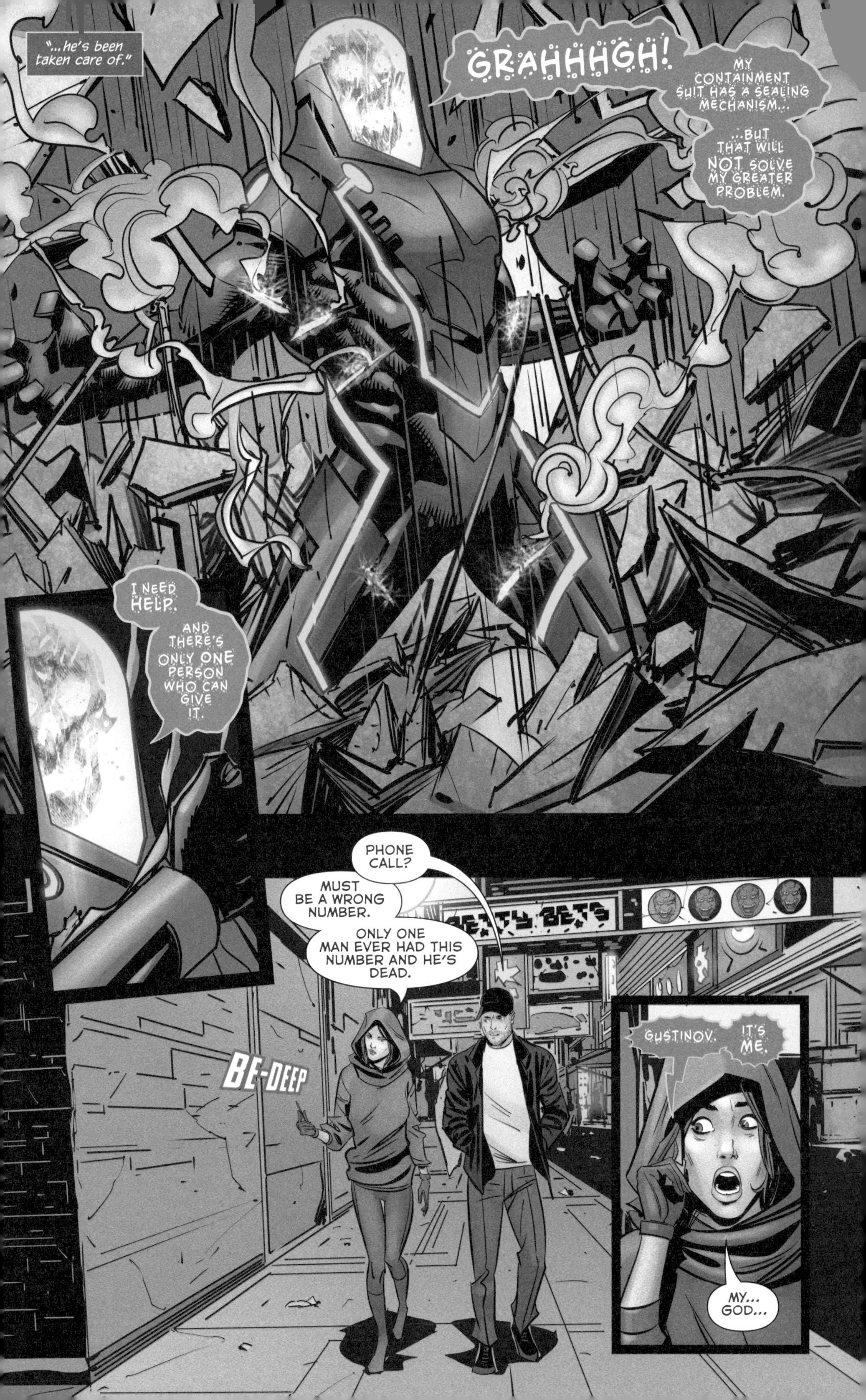
"...he's been taken care of."
GRAHHHGH!
MY CONTAINMENT SUIT HAS A SEALING MECHANISM...
...BUT THAT WILL NOT SOLVE MY GREATER PROBLEM.
I NEED HELP.
AND THERE'S ONLY ONE PERSON WHO CAN GIVE IT.
PHONE CALL?
MUST BE A WRONG NUMBER.
ONLY ONE MAN EVER HAD THIS NUMBER AND HE'S DEAD.
BE-DEEP
GUSTINOV.
IT'S ME.
MY... GOD...

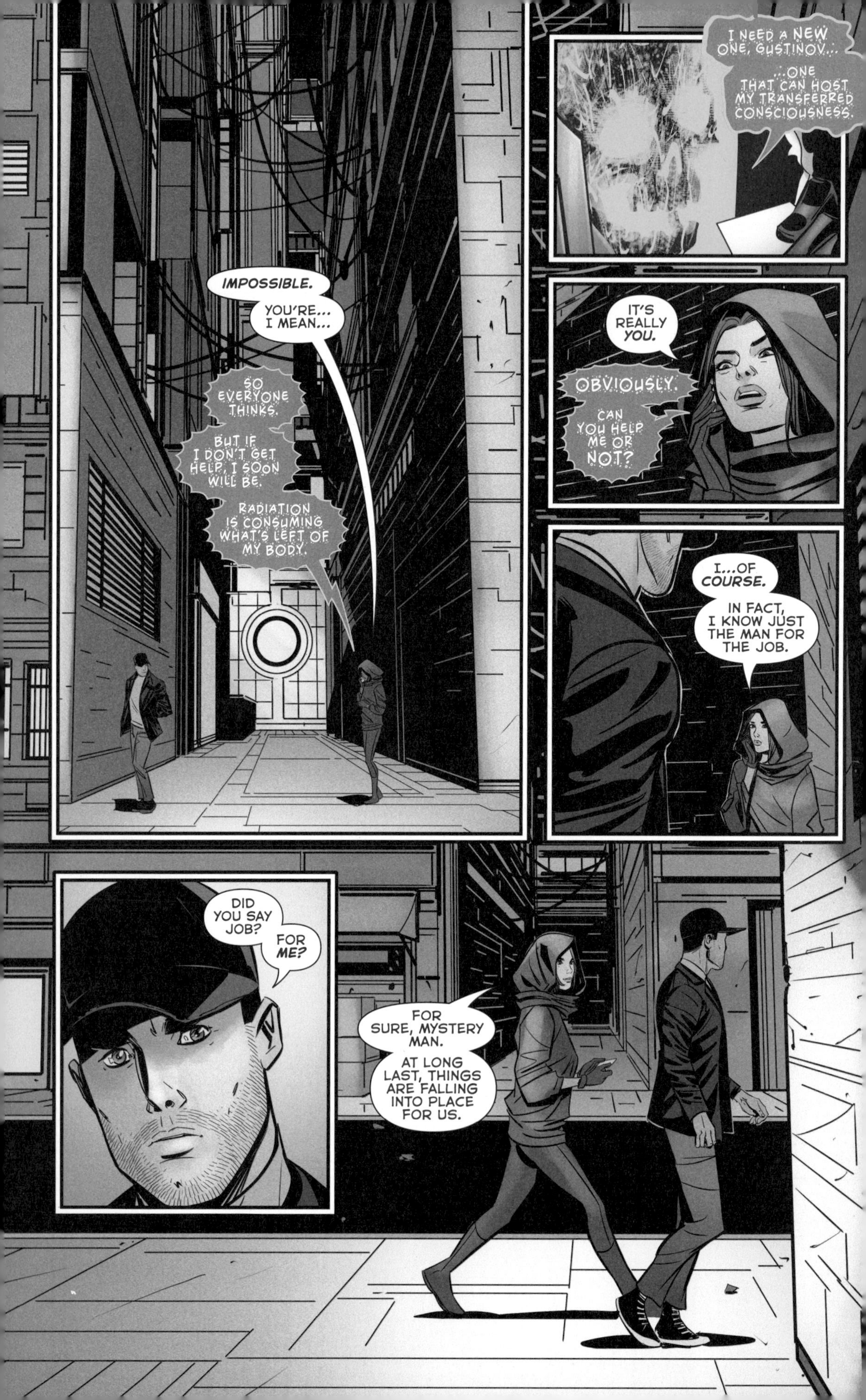
IMPOSSIBLE.
YOU'RE... I MEAN...
SO EVERYONE THINKS.
BUT IF I DON'T GET HELP, I SOON WILL BE.
RADIATION IS CONSUMING WHAT'S LEFT OF MY BODY.
I NEED A NEW ONE, GUSTINOV...
...ONE THAT CAN HOST MY TRANSFERRED CONSCIOUSNESS.
IT'S REALLY YOU.
OBVIOUSLY.
CAN YOU HELP ME OR NOT?
I...OF COURSE.
IN FACT, I KNOW JUST THE MAN FOR THE JOB.
DID YOU SAY JOB?
FOR ME?
FOR SURE, MYSTERY MAN.
AT LONG LAST, THINGS ARE FALLING INTO PLACE FOR US.

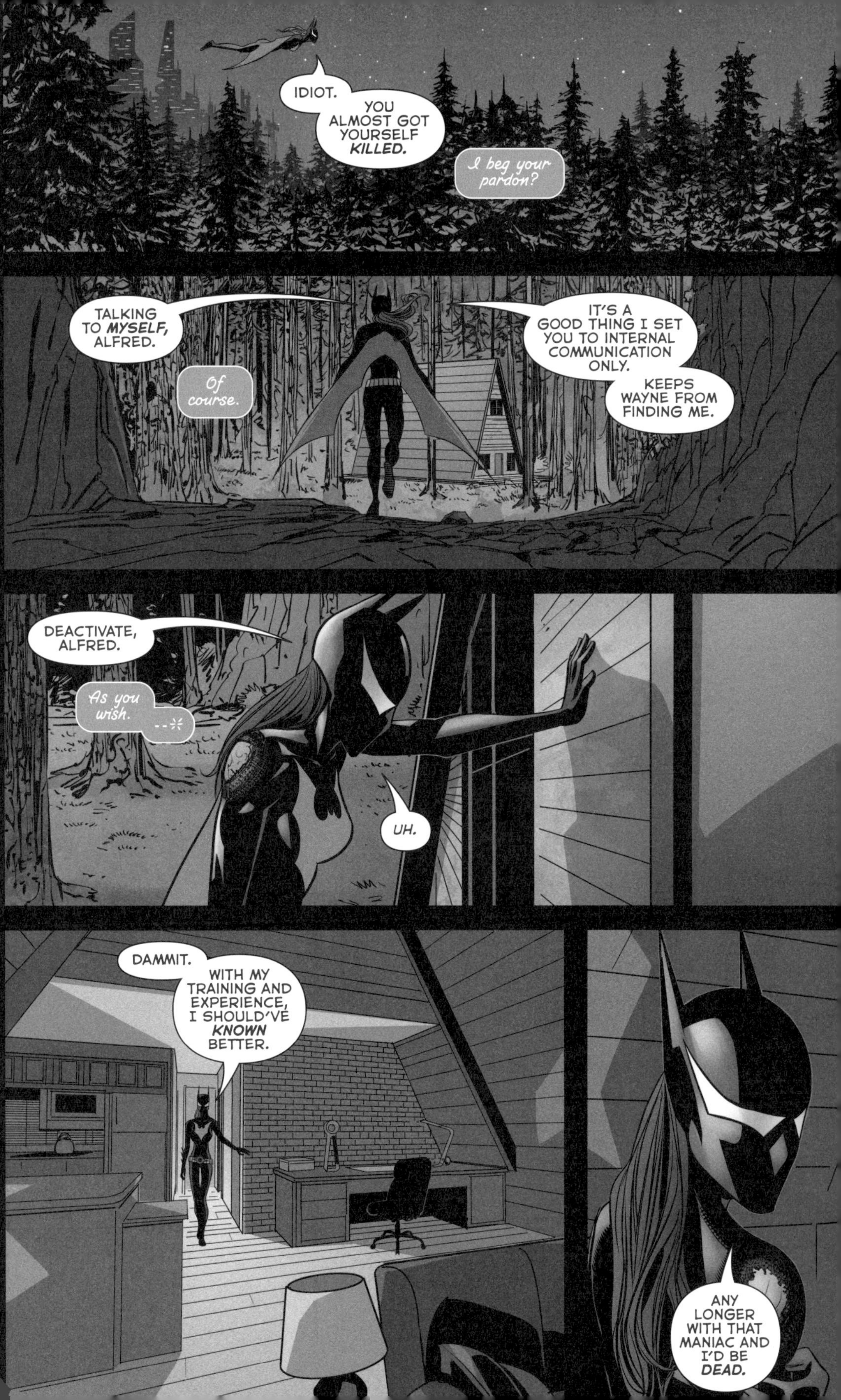

IDIOT.
YOU ALMOST GOT YOURSELF *KILLED.*
I beg your pardon?
TALKING TO *MYSELF,* ALFRED.
IT'S A GOOD THING I SET YOU TO INTERNAL COMMUNICATION ONLY.
KEEPS WAYNE FROM FINDING ME.
Of course.
DEACTIVATE, ALFRED.
As you wish.
UH.
DAMMIT.
WITH MY TRAINING AND EXPERIENCE, I SHOULD'VE *KNOWN* BETTER.
ANY LONGER WITH THAT MANIAC AND I'D BE *DEAD.*

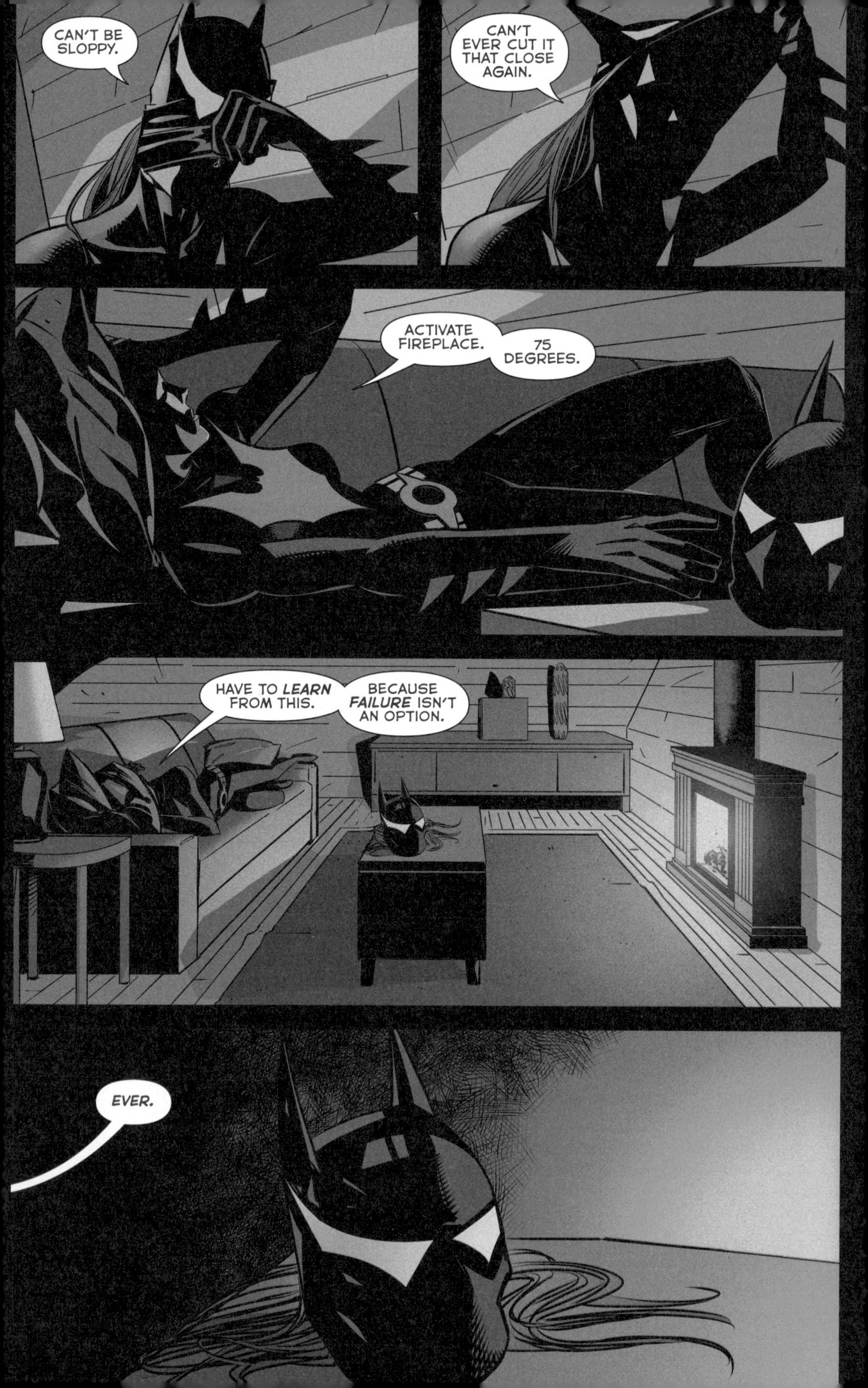

CAN'T BE SLOPPY.
CAN'T EVER CUT IT THAT CLOSE AGAIN.
ACTIVATE FIREPLACE.
75 DEGREES.
HAVE TO *LEARN* FROM THIS.
BECAUSE *FAILURE* ISN'T AN OPTION.
EVER.

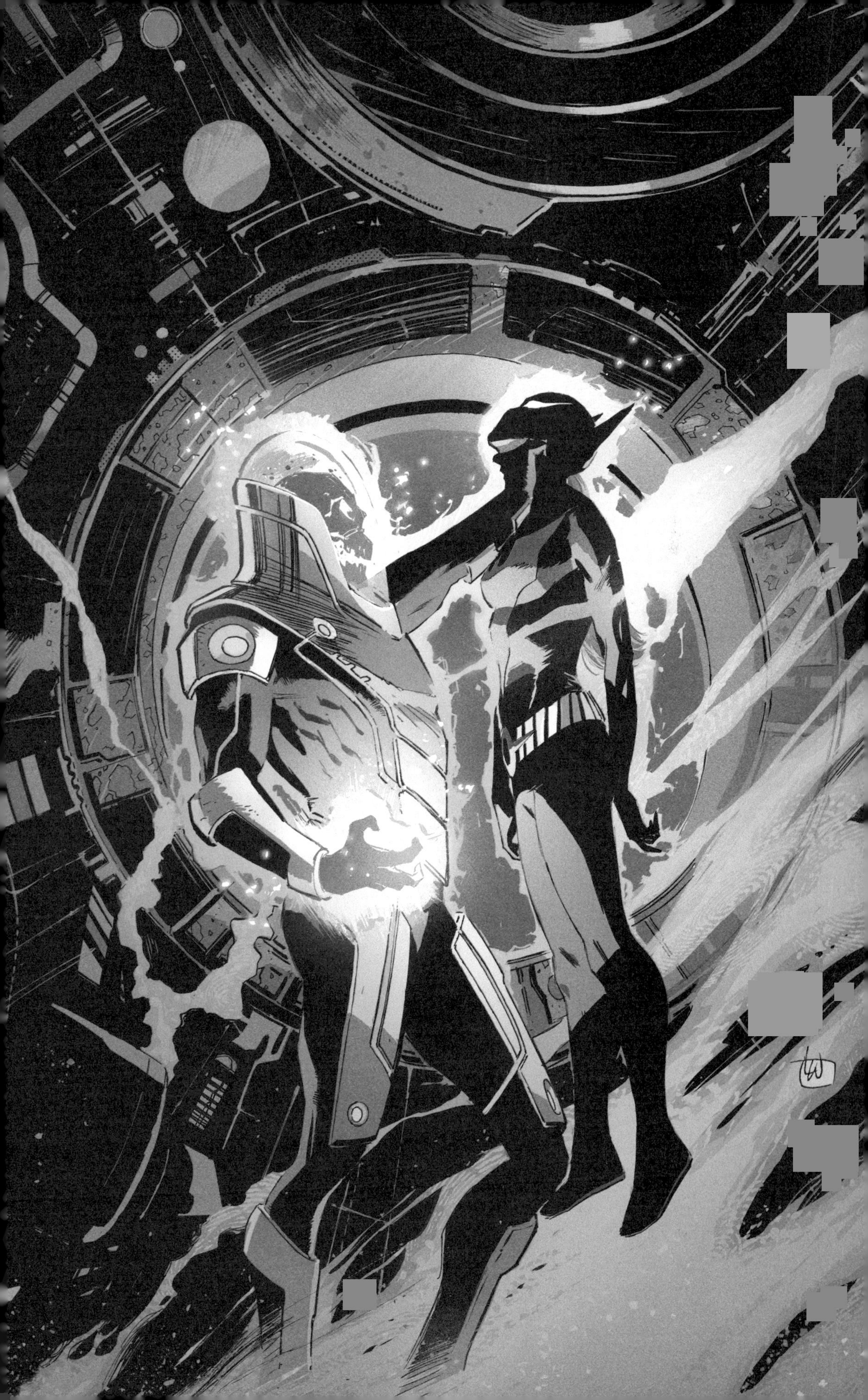

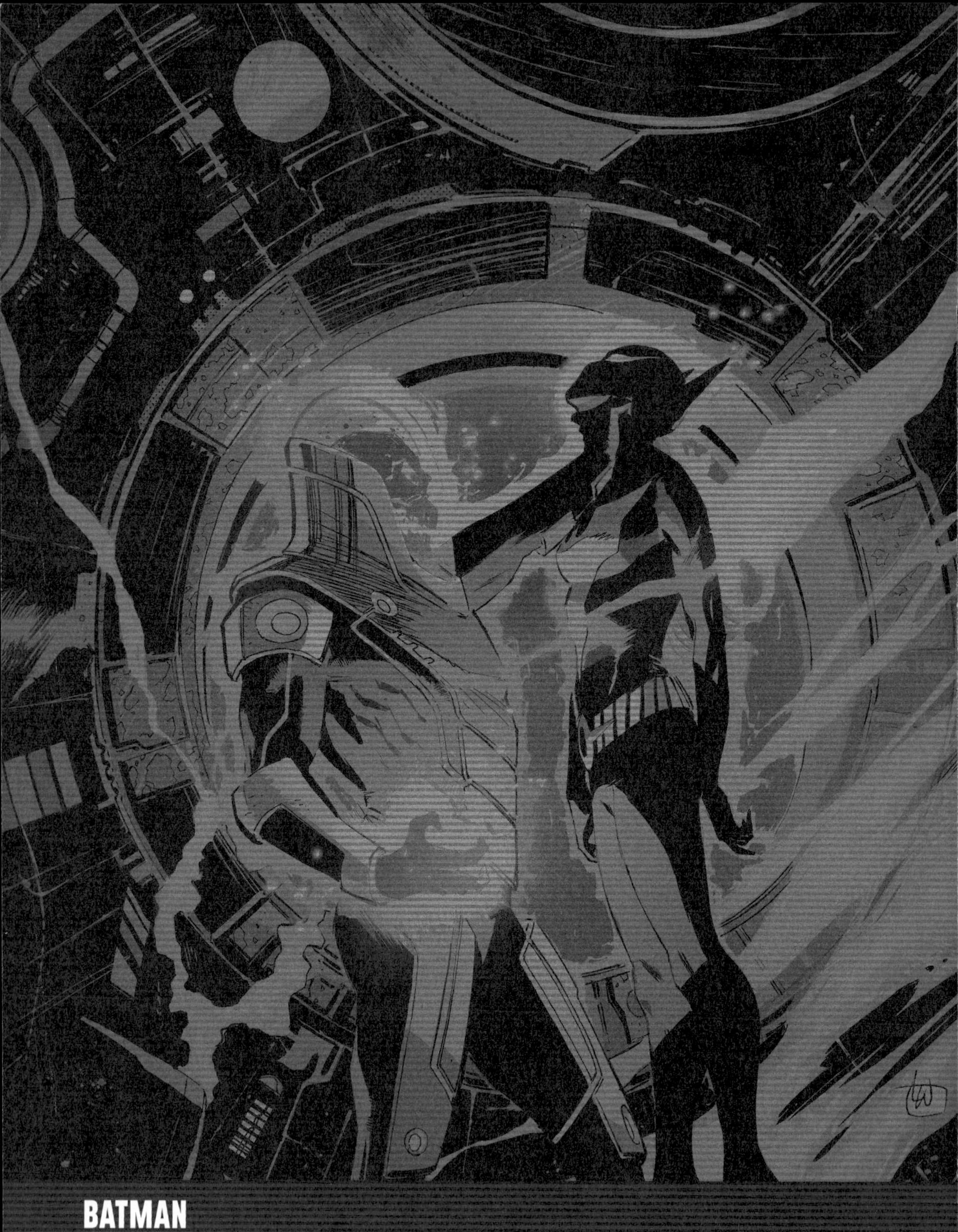

BATMAN
BEYOND
#40

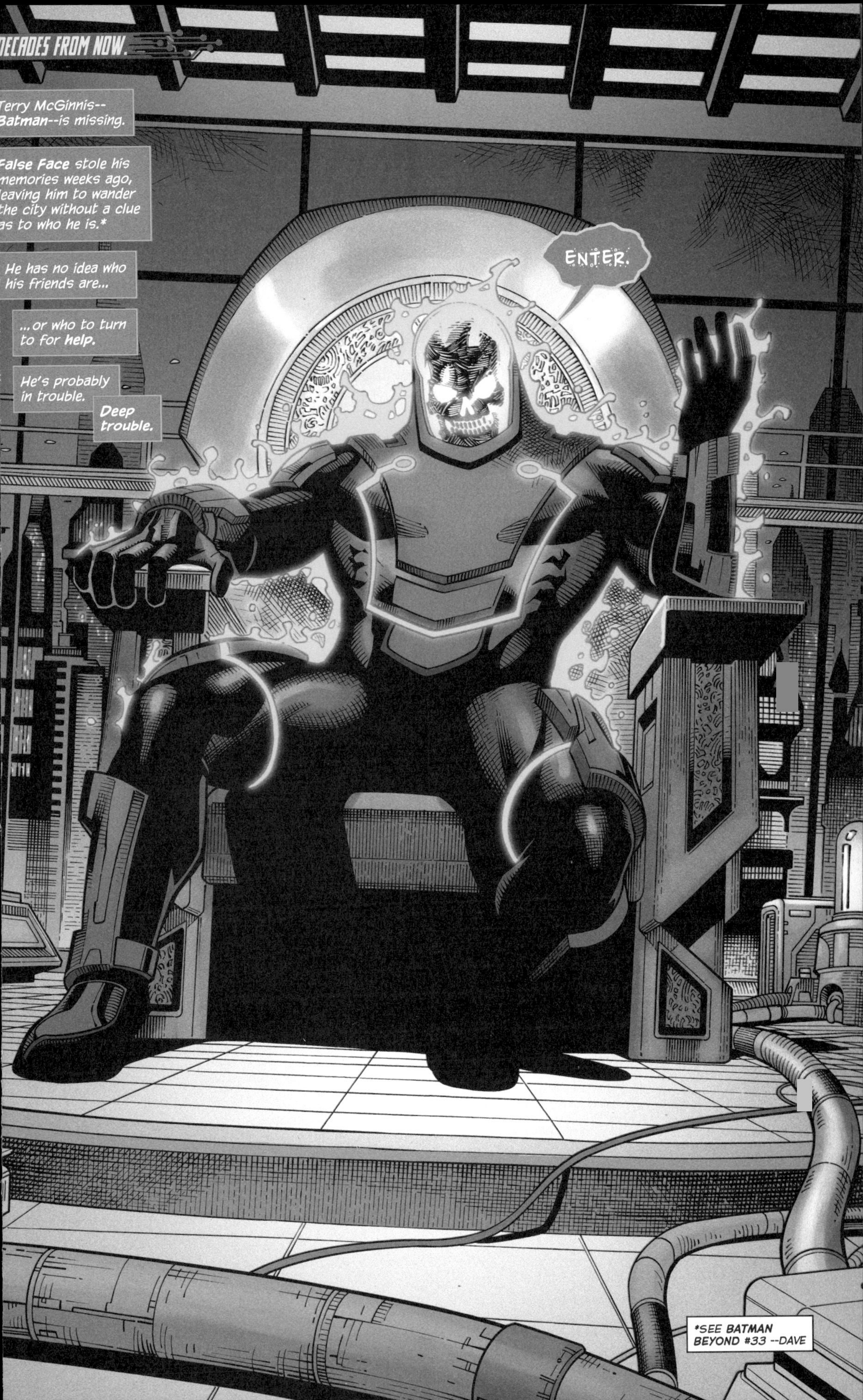

DECADES FROM NOW.
Terry McGinnis--Batman--is missing.
False Face stole his memories weeks ago, leaving him to wander the city without a clue as to who he is.*
He has no idea who his friends are...
...or who to turn to for help.
He's probably in trouble.
Deep trouble.
ENTER.
*SEE BATMAN BEYOND #33 --DAVE

DEREK. IT'S REALLY YOU. ALIVE.

IF YOU CAN CALL THIS LIVING.

I'M STILL HERE, THOUGH YOU SHOULD REMEMBER THAT, AFFLICTED AS I AM, I PREFER TO BE CALLED BLIGHT.

As if amnesia weren't enough to deal with, McGinnis is wanted for *murder*.

He can't possibly be guilty, but we can assume he's fallen in with a bad crowd.

IF I'D KNOWN YOU WERE ALIVE, I WOULD HAVE COME LOOKING FOR YOU.

BUT THE POLICE SAID YOU WERE *DEAD.*

SO THEY THOUGHT, BUT YOU CAN'T *KILL* RADIATION.

WHO'S YOUR FRIEND?

MYSTERY MAN. FOUND HIM WANDERING THE STREETS.

LOST IN A HAZE OF *AMNESIA.*

STUMBLED INTO *CONSTANCE* AND SHE'S BEEN HELPING ME EVER SINCE.

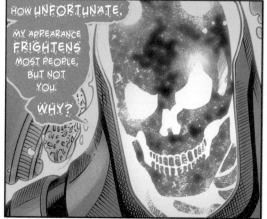

HOW *UNFORTUNATE.*

MY APPEARANCE *FRIGHTENS* MOST PEOPLE, BUT NOT YOU.

WHY?

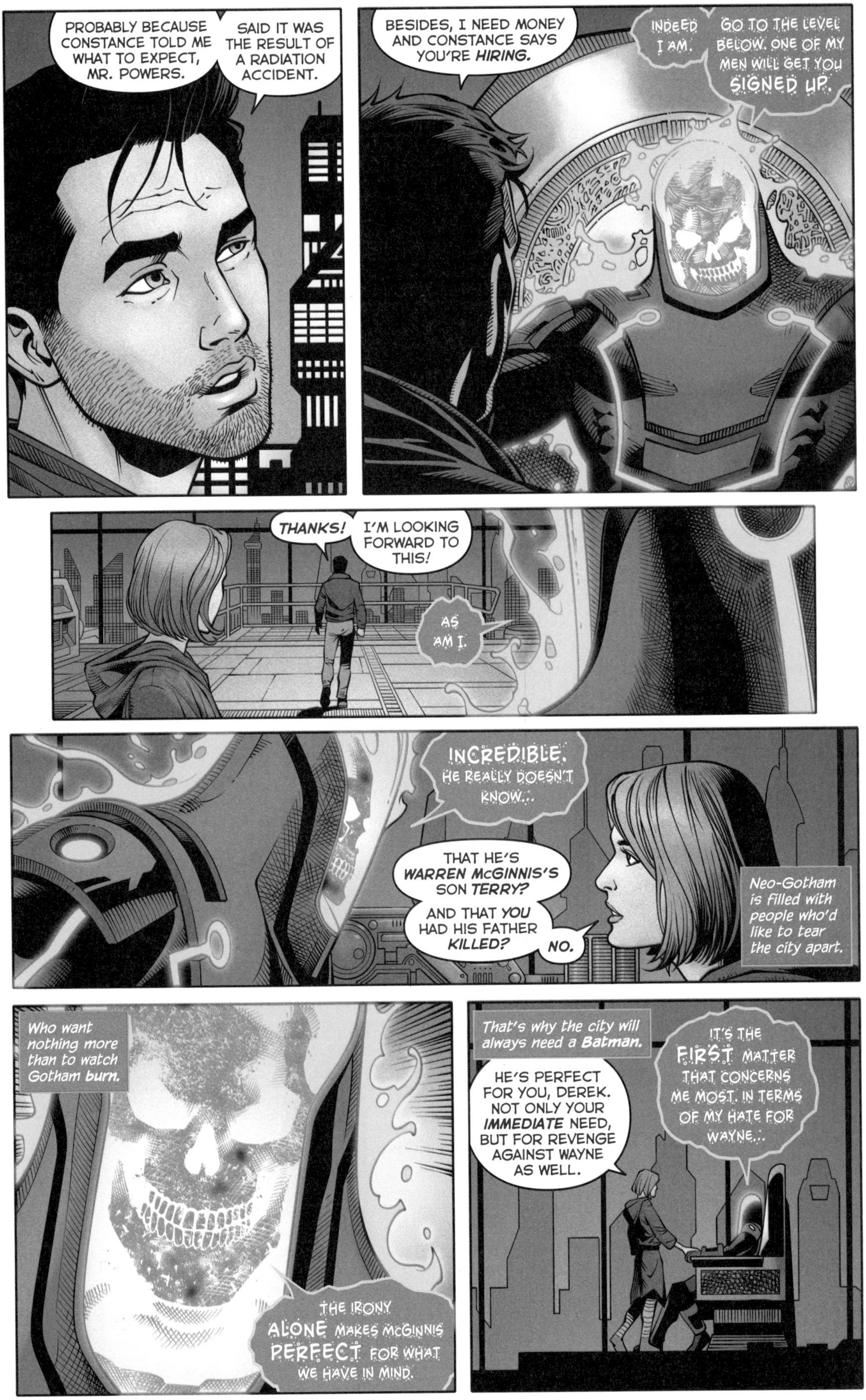
PROBABLY BECAUSE CONSTANCE TOLD ME WHAT TO EXPECT, MR. POWERS.
SAID IT WAS THE RESULT OF A RADIATION ACCIDENT.
BESIDES, I NEED MONEY AND CONSTANCE SAYS YOU'RE HIRING.
INDEED I AM.
GO TO THE LEVEL BELOW. ONE OF MY MEN WILL GET YOU SIGNED UP.
THANKS!
I'M LOOKING FORWARD TO THIS!
AS AM I.
INCREDIBLE. HE REALLY DOESN'T KNOW...
THAT HE'S WARREN McGINNIS'S SON TERRY?
AND THAT YOU HAD HIS FATHER KILLED?
NO.
Neo-Gotham is filled with people who'd like to tear the city apart.
Who want nothing more than to watch Gotham burn.
THE IRONY ALONE MAKES McGINNIS PERFECT FOR WHAT WE HAVE IN MIND.
That's why the city will always need a Batman.
HE'S PERFECT FOR YOU, DEREK. NOT ONLY YOUR IMMEDIATE NEED, BUT FOR REVENGE AGAINST WAYNE AS WELL.
IT'S THE FIRST MATTER THAT CONCERNS ME MOST, IN TERMS OF MY HATE FOR WAYNE...

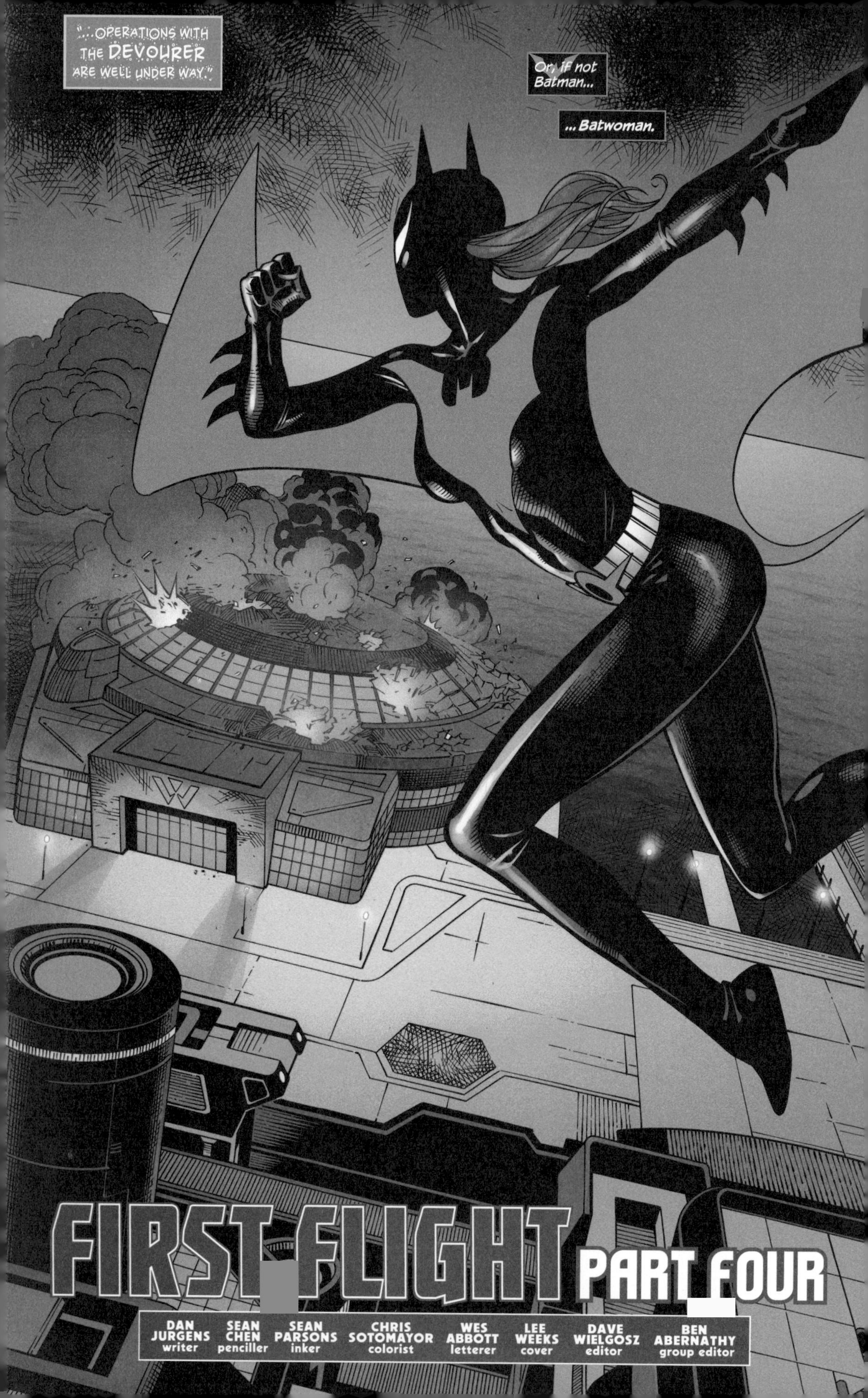
"...OPERATIONS WITH THE DEVOURER ARE WELL UNDER WAY."
Or, if not Batman...
...Batwoman.
FIRST FLIGHT PART FOUR
DAN JURGENS writer
SEAN CHEN penciller
SEAN PARSONS inker
CHRIS SOTOMAYOR colorist
WES ABBOTT letterer
LEE WEEKS cover
DAVE WIELGOSZ editor
BEN ABERNATHY group editor

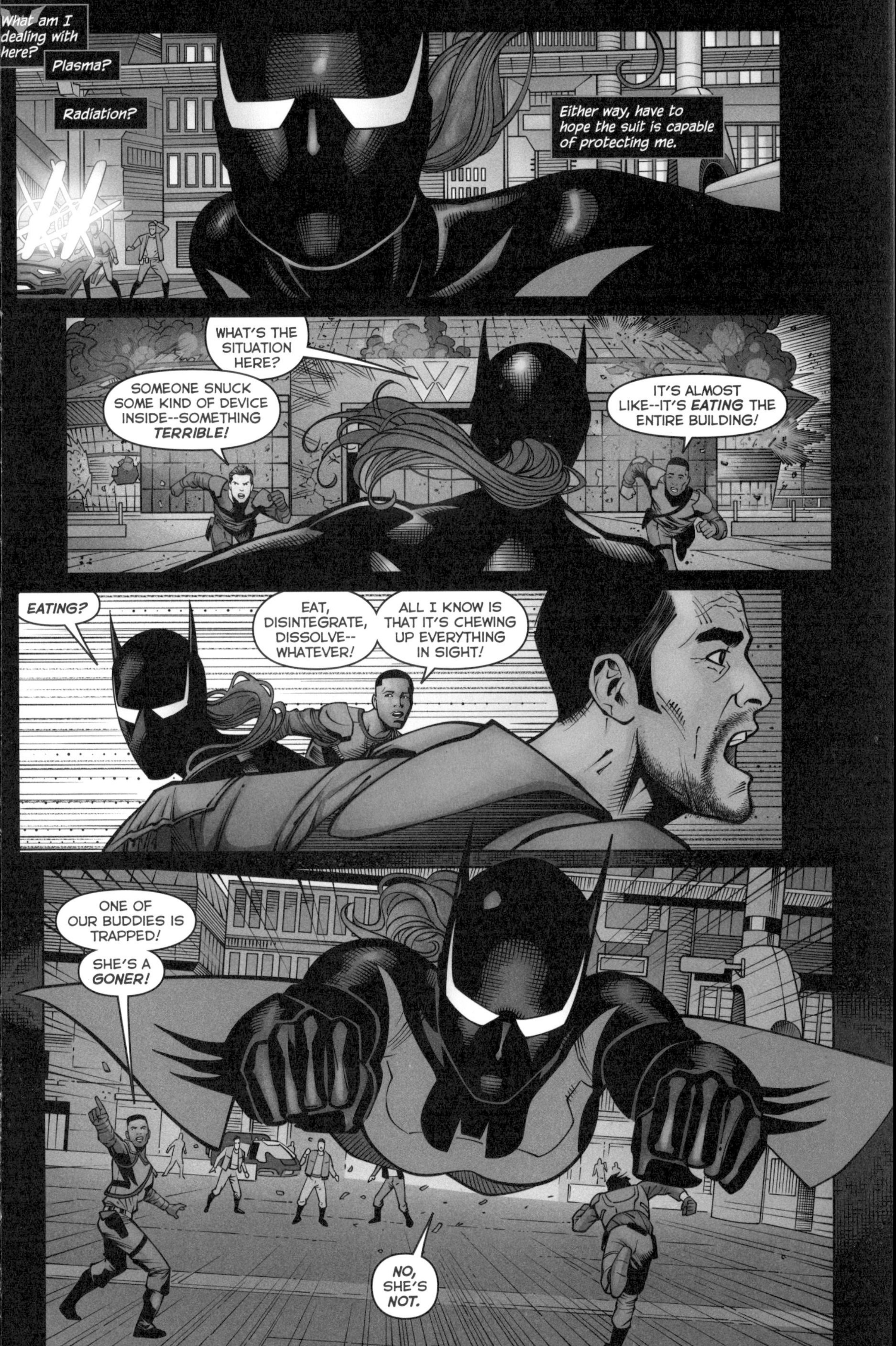
What am I dealing with here?
Plasma?
Radiation?
Either way, have to hope the suit is capable of protecting me.
WHAT'S THE SITUATION HERE?
SOMEONE SNUCK SOME KIND OF DEVICE INSIDE--SOMETHING TERRIBLE!
IT'S ALMOST LIKE--IT'S EATING THE ENTIRE BUILDING!
EATING?
EAT, DISINTEGRATE, DISSOLVE--WHATEVER!
ALL I KNOW IS THAT IT'S CHEWING UP EVERYTHING IN SIGHT!
ONE OF OUR BUDDIES IS TRAPPED!
SHE'S A GONER!
NO, SHE'S NOT.

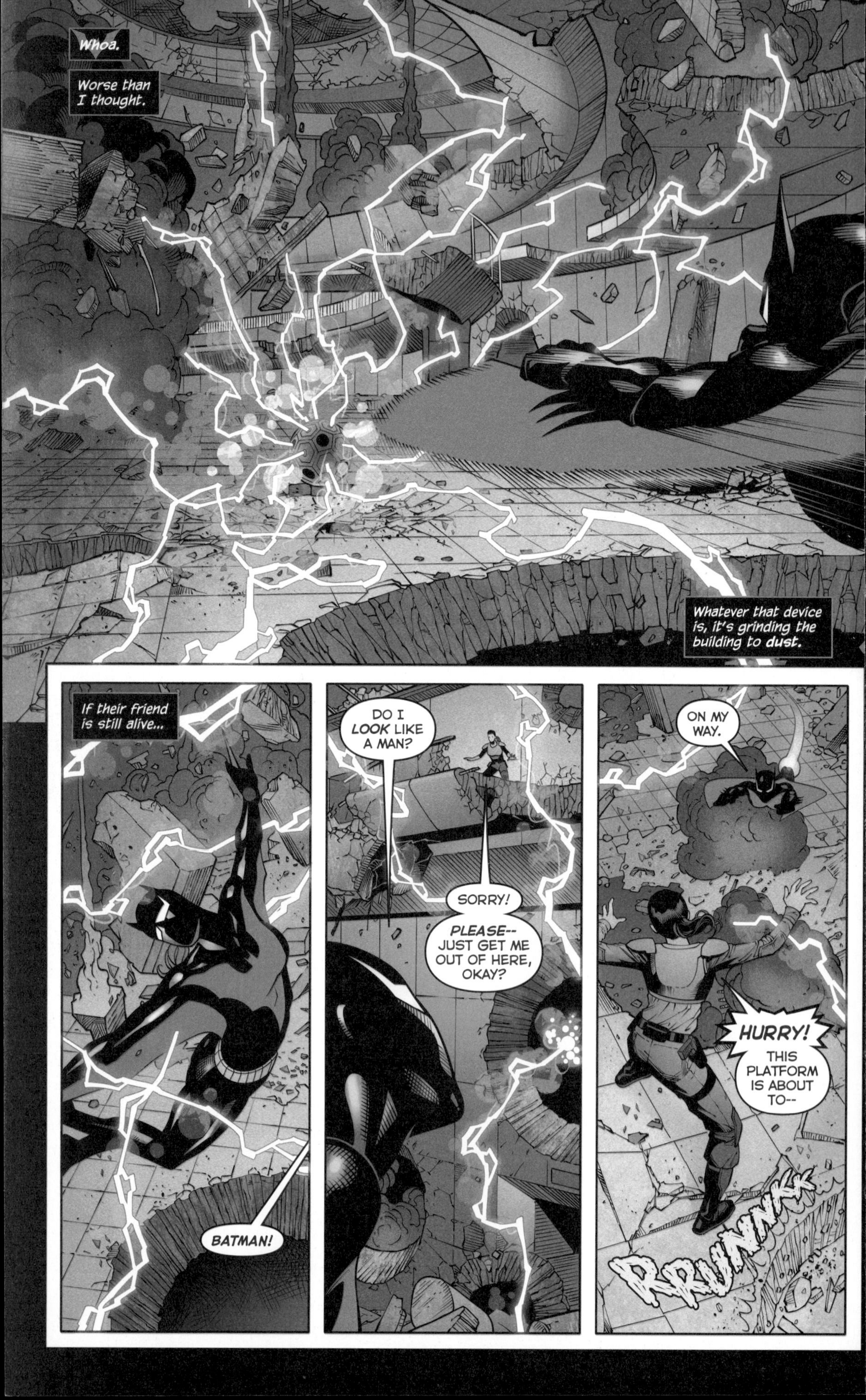

Whoa.
Worse than I thought.
Whatever that device is, it's grinding the building to dust.
If their friend is still alive...
BATMAN!
DO I LOOK LIKE A MAN?
SORRY!
PLEASE-- JUST GET ME OUT OF HERE, OKAY?
ON MY WAY.
HURRY!
THIS PLATFORM IS ABOUT TO--
RRUNNKK

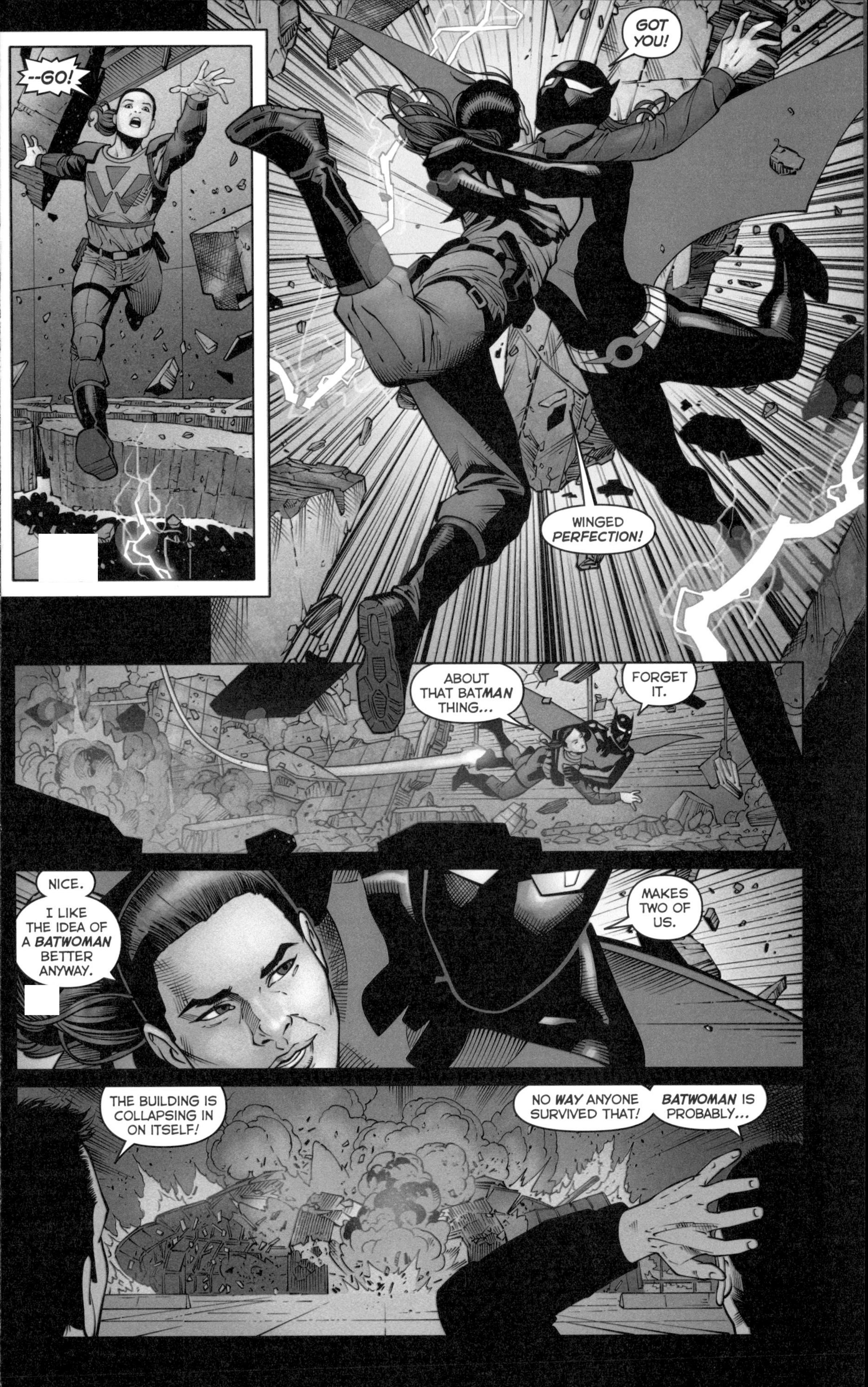
--GO!
GOT YOU!
WINGED PERFECTION!
ABOUT THAT BATMAN THING...
FORGET IT.
NICE.
I LIKE THE IDEA OF A BATWOMAN BETTER ANYWAY.
MAKES TWO OF US.
THE BUILDING IS COLLAPSING IN ON ITSELF!
NO WAY ANYONE SURVIVED THAT!
BATWOMAN IS PROBABLY...

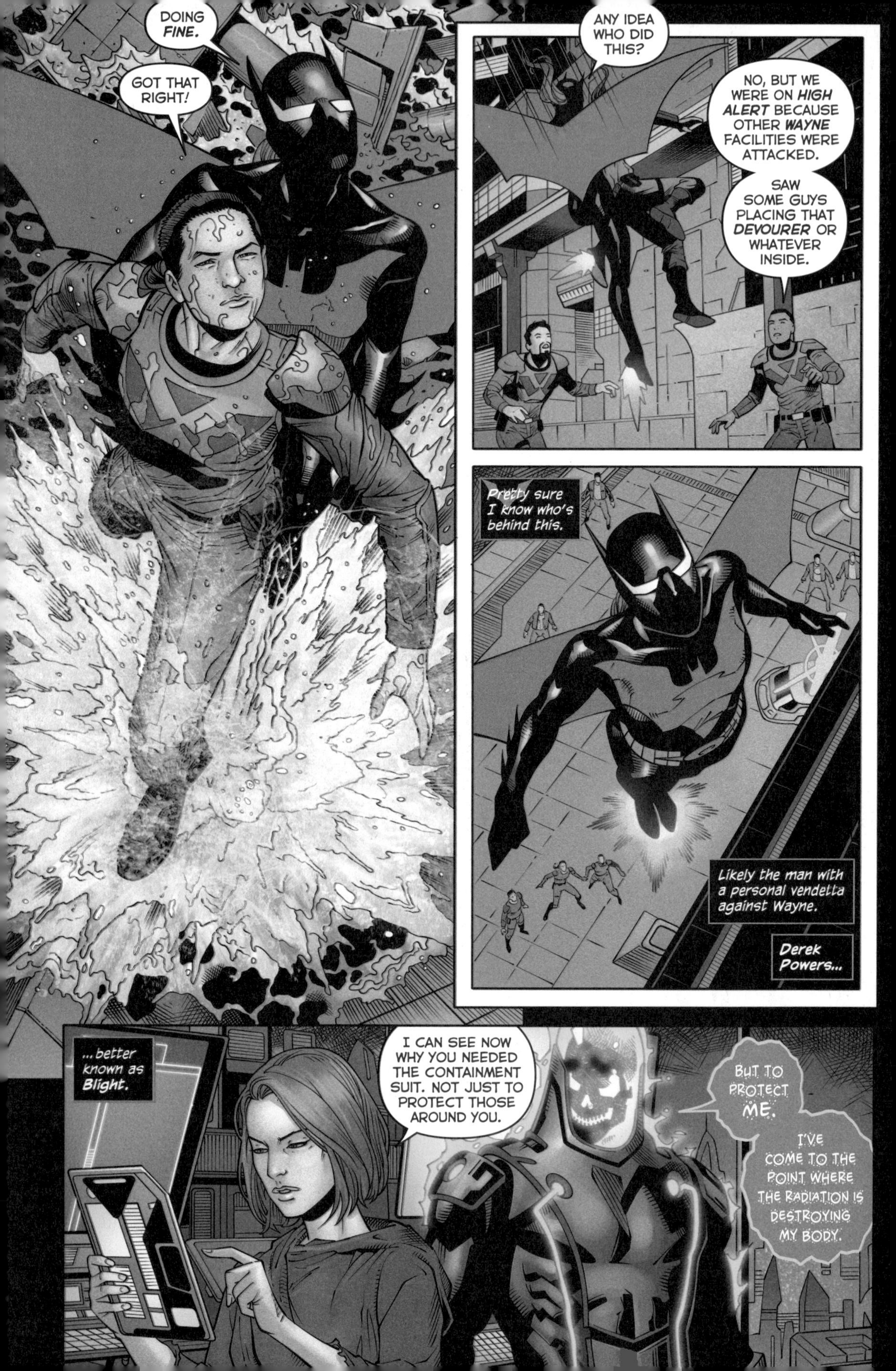
DOING FINE.
GOT THAT RIGHT!
ANY IDEA WHO DID THIS?
NO, BUT WE WERE ON HIGH ALERT BECAUSE OTHER WAYNE FACILITIES WERE ATTACKED.
SAW SOME GUYS PLACING THAT DEVOURER OR WHATEVER INSIDE.
Pretty sure I know who's behind this.
Likely the man with a personal vendetta against Wayne.
Derek Powers...
...better known as Blight.
I CAN SEE NOW WHY YOU NEEDED THE CONTAINMENT SUIT. NOT JUST TO PROTECT THOSE AROUND YOU.
BUT TO PROTECT ME.
I'VE COME TO THE POINT WHERE THE RADIATION IS DESTROYING MY BODY.

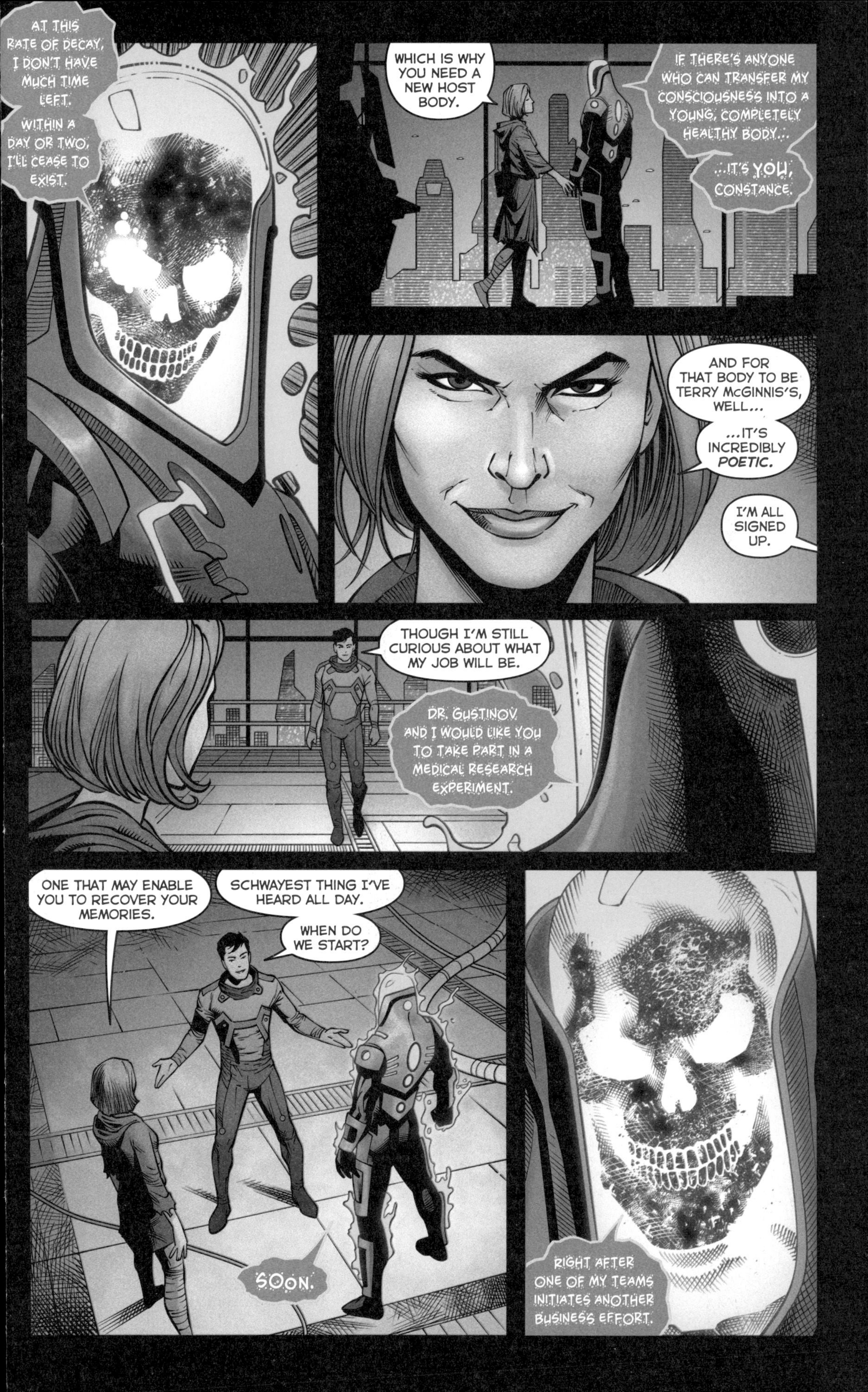
AT THIS RATE OF DECAY, I DON'T HAVE MUCH TIME LEFT.
WITHIN A DAY OR TWO, I'LL CEASE TO EXIST.
WHICH IS WHY YOU NEED A NEW HOST BODY.
IF THERE'S ANYONE WHO CAN TRANSFER MY CONSCIOUSNESS INTO A YOUNG, COMPLETELY HEALTHY BODY...
...IT'S YOU, CONSTANCE.
AND FOR THAT BODY TO BE TERRY McGINNIS'S, WELL...
...IT'S INCREDIBLY POETIC.
I'M ALL SIGNED UP.
THOUGH I'M STILL CURIOUS ABOUT WHAT MY JOB WILL BE.
DR. GUSTINOV AND I WOULD LIKE YOU TO TAKE PART IN A MEDICAL RESEARCH EXPERIMENT.
ONE THAT MAY ENABLE YOU TO RECOVER YOUR MEMORIES.
SCHWAYEST THING I'VE HEARD ALL DAY.
WHEN DO WE START?
SOON.
RIGHT AFTER ONE OF MY TEAMS INITIATES ANOTHER BUSINESS EFFORT.

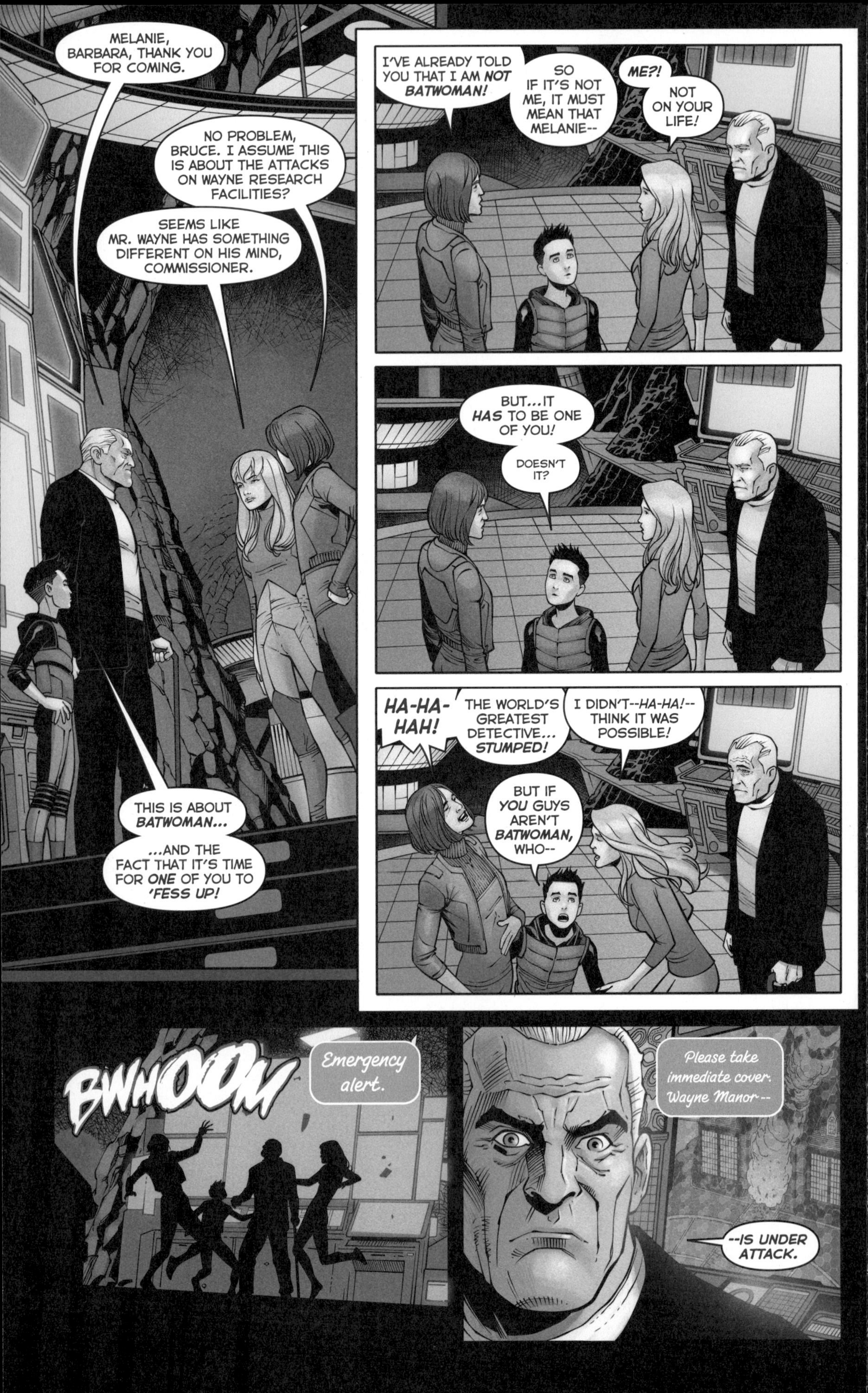
MELANIE, BARBARA, THANK YOU FOR COMING.
NO PROBLEM, BRUCE. I ASSUME THIS IS ABOUT THE ATTACKS ON WAYNE RESEARCH FACILITIES?
SEEMS LIKE MR. WAYNE HAS SOMETHING DIFFERENT ON HIS MIND, COMMISSIONER.
THIS IS ABOUT BATWOMAN...
...AND THE FACT THAT IT'S TIME FOR ONE OF YOU TO 'FESS UP!
I'VE ALREADY TOLD YOU THAT I AM NOT BATWOMAN!
SO IF IT'S NOT ME, IT MUST MEAN THAT MELANIE--
ME?!
NOT ON YOUR LIFE!
BUT...IT HAS TO BE ONE OF YOU!
DOESN'T IT?
HA-HA-HAH!
THE WORLD'S GREATEST DETECTIVE... STUMPED!
I DIDN'T--HA-HA!--THINK IT WAS POSSIBLE!
BUT IF YOU GUYS AREN'T BATWOMAN, WHO--
BWHOOOM
Emergency alert.
Please take immediate cover. Wayne Manor--
--IS UNDER ATTACK.

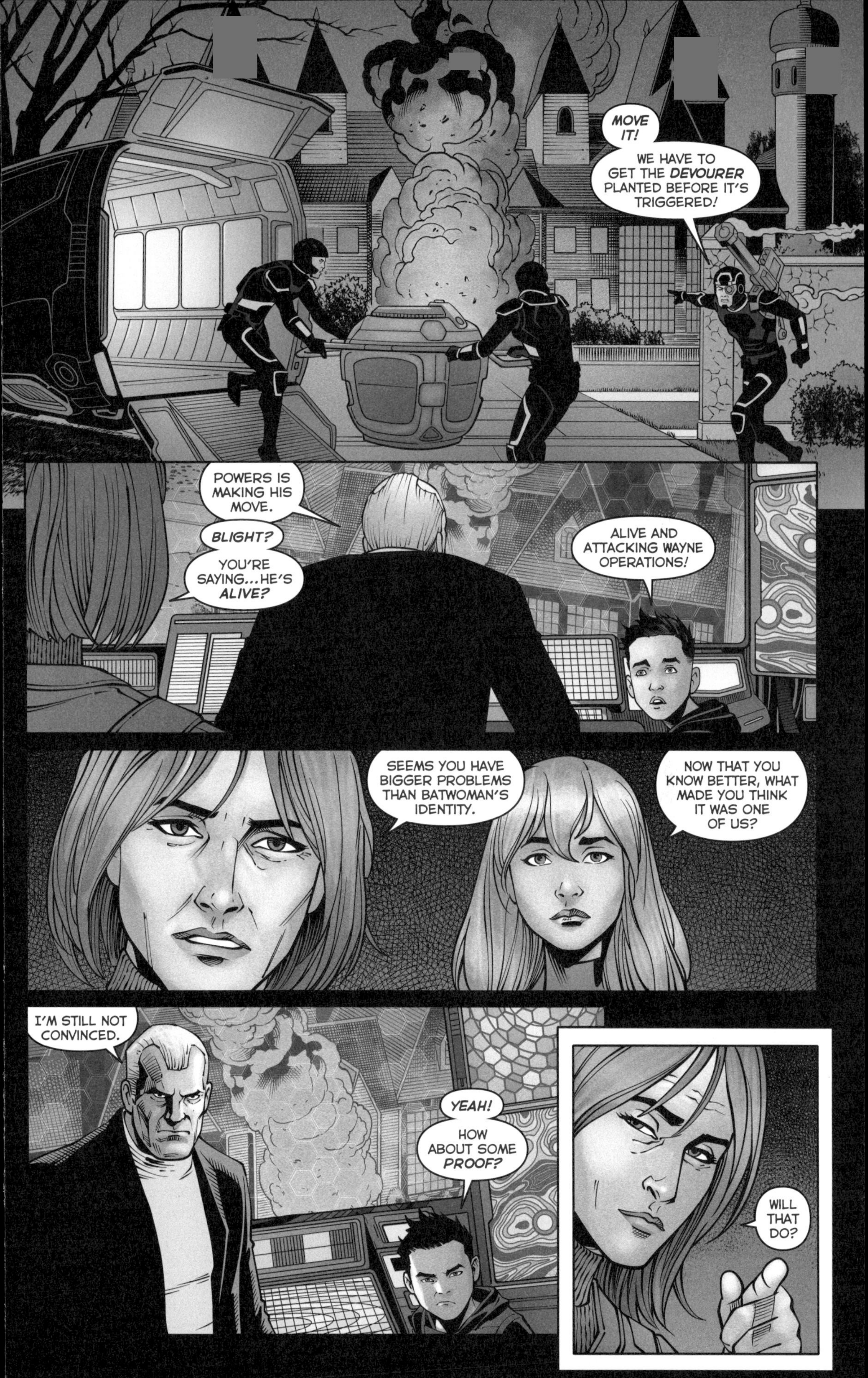
MOVE IT!
WE HAVE TO GET THE DEVOURER PLANTED BEFORE IT'S TRIGGERED!
POWERS IS MAKING HIS MOVE.
BLIGHT?
YOU'RE SAYING...HE'S ALIVE?
ALIVE AND ATTACKING WAYNE OPERATIONS!
SEEMS YOU HAVE BIGGER PROBLEMS THAN BATWOMAN'S IDENTITY.
NOW THAT YOU KNOW BETTER, WHAT MADE YOU THINK IT WAS ONE OF US?
I'M STILL NOT CONVINCED.
YEAH!
HOW ABOUT SOME PROOF?
WILL THAT DO?

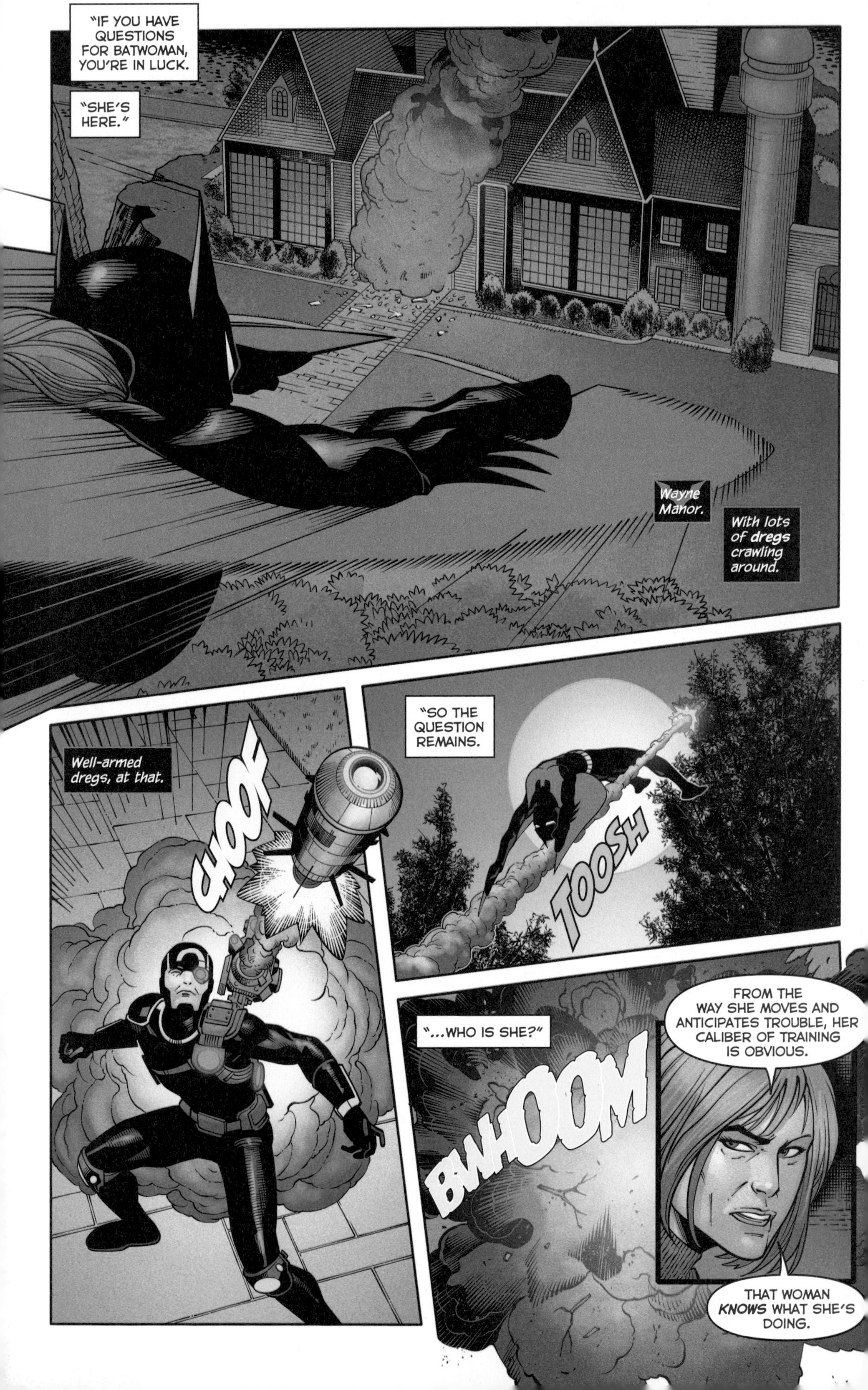
"IF YOU HAVE QUESTIONS FOR BATWOMAN, YOU'RE IN LUCK.
"SHE'S HERE."
Wayne Manor.
With lots of dregs crawling around.
Well-armed dregs, at that.
CHOOF
"SO THE QUESTION REMAINS.
TOOSH
"...WHO IS SHE?"
BWHOOM
FROM THE WAY SHE MOVES AND ANTICIPATES TROUBLE, HER CALIBER OF TRAINING IS OBVIOUS.
THAT WOMAN KNOWS WHAT SHE'S DOING.

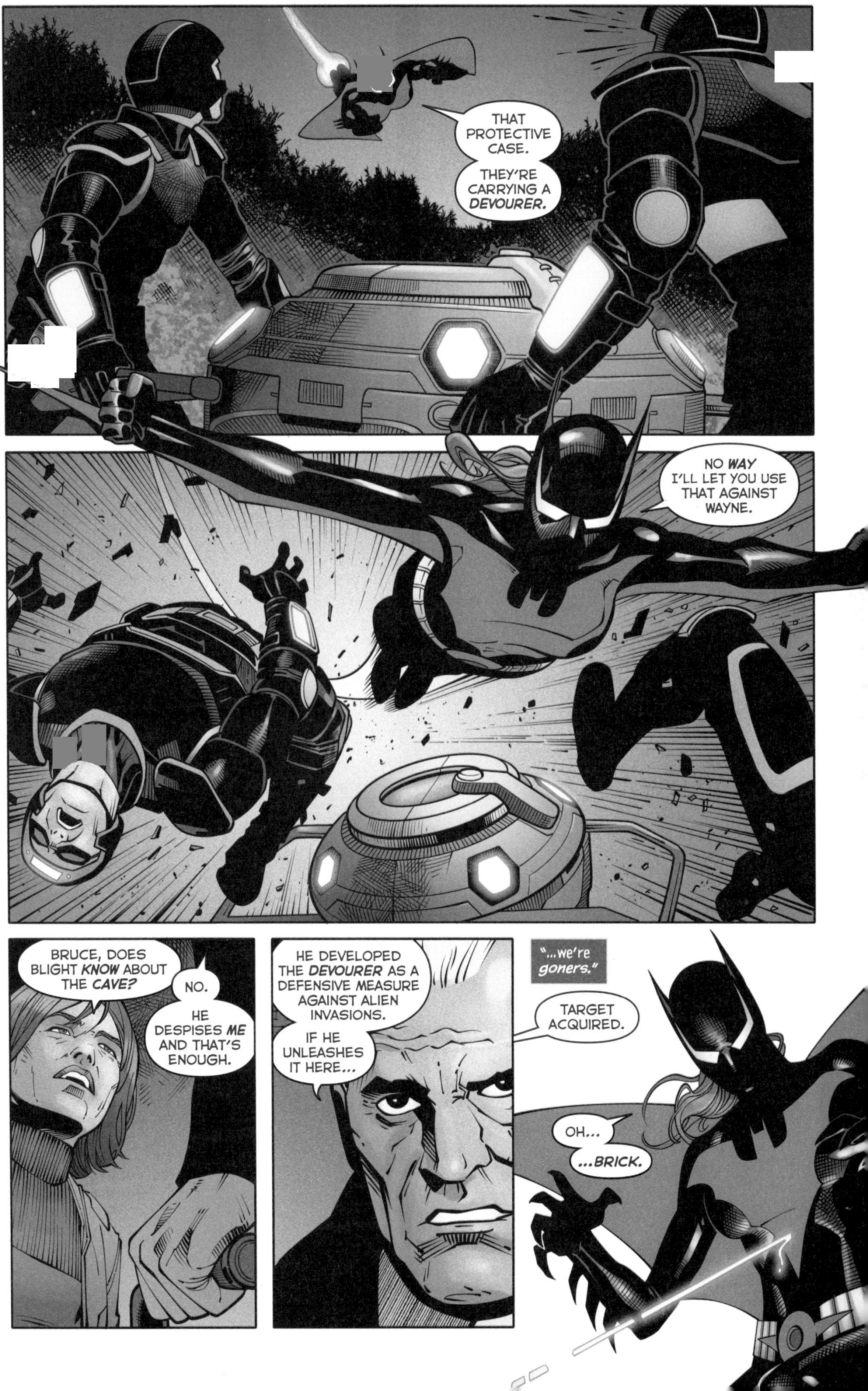
THAT PROTECTIVE CASE.
THEY'RE CARRYING A *DEVOURER.*
NO *WAY* I'LL LET YOU USE THAT AGAINST WAYNE.
BRUCE, DOES BLIGHT *KNOW* ABOUT THE *CAVE?*
NO.
HE DESPISES *ME* AND THAT'S ENOUGH.
HE DEVELOPED THE *DEVOURER* AS A DEFENSIVE MEASURE AGAINST ALIEN INVASIONS.
IF HE UNLEASHES IT HERE...
"...we're *goners.*"
TARGET ACQUIRED.
OH...
...BRICK.

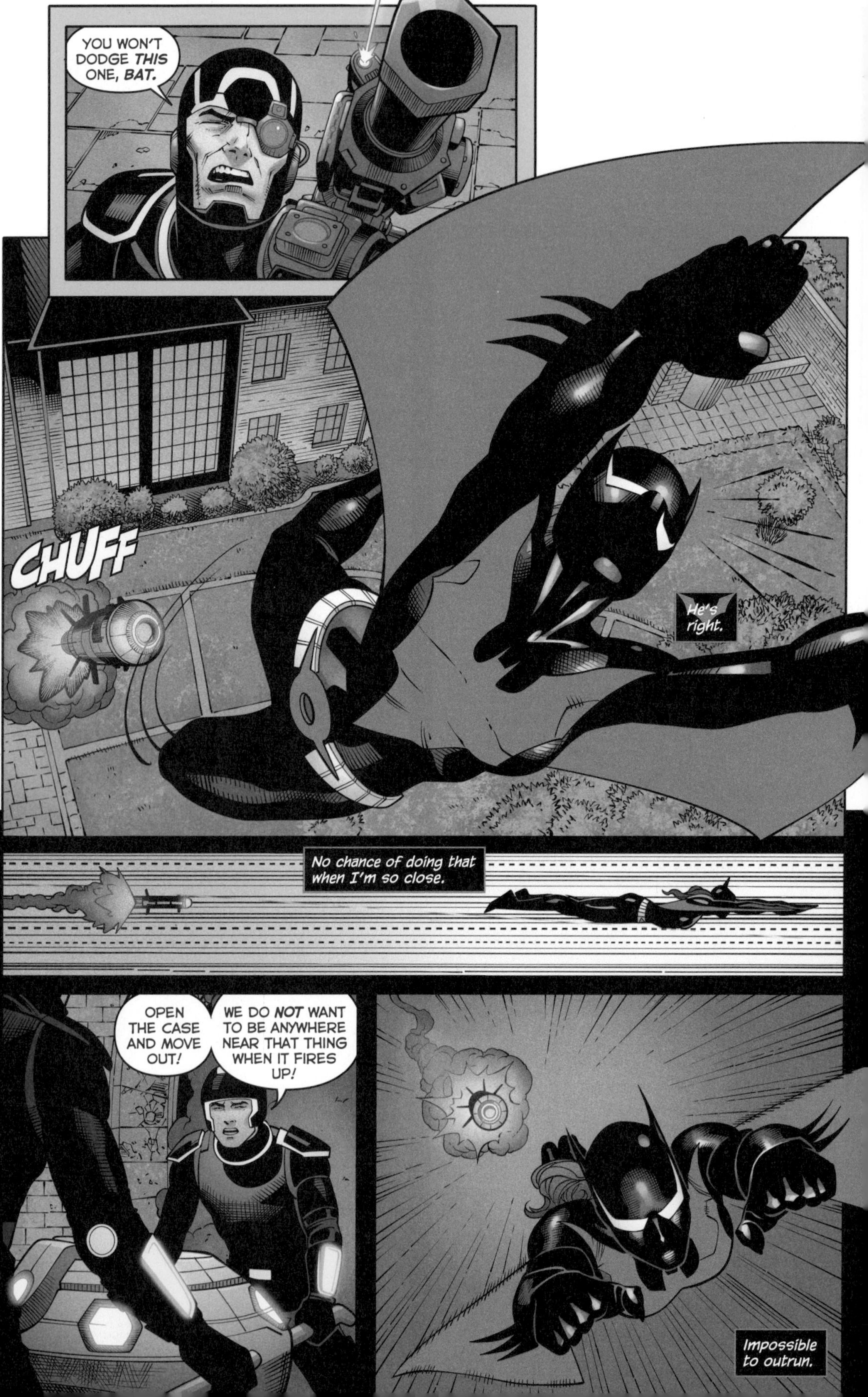
YOU WON'T DODGE THIS ONE, BAT.
CHUFF
He's right.
No chance of doing that when I'm so close.
OPEN THE CASE AND MOVE OUT!
WE DO NOT WANT TO BE ANYWHERE NEAR THAT THING WHEN IT FIRES UP!
Impossible to outrun.

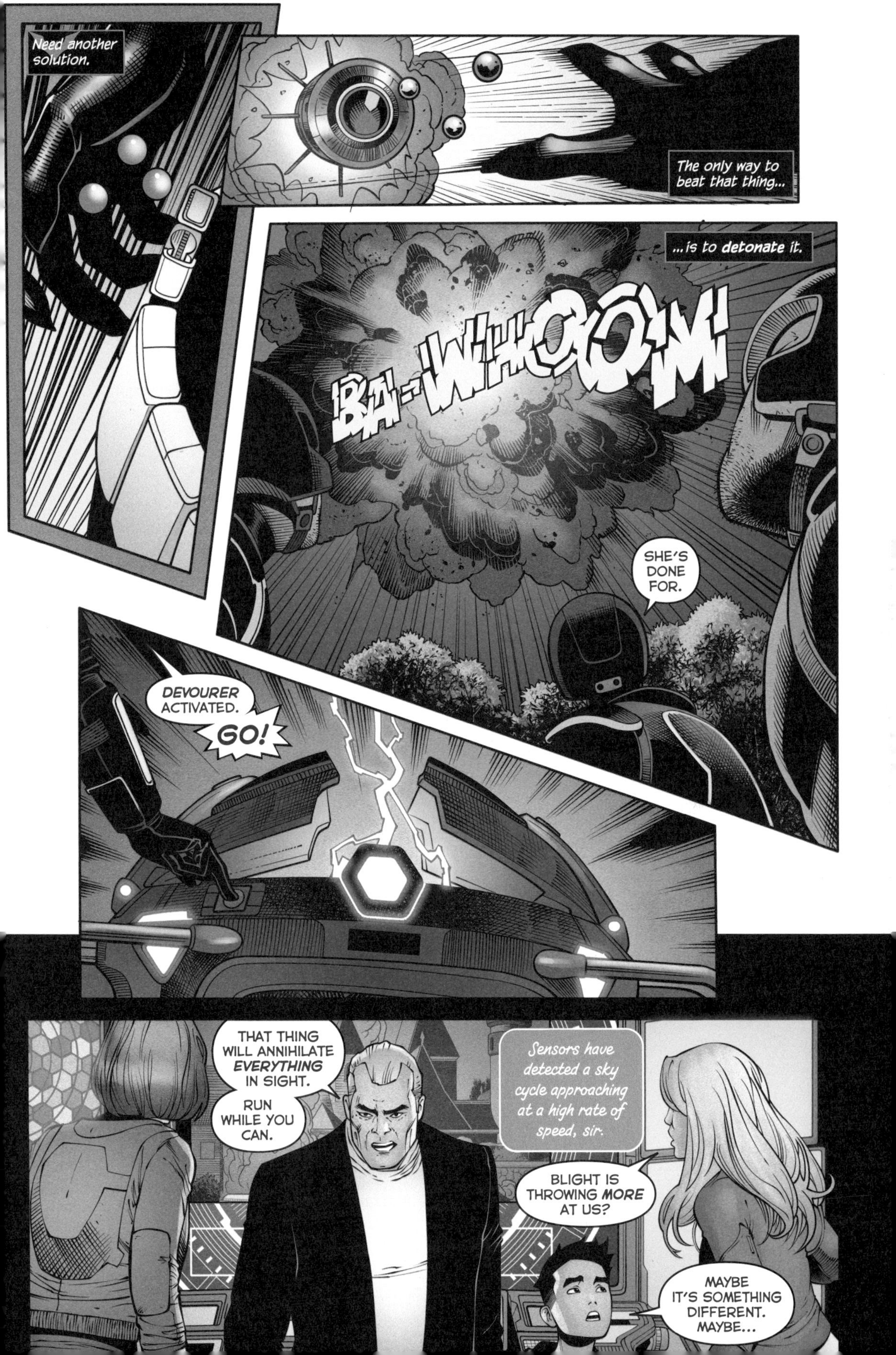

Need another solution.
The only way to beat that thing...
...is to detonate it.
BA-WHOOOM!
SHE'S DONE FOR.
DEVOURER ACTIVATED.
GO!
THAT THING WILL ANNIHILATE EVERYTHING IN SIGHT.
RUN WHILE YOU CAN.
Sensors have detected a sky cycle approaching at a high rate of speed, sir.
BLIGHT IS THROWING MORE AT US?
MAYBE IT'S SOMETHING DIFFERENT. MAYBE...

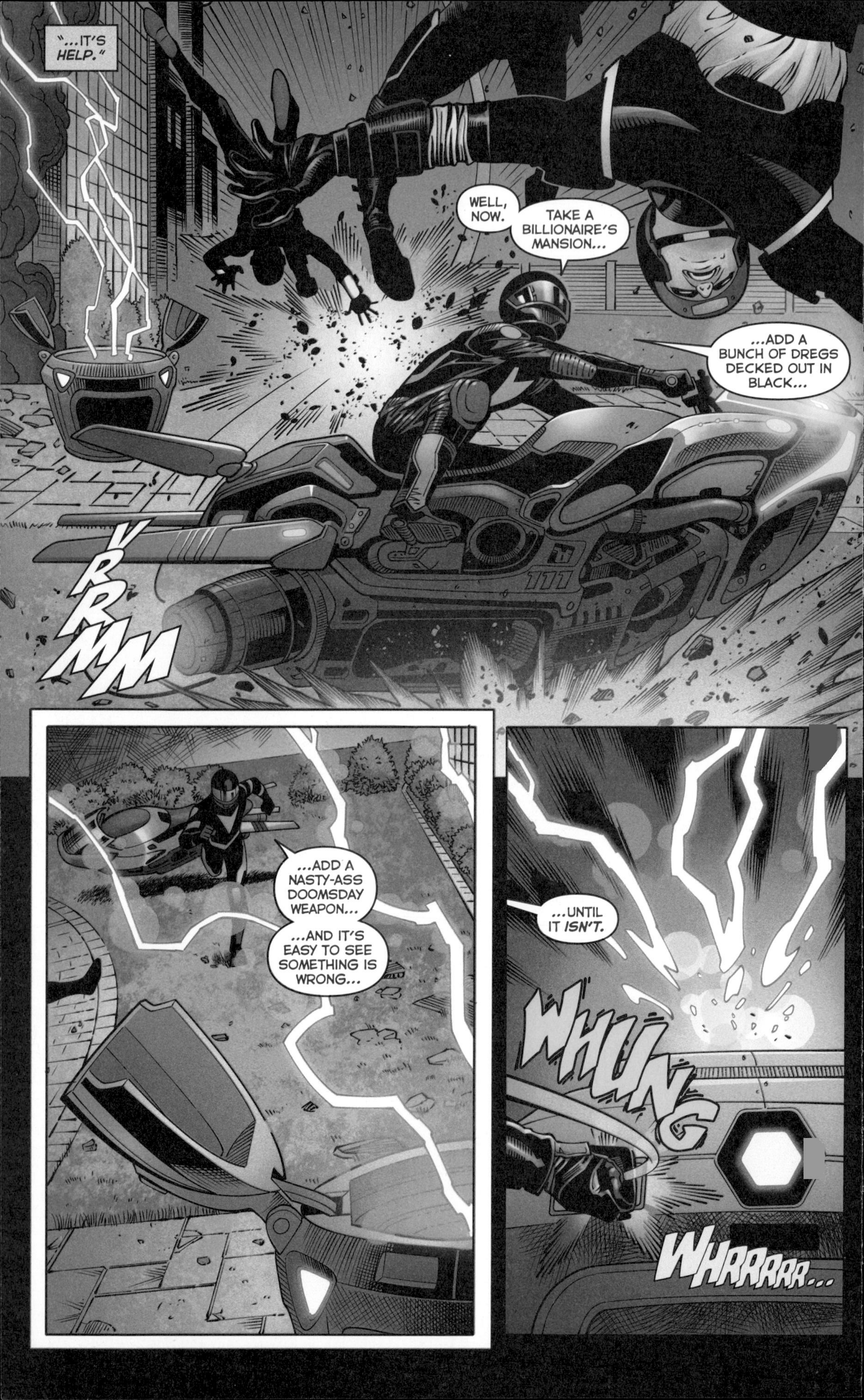
"...IT'S HELP."
WELL, NOW.
TAKE A BILLIONAIRE'S MANSION...
...ADD A BUNCH OF DREGS DECKED OUT IN BLACK...
VRRMM
...ADD A NASTY-ASS DOOMSDAY WEAPON...
...AND IT'S EASY TO SEE SOMETHING IS WRONG...
...UNTIL IT ISN'T.
WHUNG
WHRRRRR...

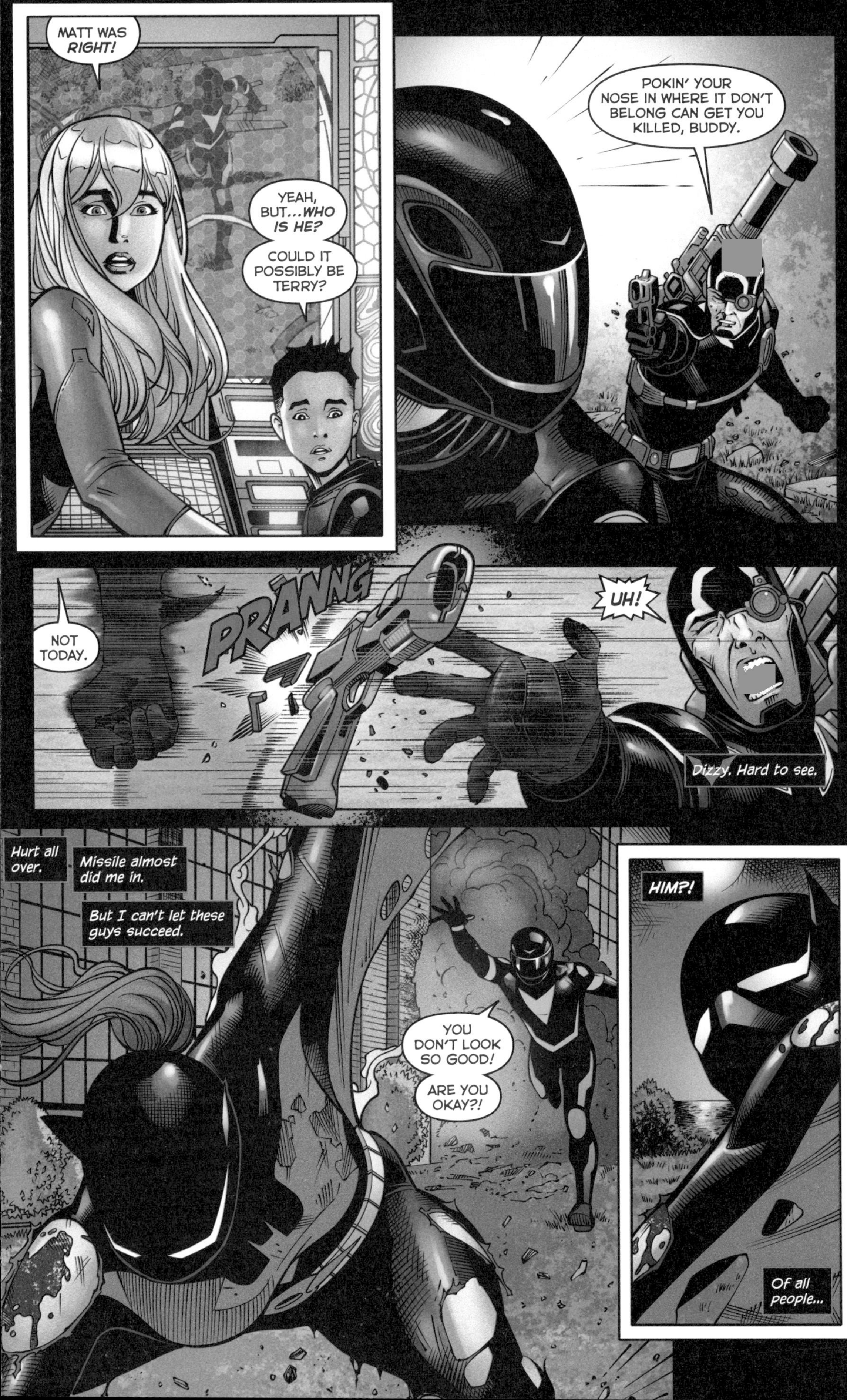
MATT WAS RIGHT!
YEAH, BUT...WHO IS HE?
COULD IT POSSIBLY BE TERRY?
POKIN' YOUR NOSE IN WHERE IT DON'T BELONG CAN GET YOU KILLED, BUDDY.
NOT TODAY.
PRANNG
UH!
Dizzy. Hard to see.
Hurt all over.
Missile almost did me in.
But I can't let these guys succeed.
YOU DON'T LOOK SO GOOD!
ARE YOU OKAY?!
HIM?!
Of all people...

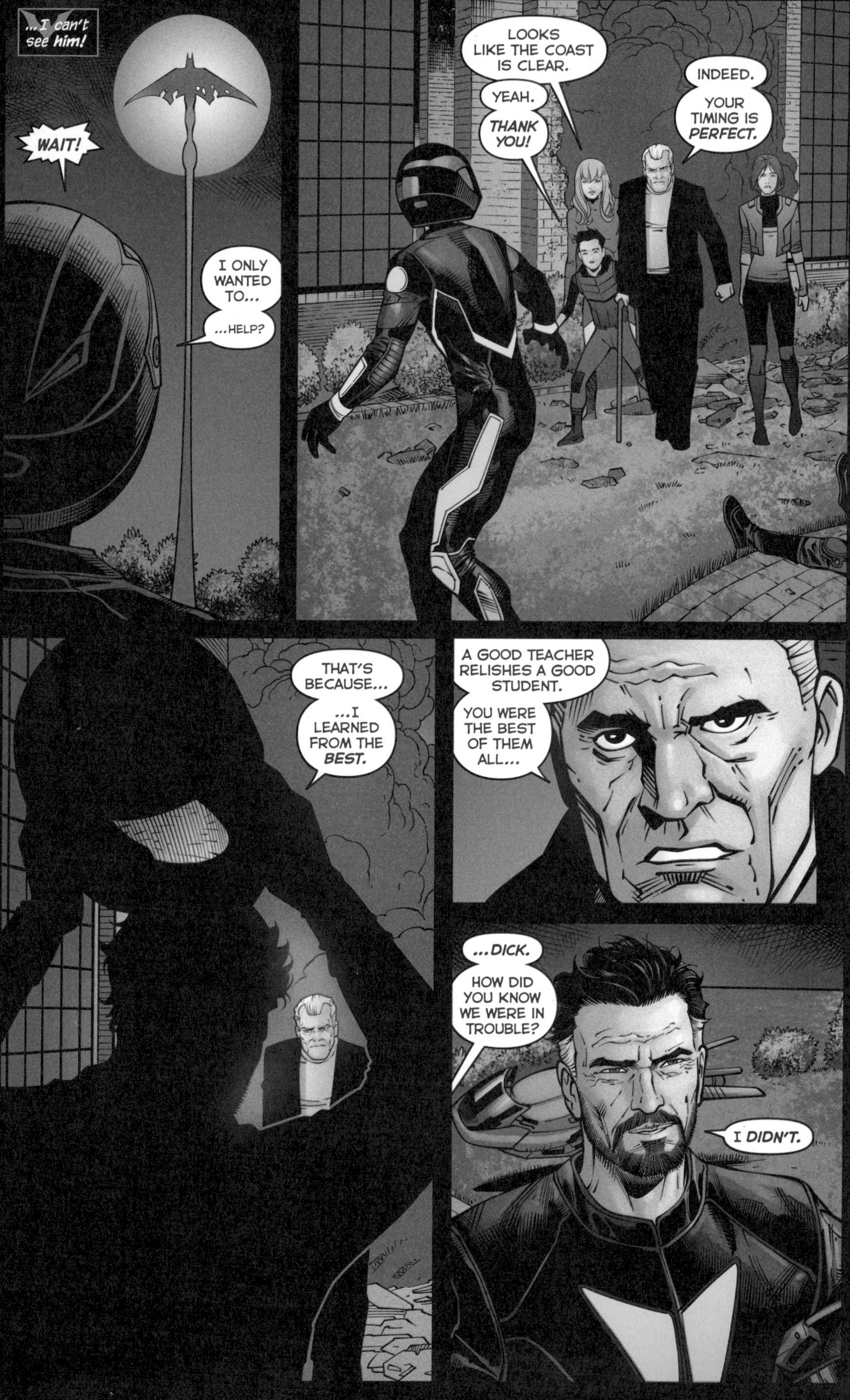
...I can't see him!
WAIT!
I ONLY WANTED TO...
...HELP?
LOOKS LIKE THE COAST IS CLEAR.
YEAH.
THANK YOU!
INDEED.
YOUR TIMING IS PERFECT.
THAT'S BECAUSE...
...I LEARNED FROM THE BEST.
A GOOD TEACHER RELISHES A GOOD STUDENT.
YOU WERE THE BEST OF THEM ALL...
...DICK.
HOW DID YOU KNOW WE WERE IN TROUBLE?
I DIDN'T.

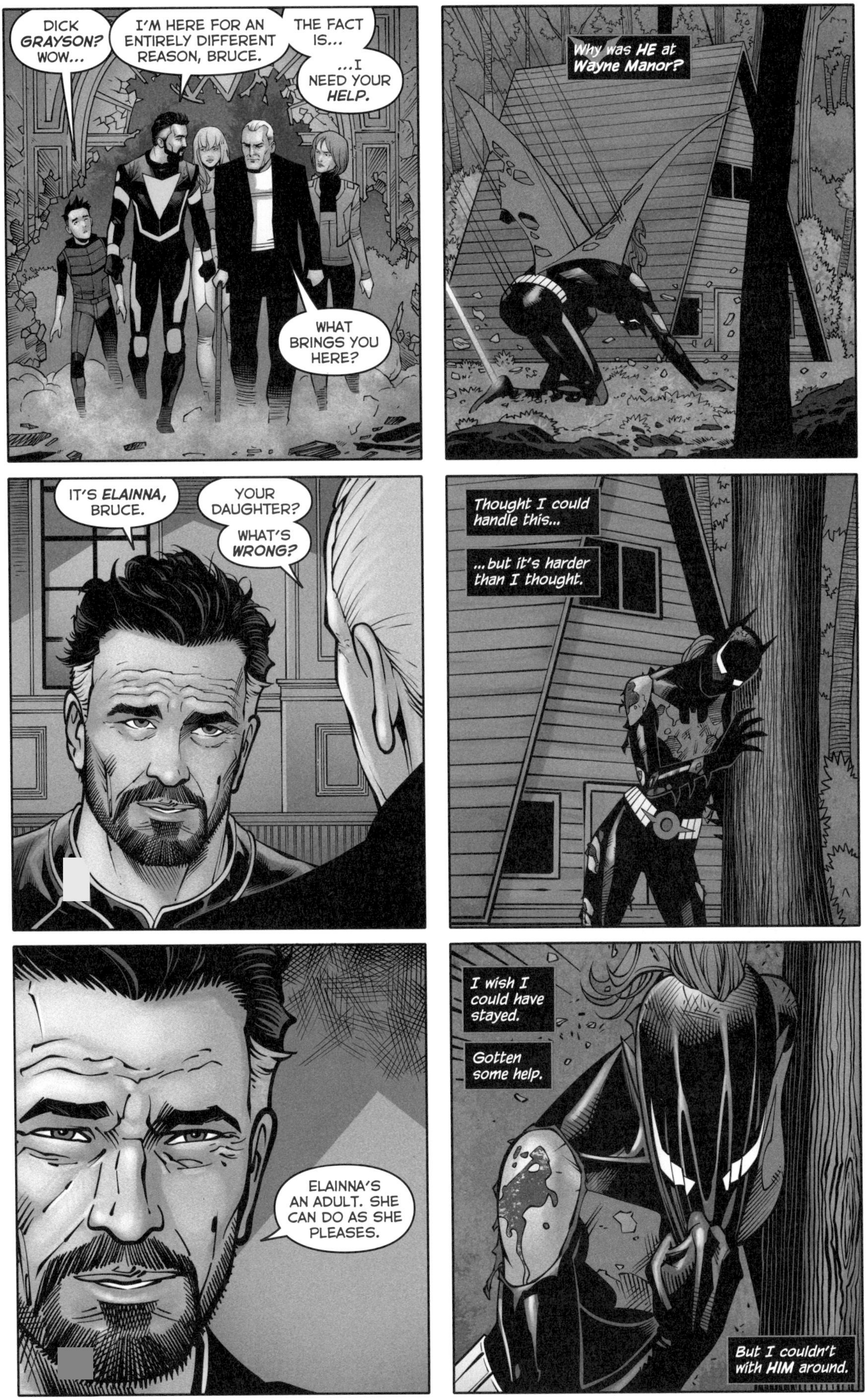

DICK GRAYSON? WOW...
I'M HERE FOR AN ENTIRELY DIFFERENT REASON, BRUCE.
THE FACT IS...
...I NEED YOUR HELP.
WHAT BRINGS YOU HERE?
Why was HE at Wayne Manor?
IT'S ELAINNA, BRUCE.
YOUR DAUGHTER?
WHAT'S WRONG?
Thought I could handle this...
...but it's harder than I thought.
ELAINNA'S AN ADULT. SHE CAN DO AS SHE PLEASES.
I wish I could have stayed.
Gotten some help.
But I couldn't with HIM around.

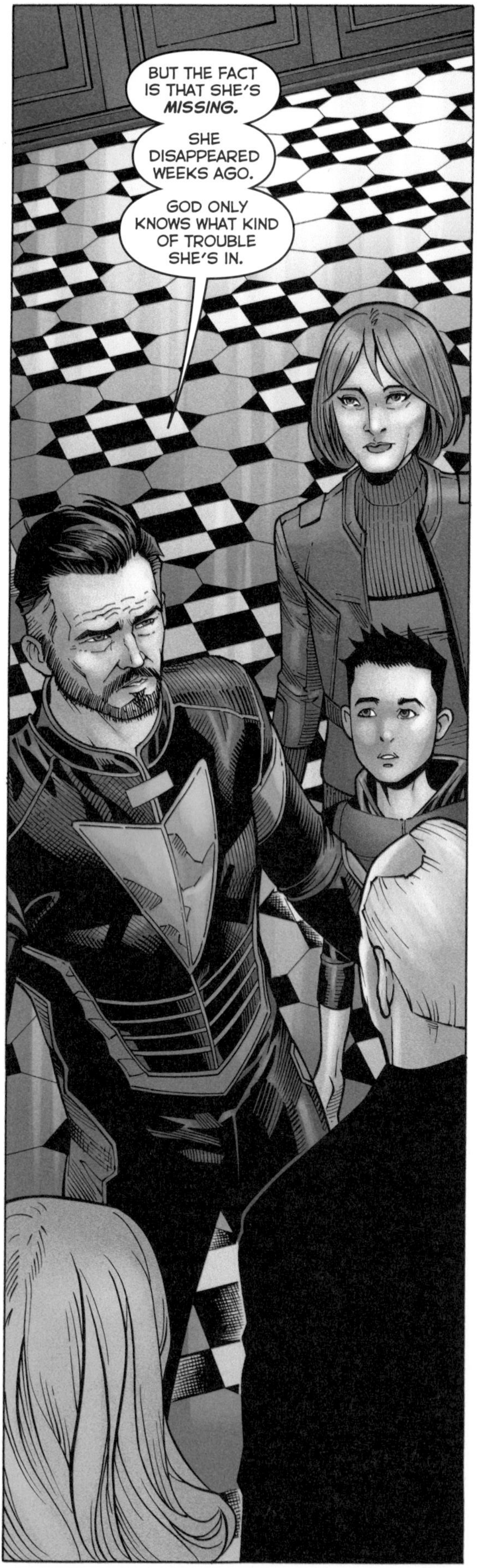
BUT THE FACT IS THAT SHE'S *MISSING.*
SHE DISAPPEARED WEEKS AGO.
GOD ONLY KNOWS WHAT KIND OF TROUBLE SHE'S IN.

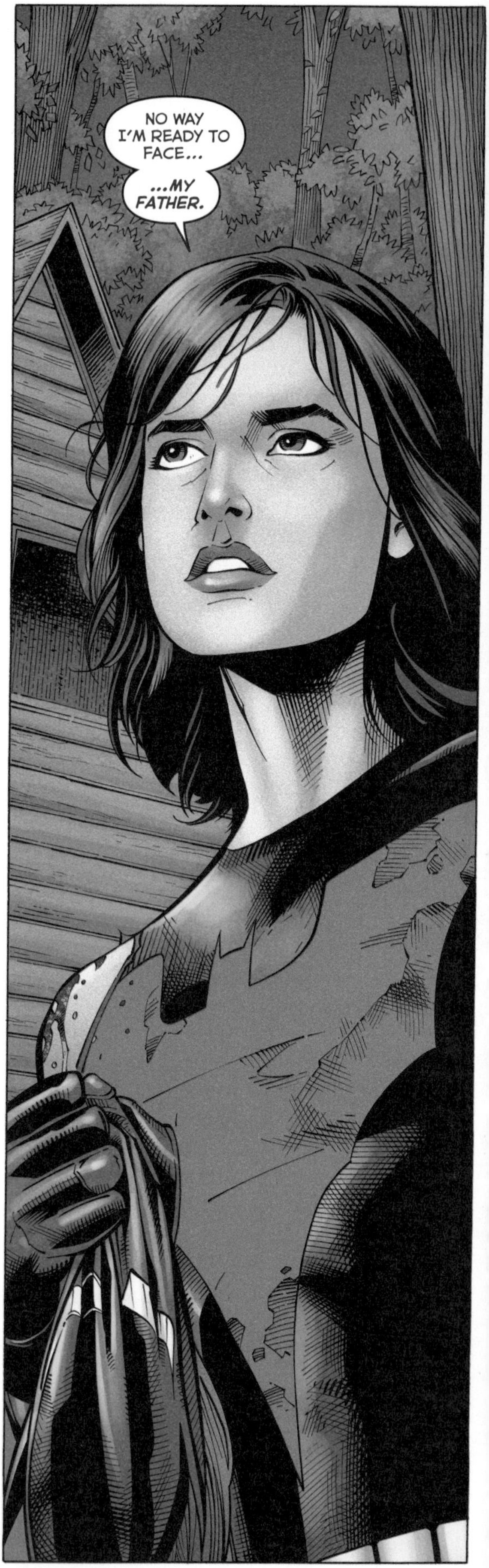
NO WAY I'M READY TO FACE...
...MY FATHER.

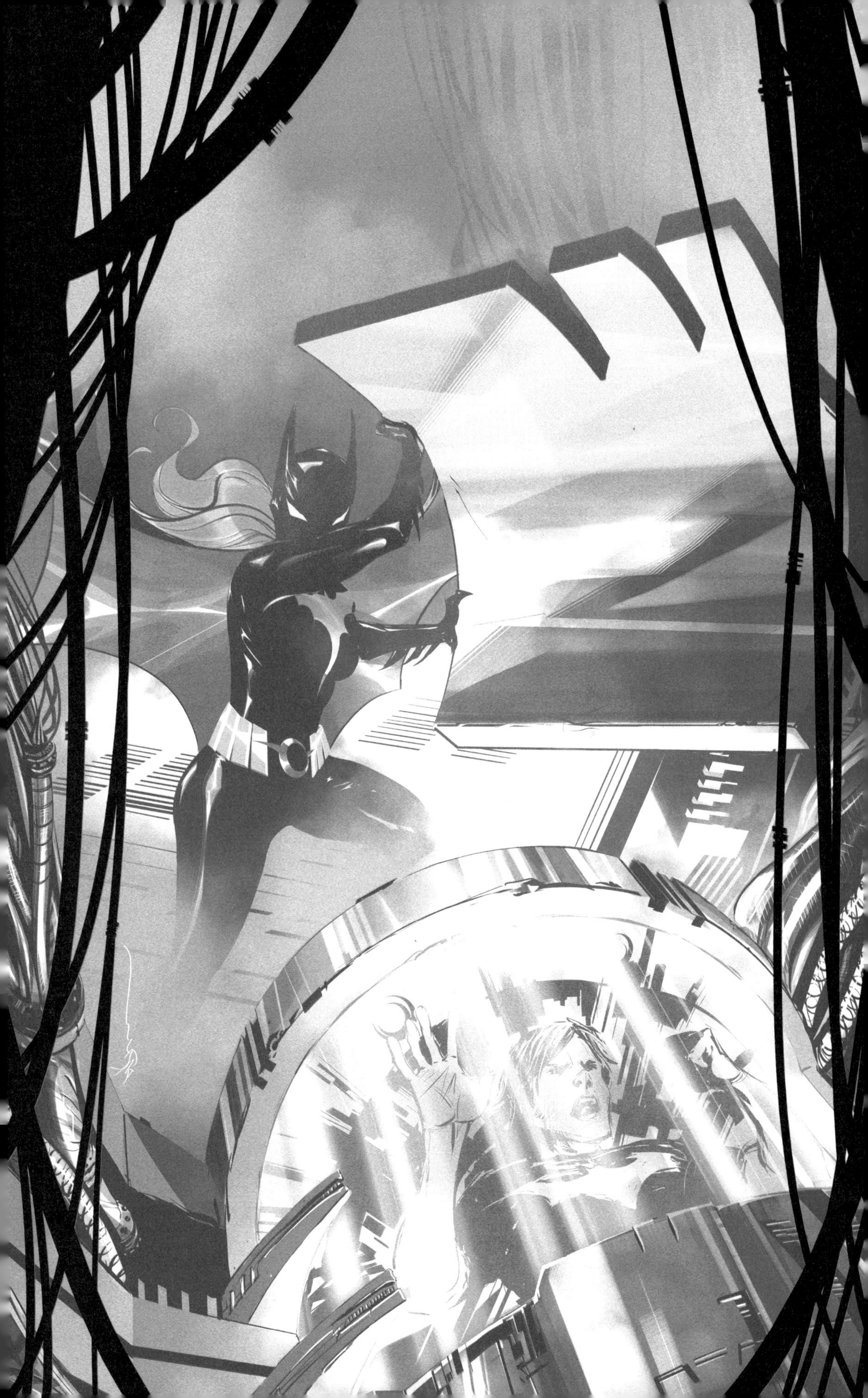

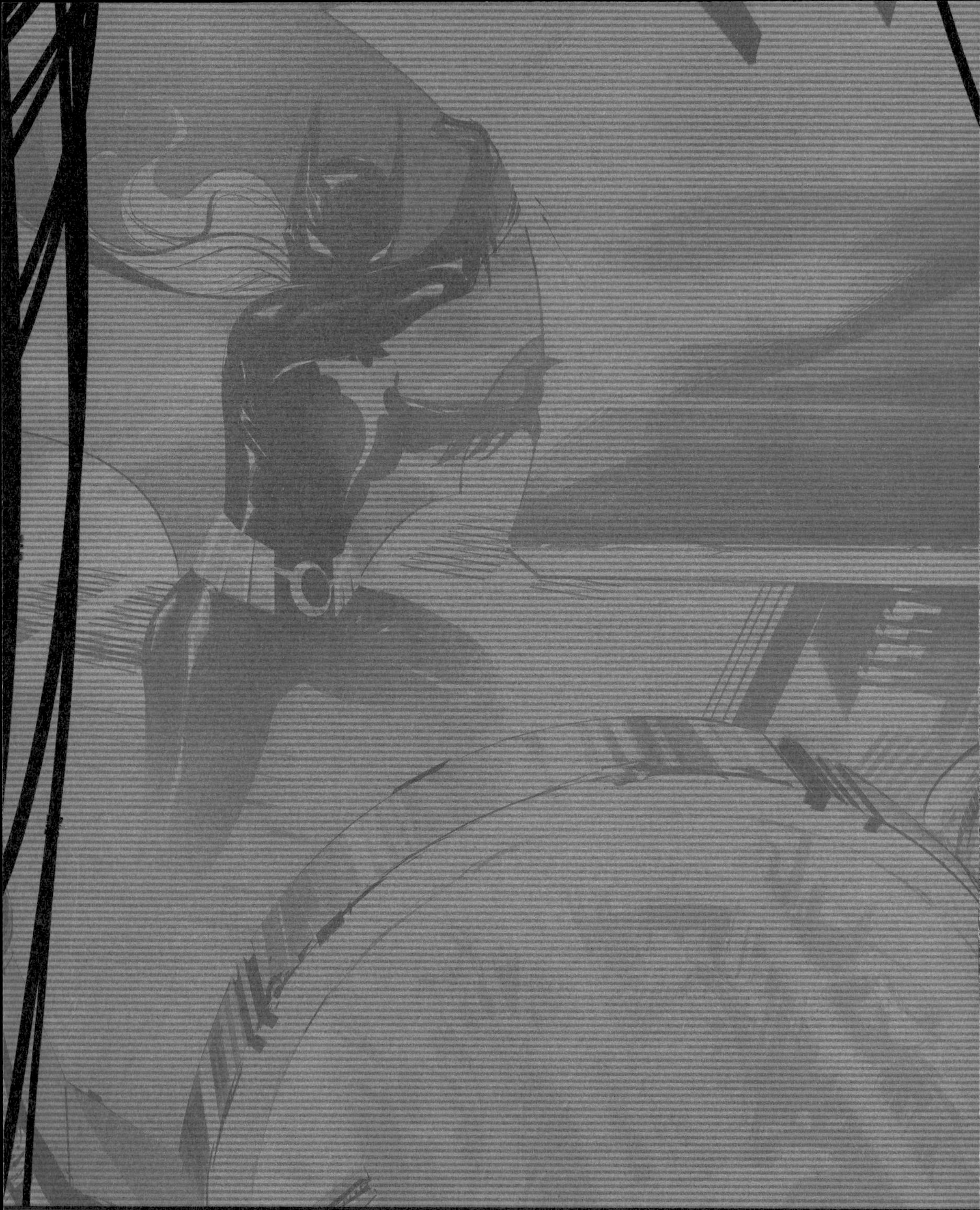

BATMAN BEYOND
#41

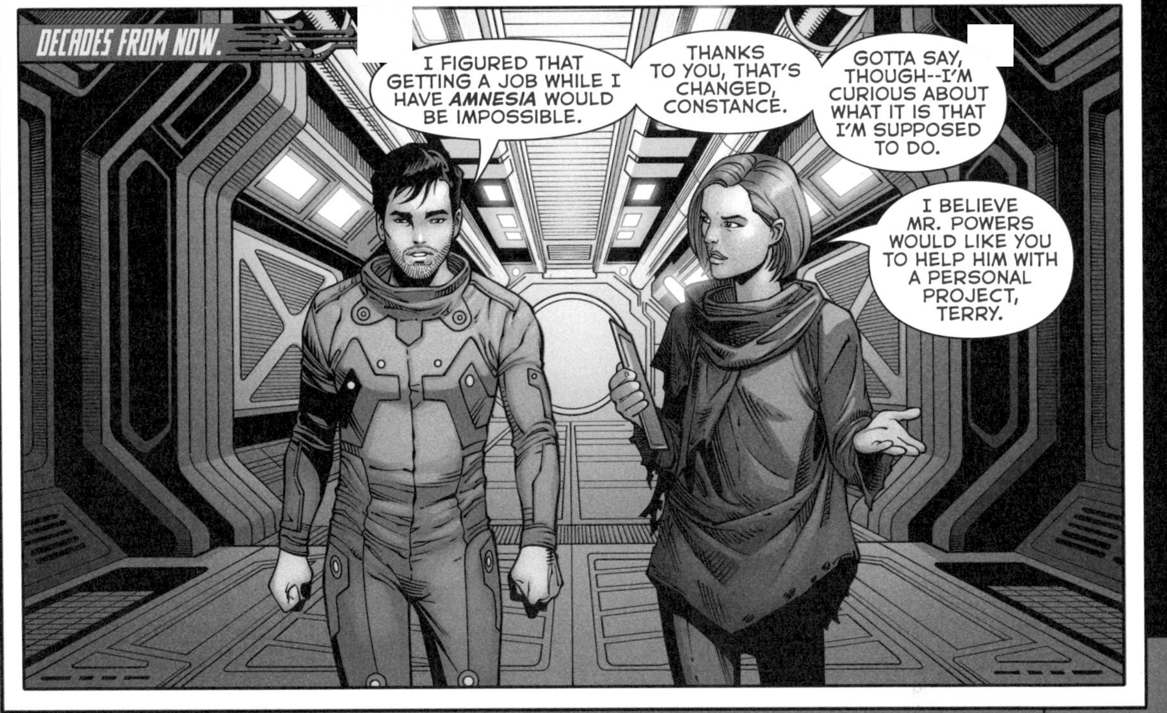
DECADES FROM NOW.
I FIGURED THAT GETTING A JOB WHILE I HAVE AMNESIA WOULD BE IMPOSSIBLE.
THANKS TO YOU, THAT'S CHANGED, CONSTANCE.
GOTTA SAY, THOUGH--I'M CURIOUS ABOUT WHAT IT IS THAT I'M SUPPOSED TO DO.
I BELIEVE MR. POWERS WOULD LIKE YOU TO HELP HIM WITH A PERSONAL PROJECT, TERRY.

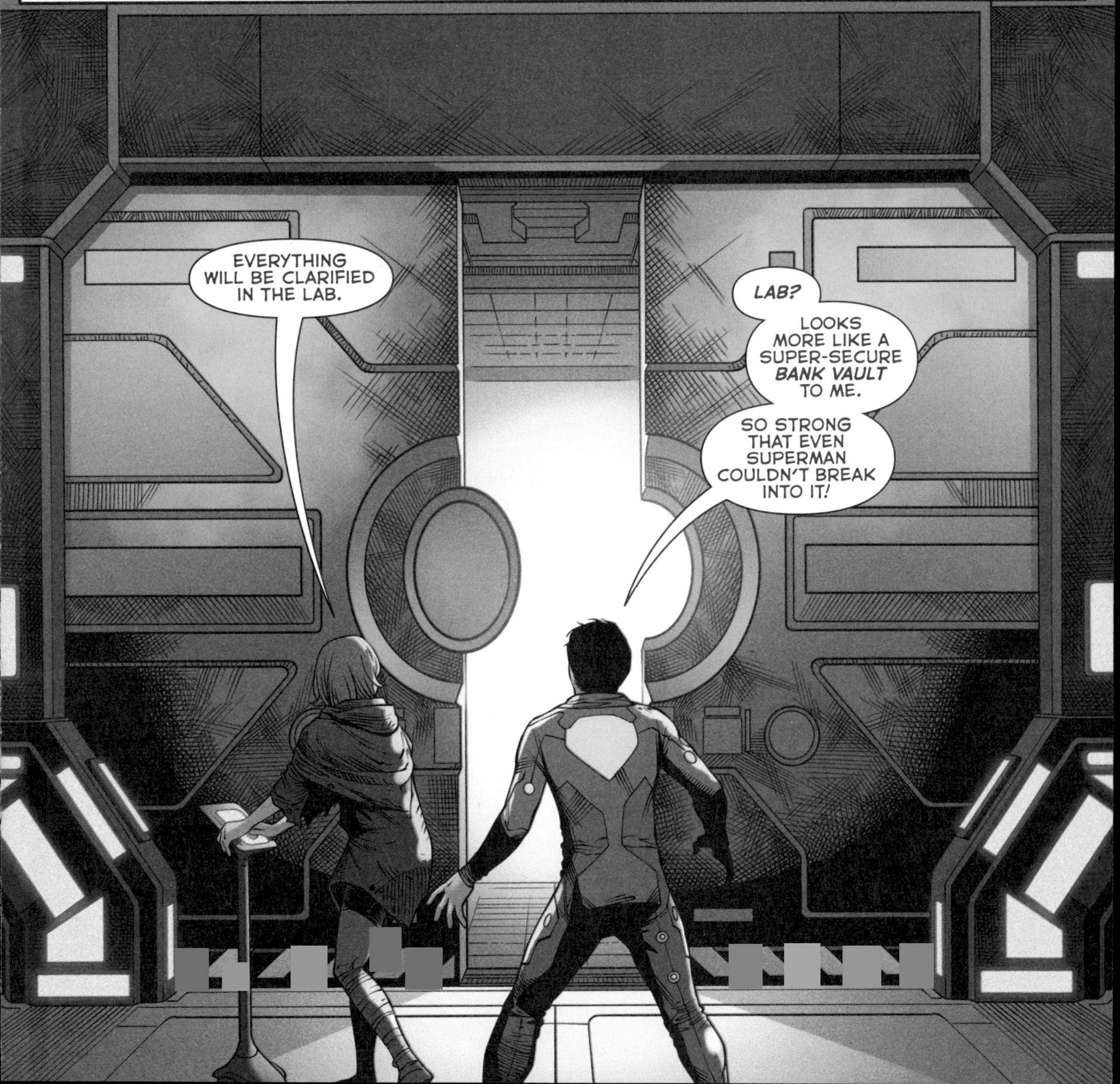
EVERYTHING WILL BE CLARIFIED IN THE LAB.
LAB?
LOOKS MORE LIKE A SUPER-SECURE BANK VAULT TO ME.
SO STRONG THAT EVEN SUPERMAN COULDN'T BREAK INTO IT!

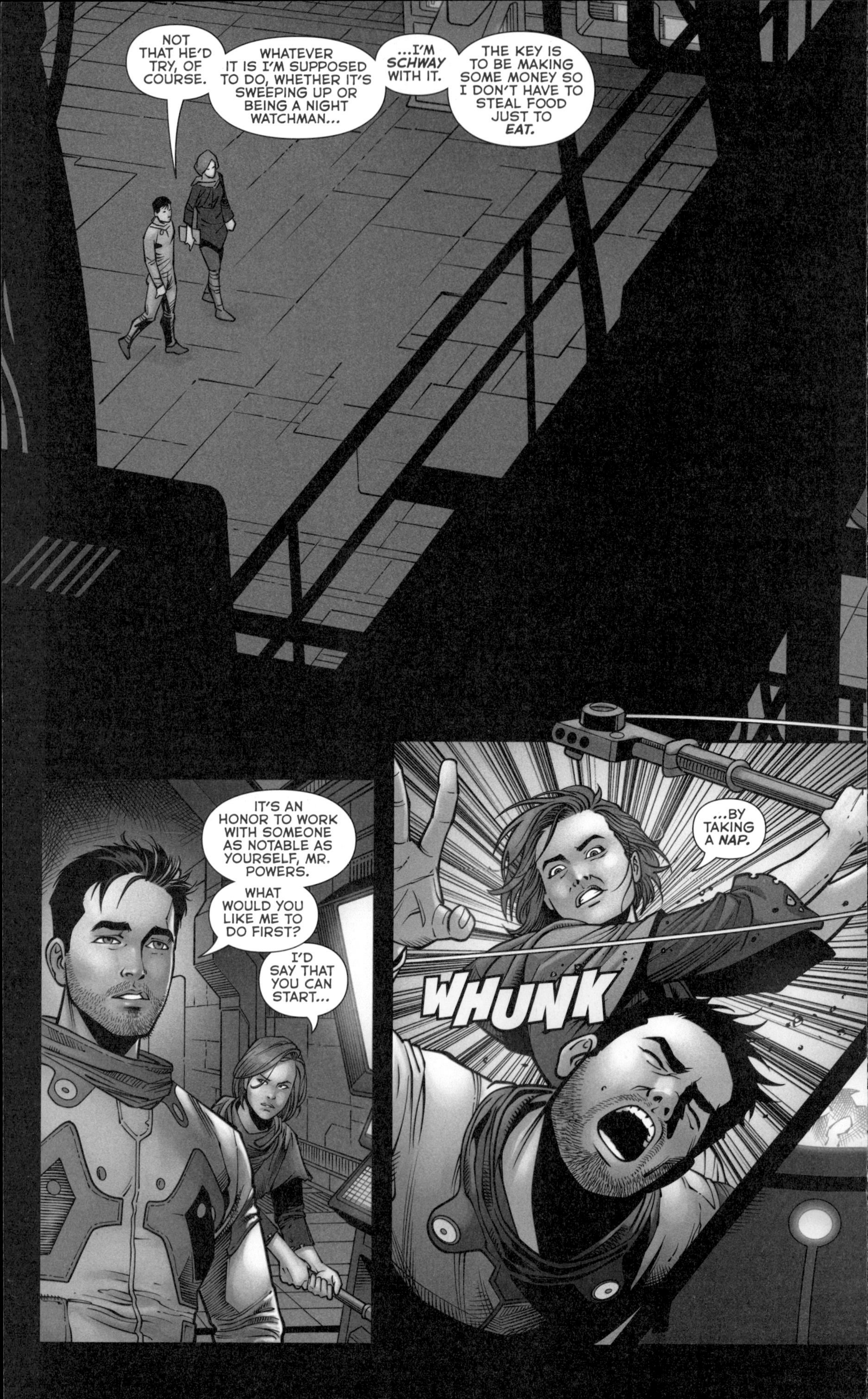
NOT THAT HE'D TRY, OF COURSE.
WHATEVER IT IS I'M SUPPOSED TO DO, WHETHER IT'S SWEEPING UP OR BEING A NIGHT WATCHMAN...
...I'M SCHWAY WITH IT.
THE KEY IS TO BE MAKING SOME MONEY SO I DON'T HAVE TO STEAL FOOD JUST TO EAT.
IT'S AN HONOR TO WORK WITH SOMEONE AS NOTABLE AS YOURSELF, MR. POWERS.
WHAT WOULD YOU LIKE ME TO DO FIRST?
I'D SAY THAT YOU CAN START...
...BY TAKING A NAP.
WHUNK

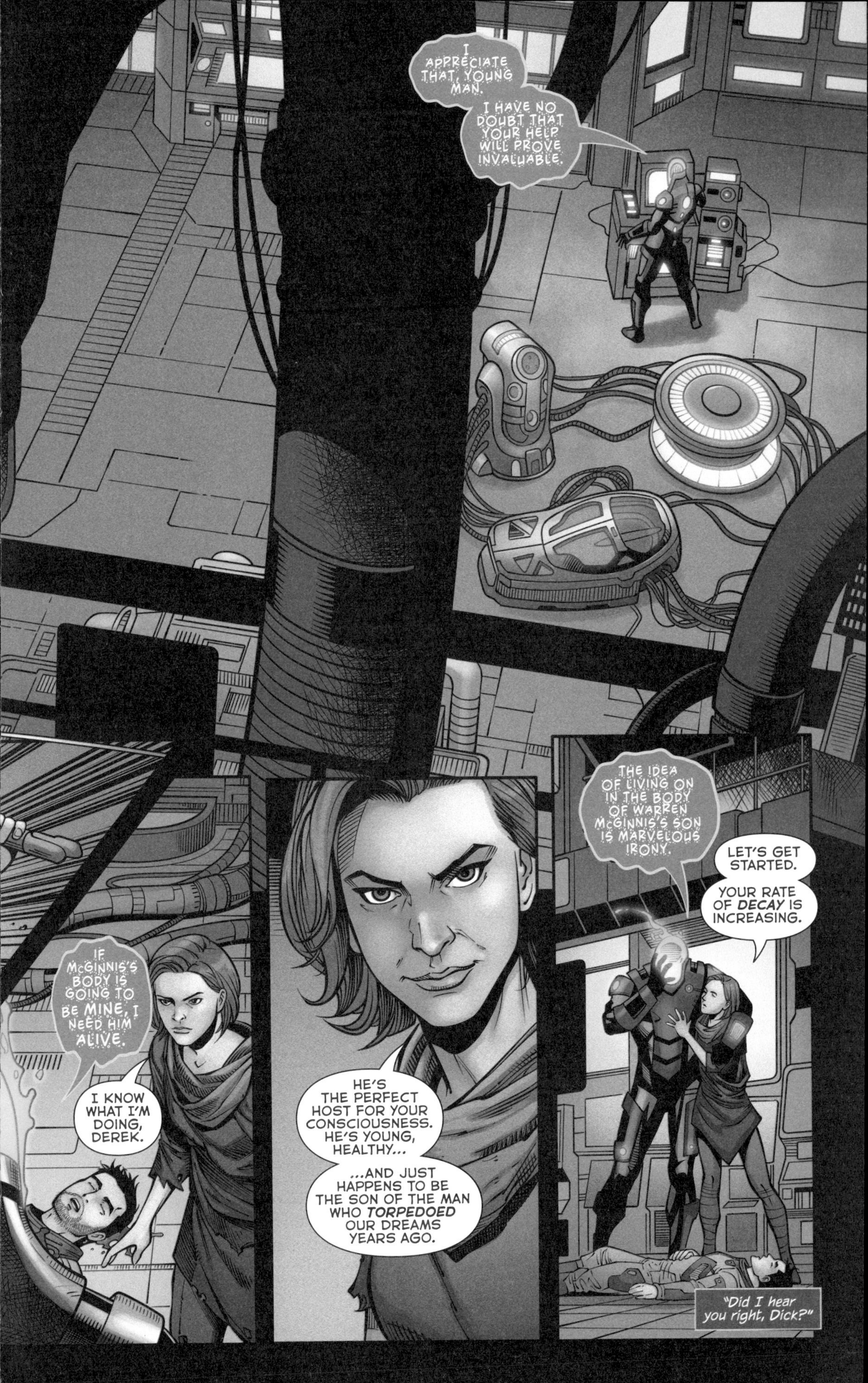
I APPRECIATE THAT, YOUNG MAN.
I HAVE NO DOUBT THAT YOUR HELP WILL PROVE INVALUABLE.
IF McGINNIS'S BODY IS GOING TO BE MINE, I NEED HIM ALIVE.
I KNOW WHAT I'M DOING, DEREK.
HE'S THE PERFECT HOST FOR YOUR CONSCIOUSNESS. HE'S YOUNG, HEALTHY...
...AND JUST HAPPENS TO BE THE SON OF THE MAN WHO TORPEDOED OUR DREAMS YEARS AGO.
THE IDEA OF LIVING ON IN THE BODY OF WARREN McGINNIS'S SON IS MARVELOUS IRONY.
LET'S GET STARTED.
YOUR RATE OF DECAY IS INCREASING.
"Did I hear you right, Dick?"

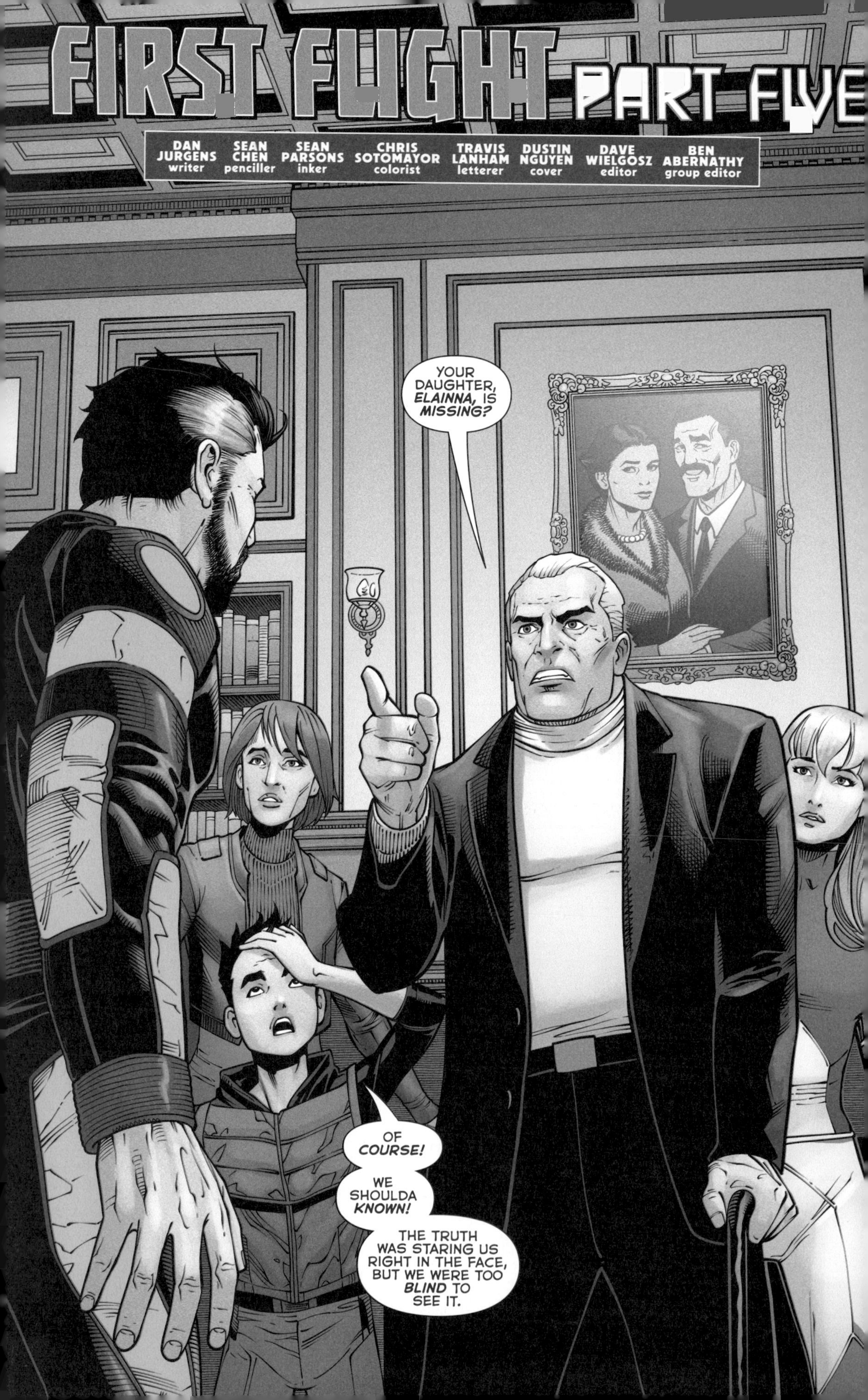
FIRST FLIGHT PART FIVE
DAN JURGENS writer
SEAN CHEN penciller
SEAN PARSONS inker
CHRIS SOTOMAYOR colorist
TRAVIS LANHAM letterer
DUSTIN NGUYEN cover
DAVE WIELGOSZ editor
BEN ABERNATHY group editor
YOUR DAUGHTER, ELAINNA, IS MISSING?
OF COURSE!
WE SHOULDA KNOWN!
THE TRUTH WAS STARING US RIGHT IN THE FACE, BUT WE WERE TOO BLIND TO SEE IT.

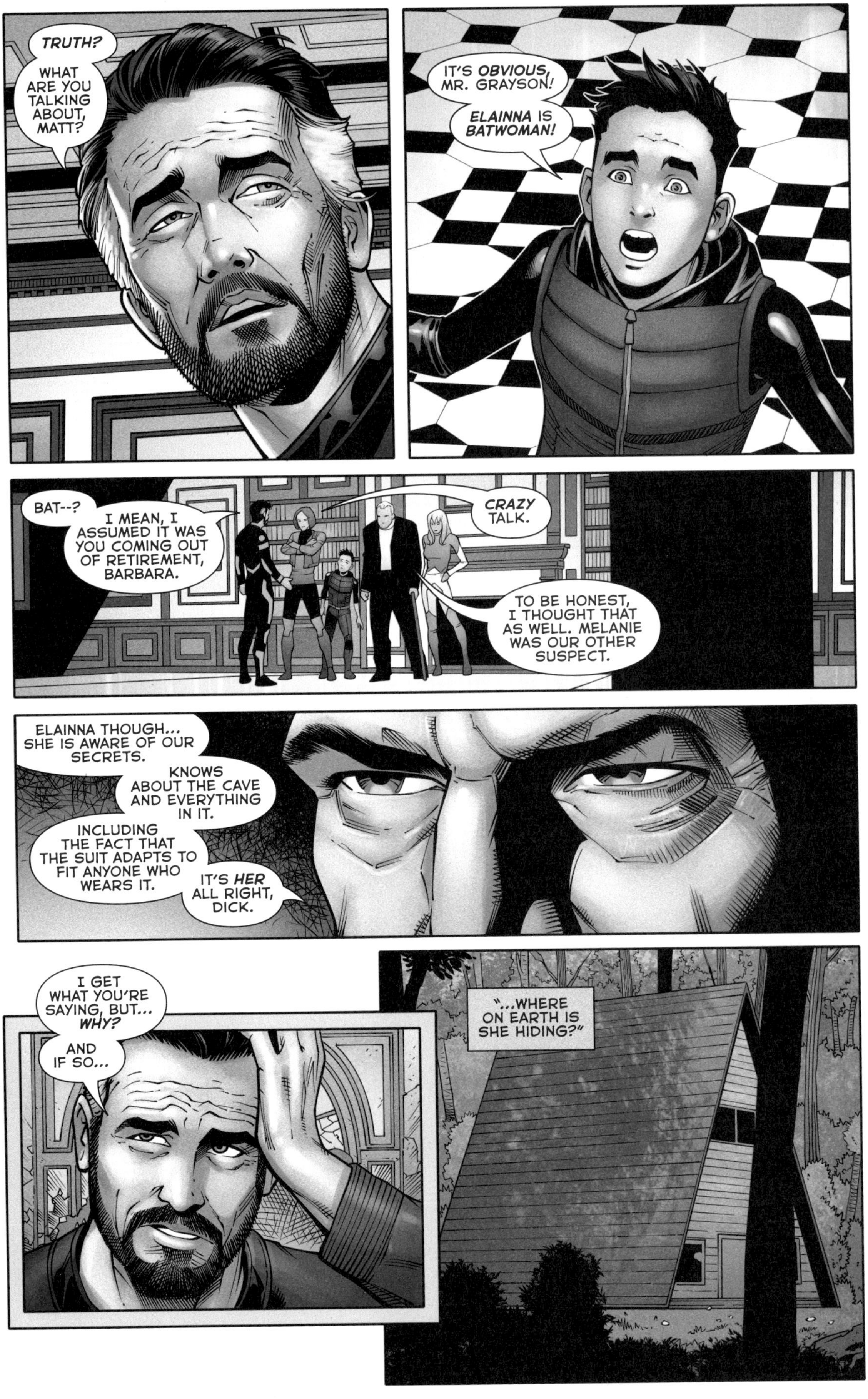
TRUTH?
WHAT ARE YOU TALKING ABOUT, MATT?
IT'S OBVIOUS, MR. GRAYSON!
ELAINNA IS BATWOMAN!
BAT--?
I MEAN, I ASSUMED IT WAS YOU COMING OUT OF RETIREMENT, BARBARA.
CRAZY TALK.
TO BE HONEST, I THOUGHT THAT AS WELL. MELANIE WAS OUR OTHER SUSPECT.
ELAINNA THOUGH... SHE IS AWARE OF OUR SECRETS.
KNOWS ABOUT THE CAVE AND EVERYTHING IN IT.
INCLUDING THE FACT THAT THE SUIT ADAPTS TO FIT ANYONE WHO WEARS IT.
IT'S HER ALL RIGHT, DICK.
I GET WHAT YOU'RE SAYING, BUT... WHY?
AND IF SO...
"...WHERE ON EARTH IS SHE HIDING?"

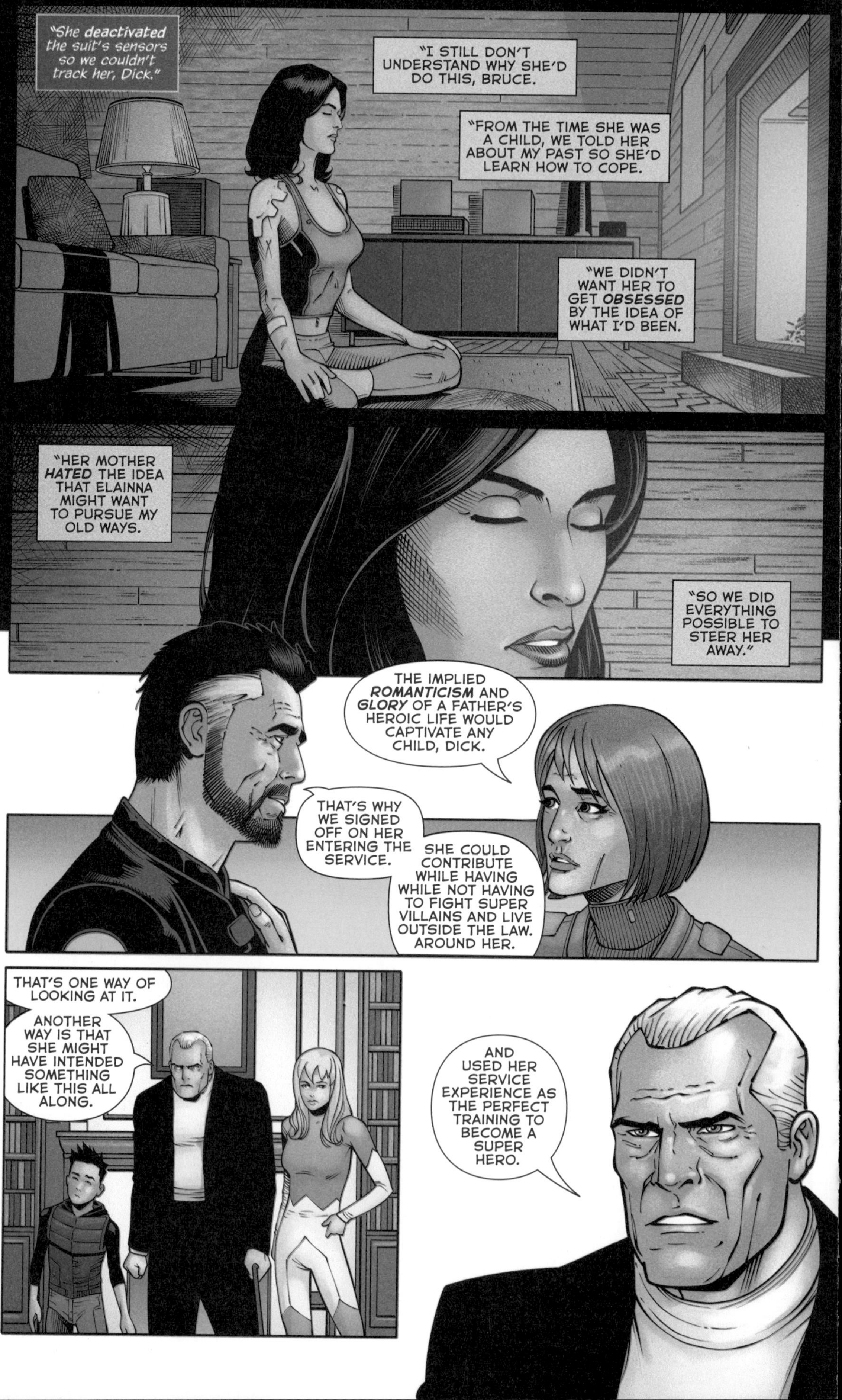
"She deactivated the suit's sensors so we couldn't track her, Dick."
"I STILL DON'T UNDERSTAND WHY SHE'D DO THIS, BRUCE.
"FROM THE TIME SHE WAS A CHILD, WE TOLD HER ABOUT MY PAST SO SHE'D LEARN HOW TO COPE.
"WE DIDN'T WANT HER TO GET OBSESSED BY THE IDEA OF WHAT I'D BEEN.
"HER MOTHER HATED THE IDEA THAT ELAINNA MIGHT WANT TO PURSUE MY OLD WAYS.
"SO WE DID EVERYTHING POSSIBLE TO STEER HER AWAY."
THE IMPLIED ROMANTICISM AND GLORY OF A FATHER'S HEROIC LIFE WOULD CAPTIVATE ANY CHILD, DICK.
THAT'S WHY WE SIGNED OFF ON HER ENTERING THE SERVICE.
SHE COULD CONTRIBUTE WHILE HAVING WHILE NOT HAVING TO FIGHT SUPER VILLAINS AND LIVE OUTSIDE THE LAW. AROUND HER.
THAT'S ONE WAY OF LOOKING AT IT.
ANOTHER WAY IS THAT SHE MIGHT HAVE INTENDED SOMETHING LIKE THIS ALL ALONG.
AND USED HER SERVICE EXPERIENCE AS THE PERFECT TRAINING TO BECOME A SUPER HERO.

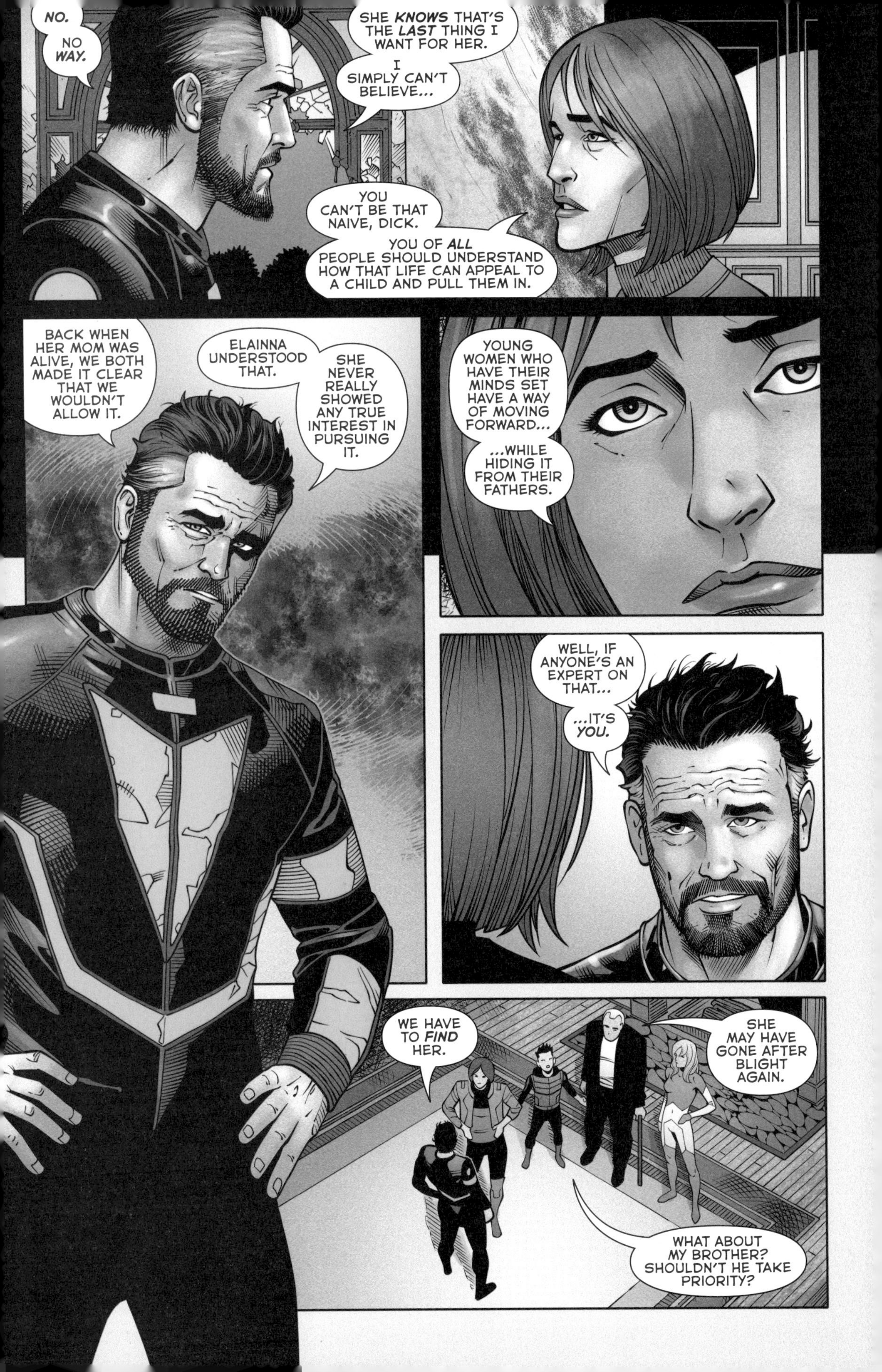

NO.
NO WAY.
SHE KNOWS THAT'S THE LAST THING I WANT FOR HER.
I SIMPLY CAN'T BELIEVE...
YOU CAN'T BE THAT NAIVE, DICK.
YOU OF ALL PEOPLE SHOULD UNDERSTAND HOW THAT LIFE CAN APPEAL TO A CHILD AND PULL THEM IN.
BACK WHEN HER MOM WAS ALIVE, WE BOTH MADE IT CLEAR THAT WE WOULDN'T ALLOW IT.
ELAINNA UNDERSTOOD THAT.
SHE NEVER REALLY SHOWED ANY TRUE INTEREST IN PURSUING IT.
YOUNG WOMEN WHO HAVE THEIR MINDS SET HAVE A WAY OF MOVING FORWARD...
...WHILE HIDING IT FROM THEIR FATHERS.
WELL, IF ANYONE'S AN EXPERT ON THAT...
...IT'S YOU.
WE HAVE TO FIND HER.
SHE MAY HAVE GONE AFTER BLIGHT AGAIN.
WHAT ABOUT MY BROTHER? SHOULDN'T HE TAKE PRIORITY?

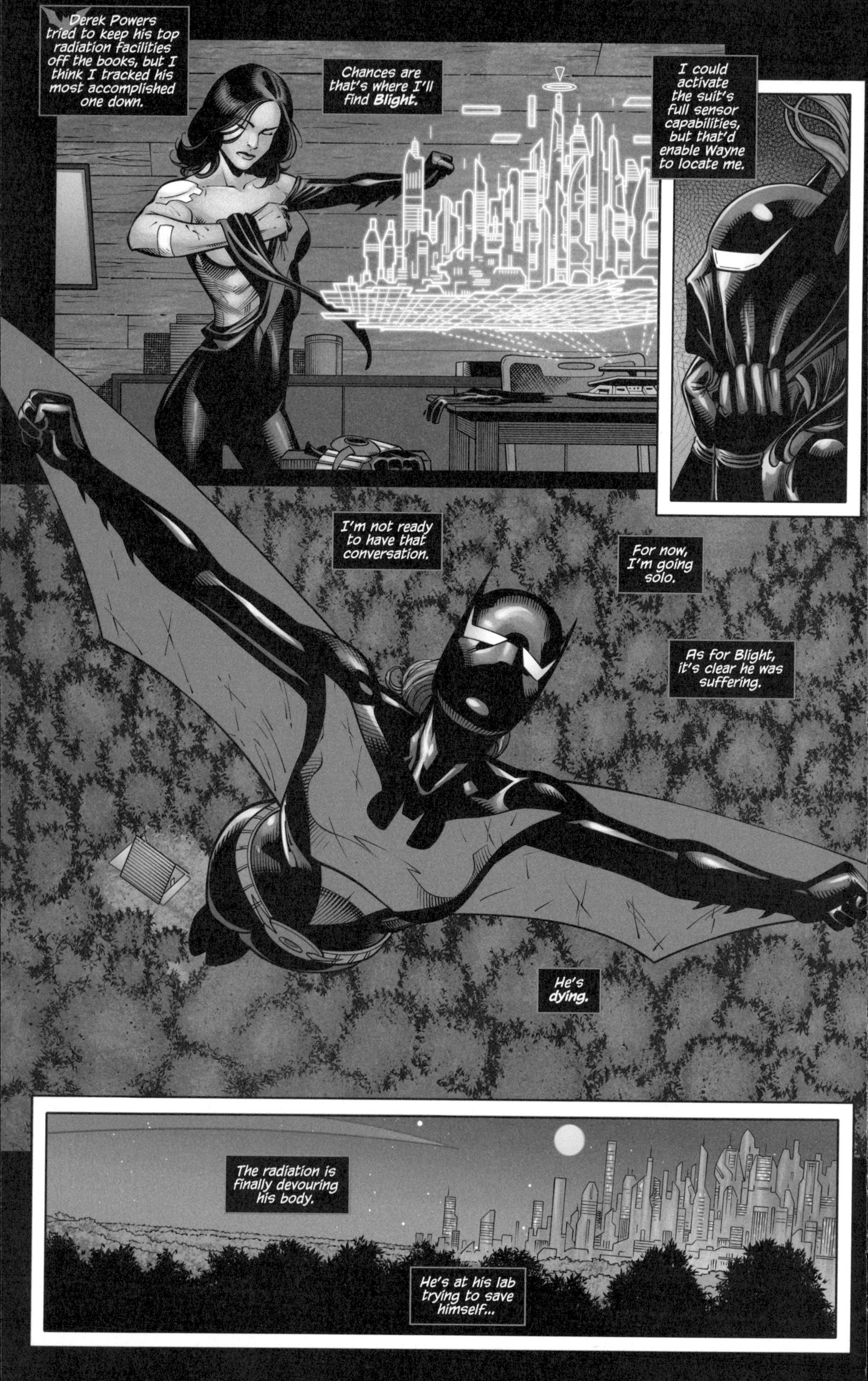

Derek Powers tried to keep his top radiation facilities off the books, but I think I tracked his most accomplished one down.
Chances are that's where I'll find **Blight.**
I could activate the suit's full sensor capabilities, but that'd enable Wayne to locate me.
I'm not ready to have that conversation.
For now, I'm going solo.
As for Blight, it's clear he was suffering.
He's **dying.**
The radiation is finally devouring his body.
He's at his lab trying to save himself...

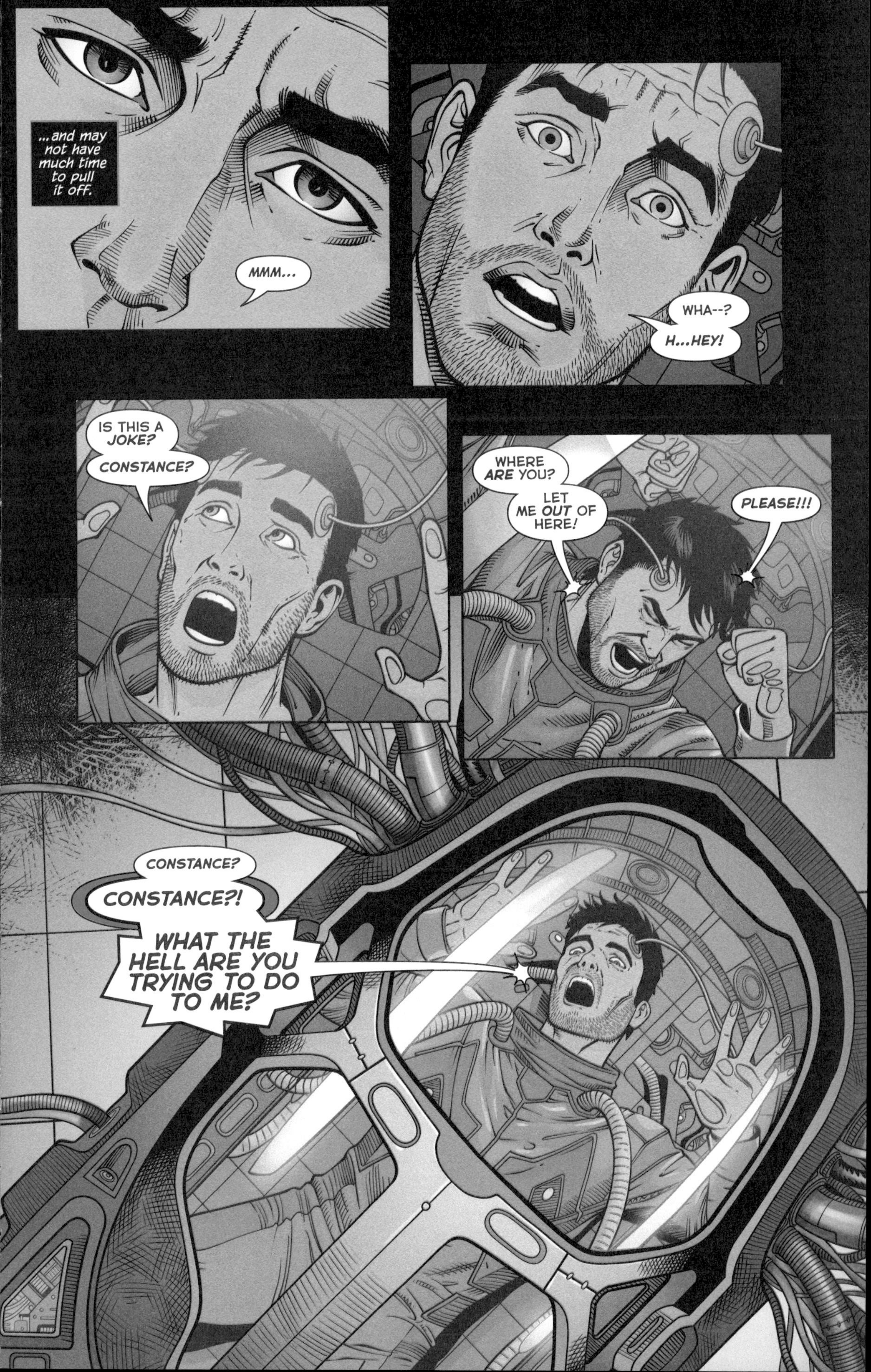
...and may not have much time to pull it off.
MMM...
WHA--?
H...HEY!
IS THIS A JOKE?
CONSTANCE?
WHERE ARE YOU?
LET ME OUT OF HERE!
PLEASE!!!
CONSTANCE?
CONSTANCE?!
WHAT THE HELL ARE YOU TRYING TO DO TO ME?

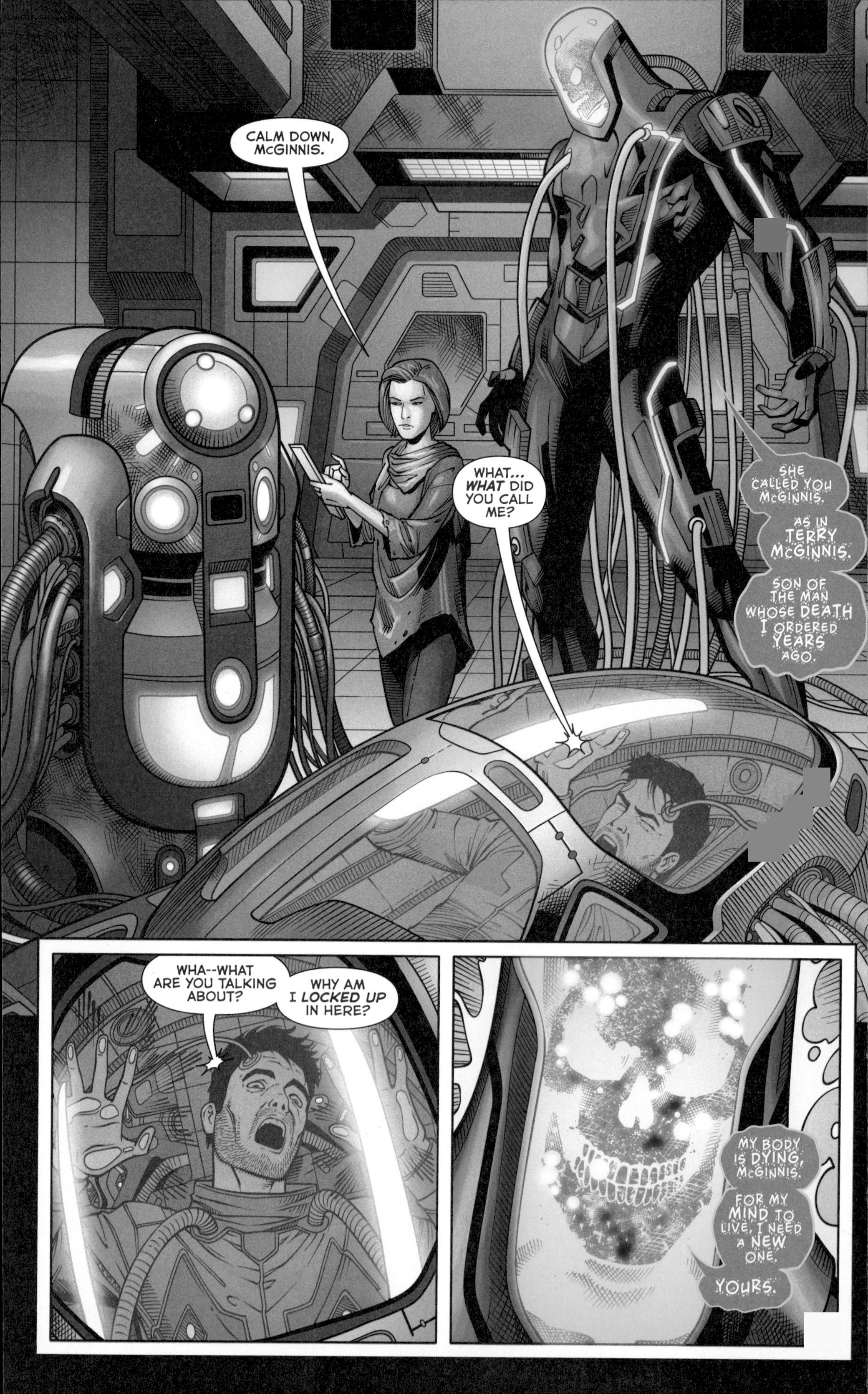
CALM DOWN, McGINNIS.
WHAT... WHAT DID YOU CALL ME?
SHE CALLED YOU McGINNIS.
AS IN TERRY McGINNIS.
SON OF THE MAN WHOSE DEATH I ORDERED YEARS AGO.
WHA--WHAT ARE YOU TALKING ABOUT?
WHY AM I LOCKED UP IN HERE?
MY BODY IS DYING, McGINNIS.
FOR MY MIND TO LIVE, I NEED A NEW ONE.
YOURS.

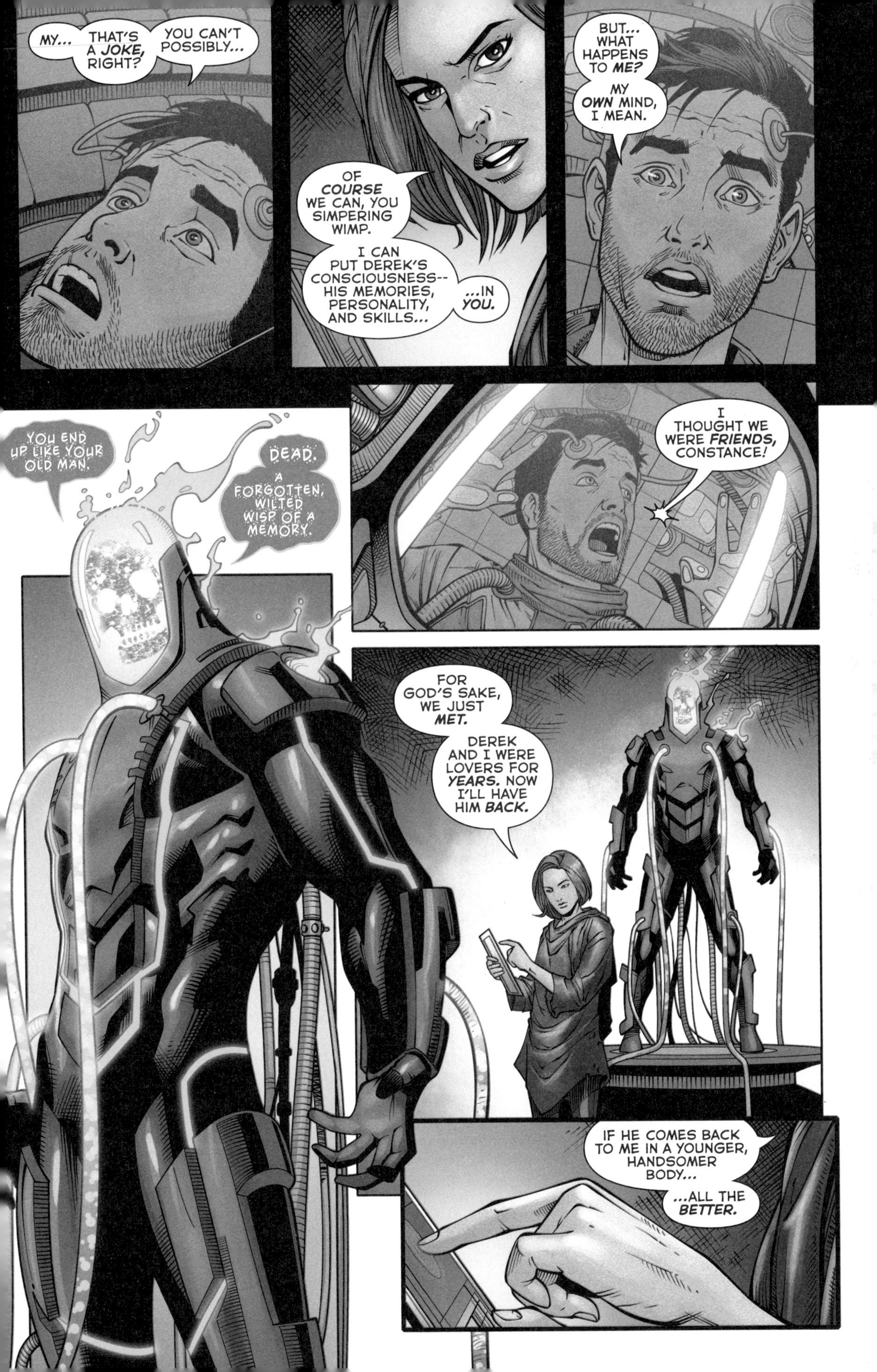
MY...
THAT'S A *JOKE,* RIGHT?
YOU CAN'T POSSIBLY...
OF *COURSE* WE CAN, YOU SIMPERING WIMP.
I CAN PUT DEREK'S CONSCIOUSNESS-- HIS MEMORIES, PERSONALITY, AND SKILLS...
...IN *YOU.*
BUT... WHAT HAPPENS TO *ME?*
MY *OWN* MIND, I MEAN.
YOU END UP LIKE YOUR OLD MAN.
DEAD.
A FORGOTTEN, WILTED WISP OF A MEMORY.
I THOUGHT WE WERE *FRIENDS,* CONSTANCE!
FOR GOD'S SAKE, WE JUST *MET.*
DEREK AND I WERE LOVERS FOR *YEARS.* NOW I'LL HAVE HIM *BACK.*
IF HE COMES BACK TO ME IN A YOUNGER, HANDSOMER BODY...
...ALL THE *BETTER.*

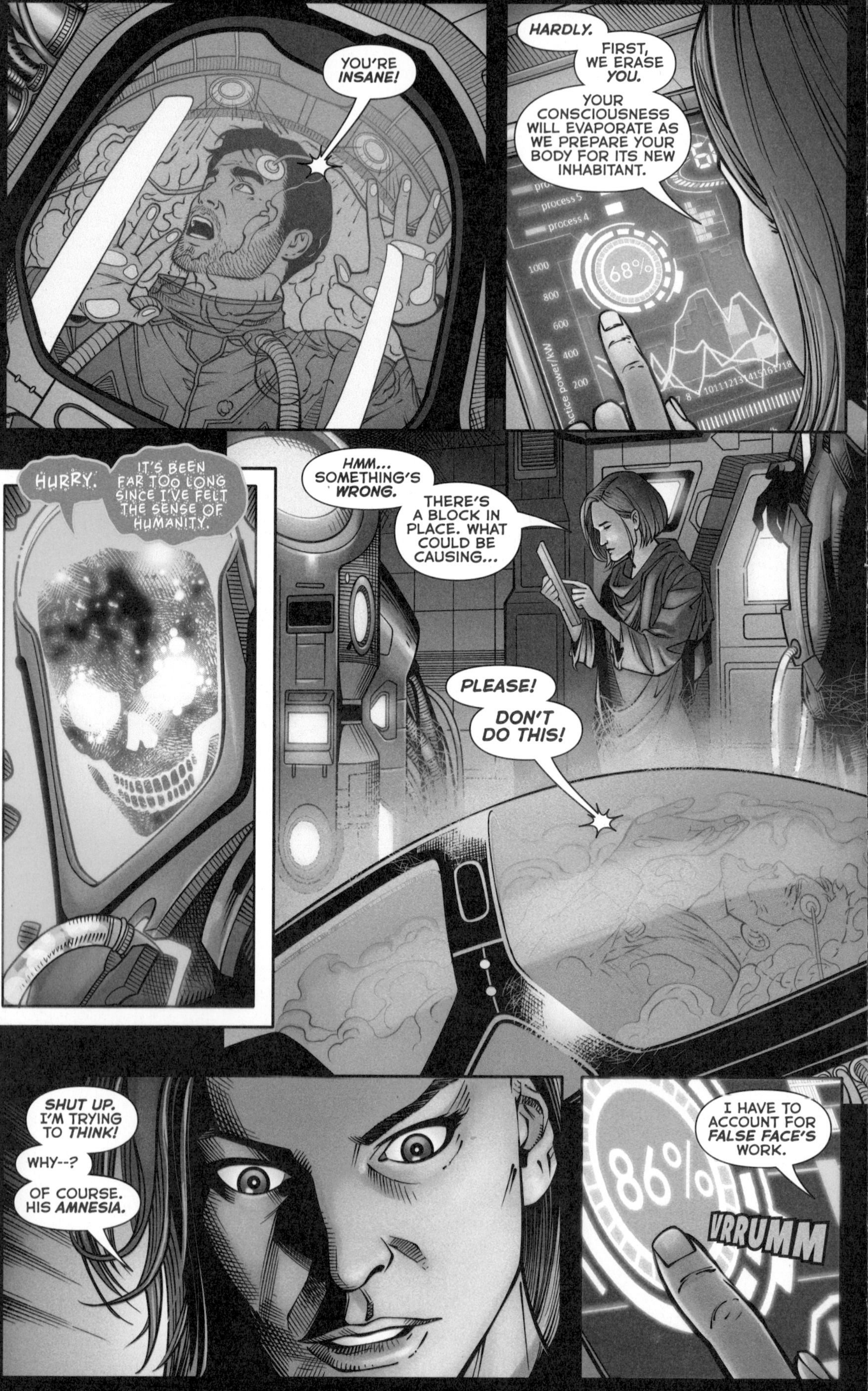
YOU'RE INSANE!
HARDLY.
FIRST, WE ERASE YOU.
YOUR CONSCIOUSNESS WILL EVAPORATE AS WE PREPARE YOUR BODY FOR ITS NEW INHABITANT.
68%
HURRY.
IT'S BEEN FAR TOO LONG SINCE I'VE FELT THE SENSE OF HUMANITY.
HMM... SOMETHING'S WRONG.
THERE'S A BLOCK IN PLACE. WHAT COULD BE CAUSING...
PLEASE!
DON'T DO THIS!
SHUT UP. I'M TRYING TO THINK!
WHY--?
OF COURSE. HIS AMNESIA.
I HAVE TO ACCOUNT FOR FALSE FACE'S WORK.
86%
VRRUMM

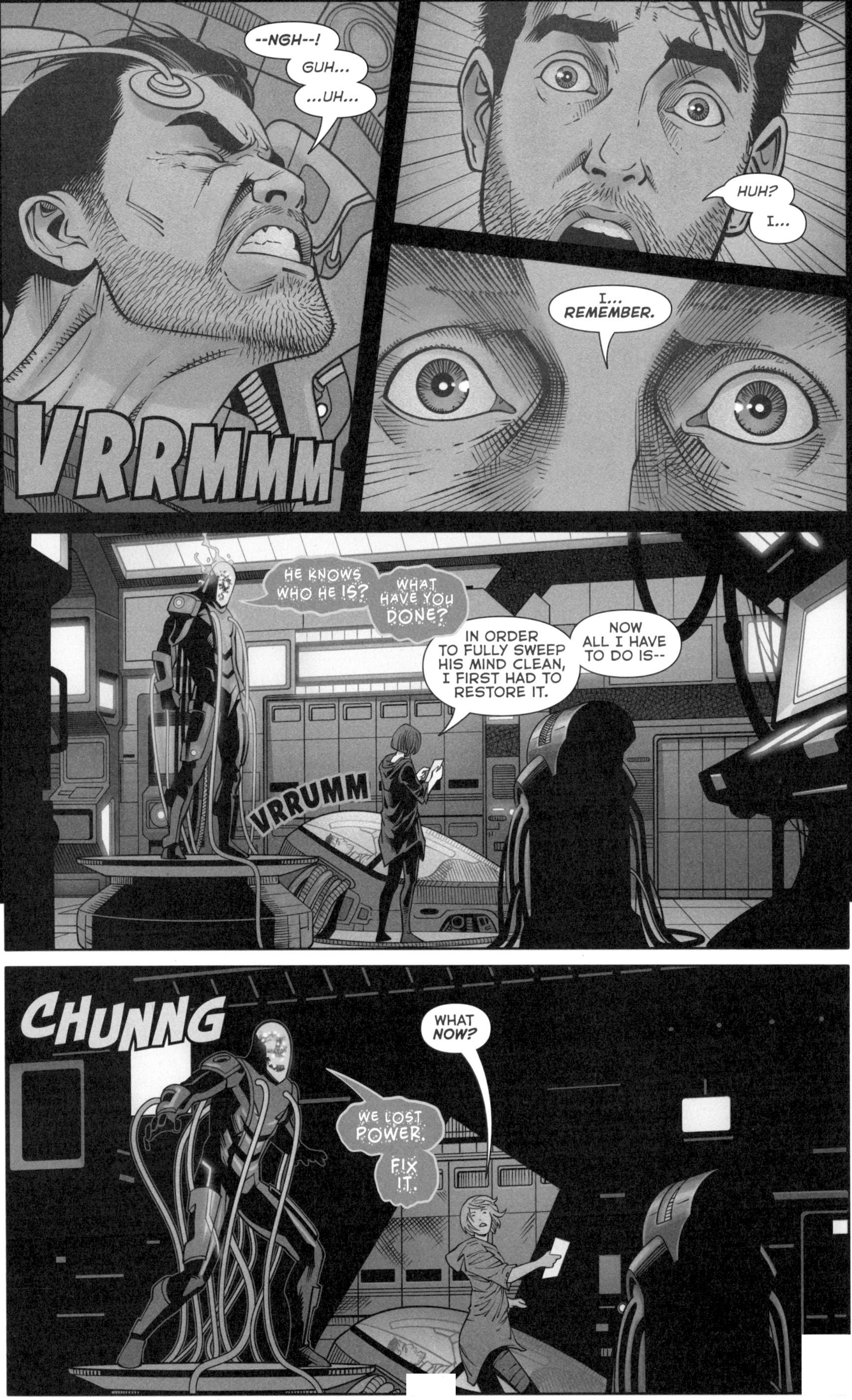
--NGH--!
GUH...
...UH...
VRRMMM
HUH?
I...
I... REMEMBER.
HE KNOWS WHO HE IS?
WHAT HAVE YOU DONE?
IN ORDER TO FULLY SWEEP HIS MIND CLEAN, I FIRST HAD TO RESTORE IT.
NOW ALL I HAVE TO DO IS--
VRRUMM
CHUNNG
WHAT NOW?
WE LOST POWER.
FIX IT.

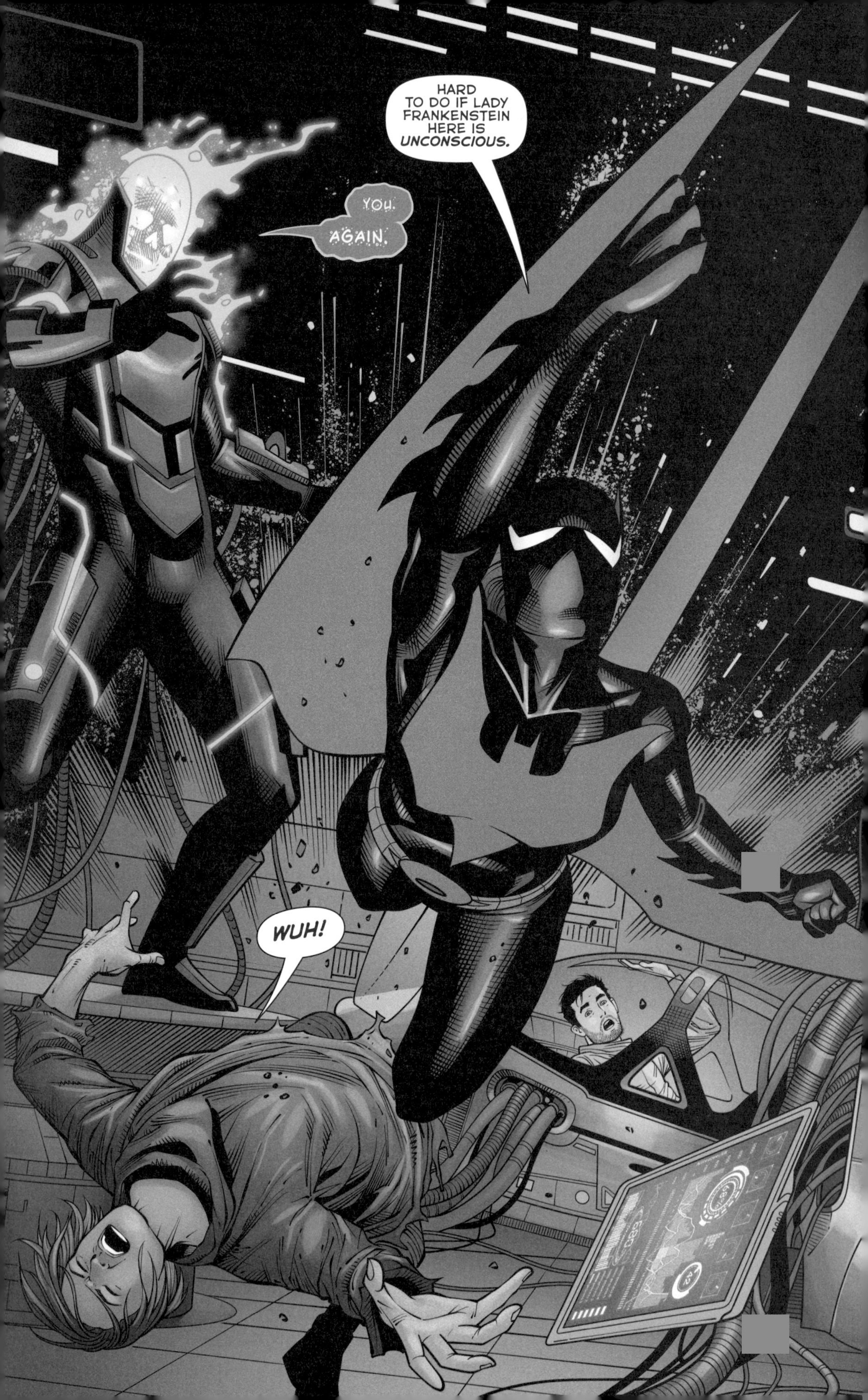
YOU. AGAIN.
HARD TO DO IF LADY FRANKENSTEIN HERE IS *UNCONSCIOUS.*
WUH!

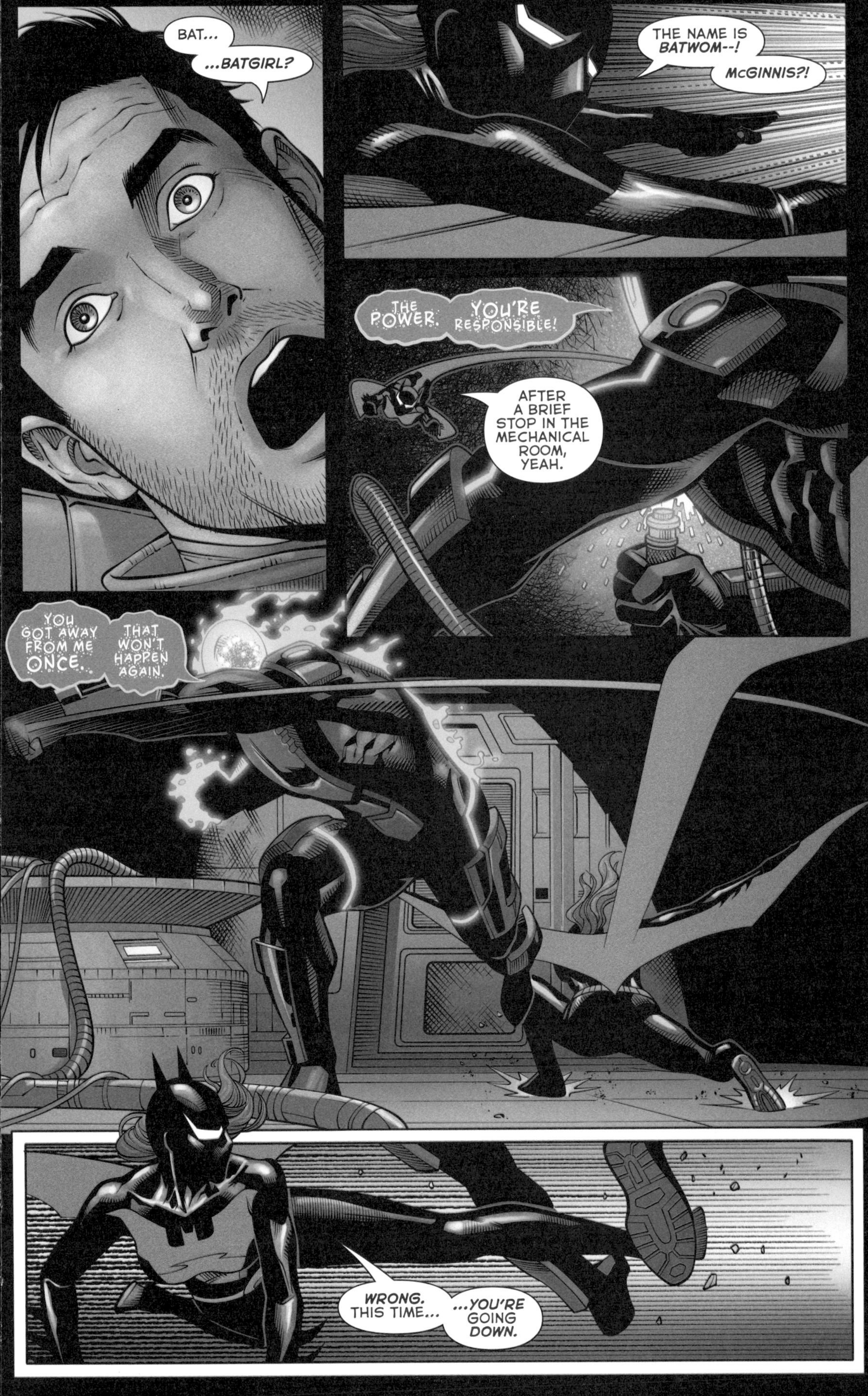
BAT...
...BATGIRL?
THE NAME IS BATWOM--!
McGINNIS?!
THE POWER.
YOU'RE RESPONSIBLE!
AFTER A BRIEF STOP IN THE MECHANICAL ROOM, YEAH.
YOU GOT AWAY FROM ME ONCE.
THAT WON'T HAPPEN AGAIN.
WRONG. THIS TIME...
...YOU'RE GOING DOWN.

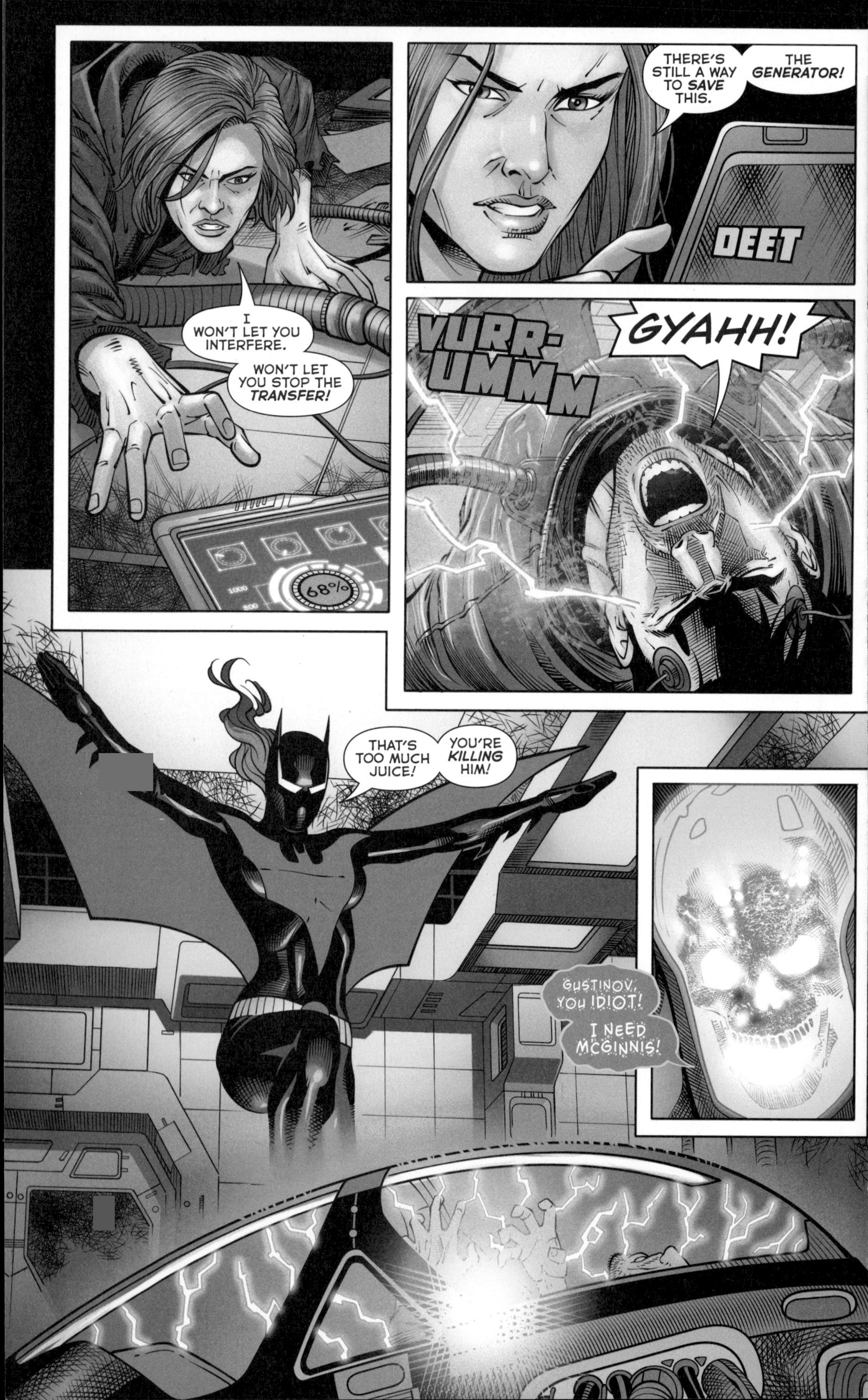
I WON'T LET YOU INTERFERE.
WON'T LET YOU STOP THE *TRANSFER!*
68%
1000
800
THERE'S STILL A WAY TO *SAVE* THIS.
THE *GENERATOR!*
DEET
VURR-UMMM
GYAHH!
THAT'S TOO MUCH JUICE!
YOU'RE *KILLING* HIM!
GUSTINOV, YOU IDIOT!
I NEED MCGINNIS!

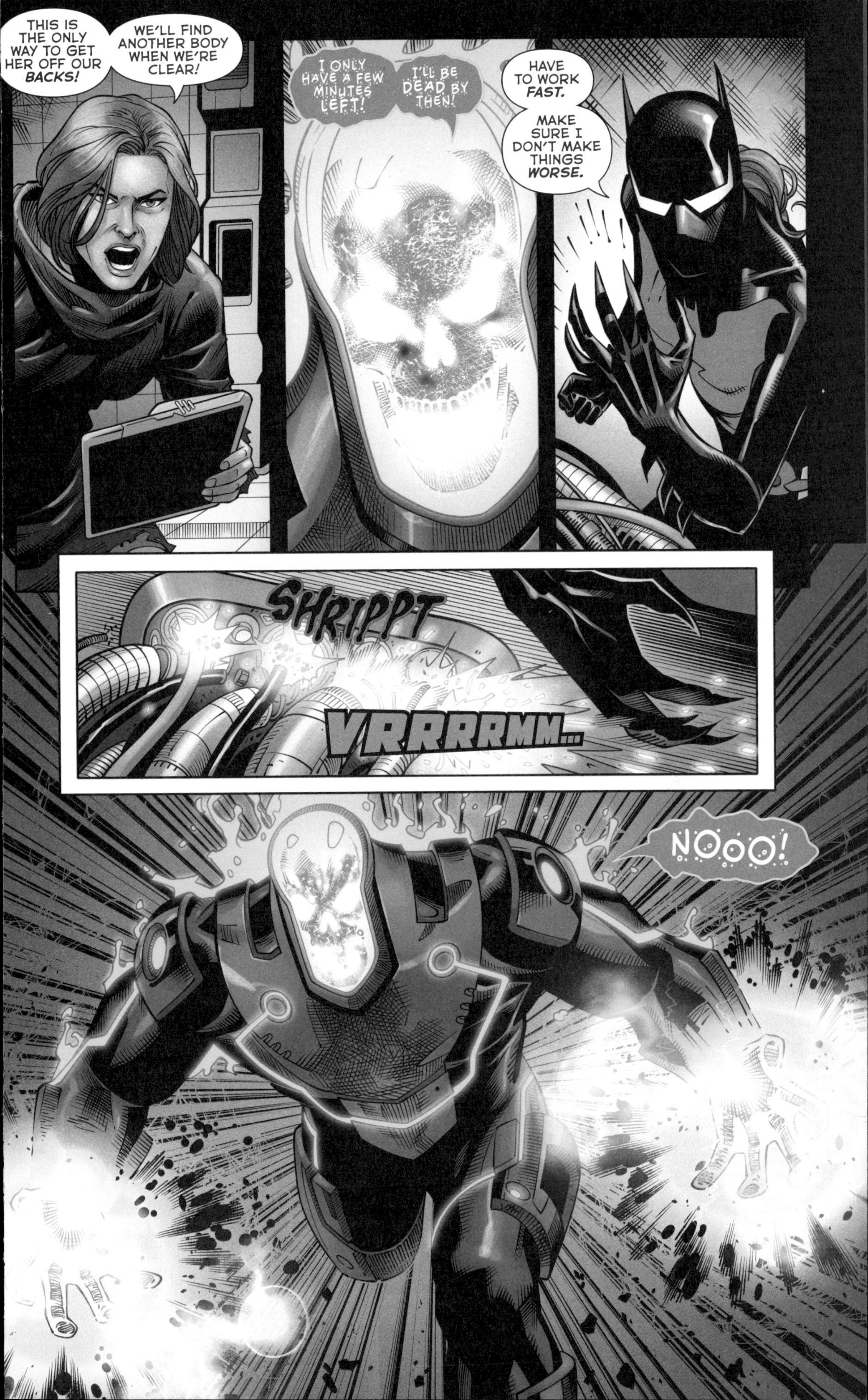

THIS IS THE ONLY WAY TO GET HER OFF OUR *BACKS!*
WE'LL FIND ANOTHER BODY WHEN WE'RE CLEAR!
I ONLY HAVE A FEW MINUTES LEFT!
I'LL BE DEAD BY THEN!
HAVE TO WORK *FAST.*
MAKE SURE I DON'T MAKE THINGS *WORSE.*
SHRIPPT
VRRRRMM...
NOOO!

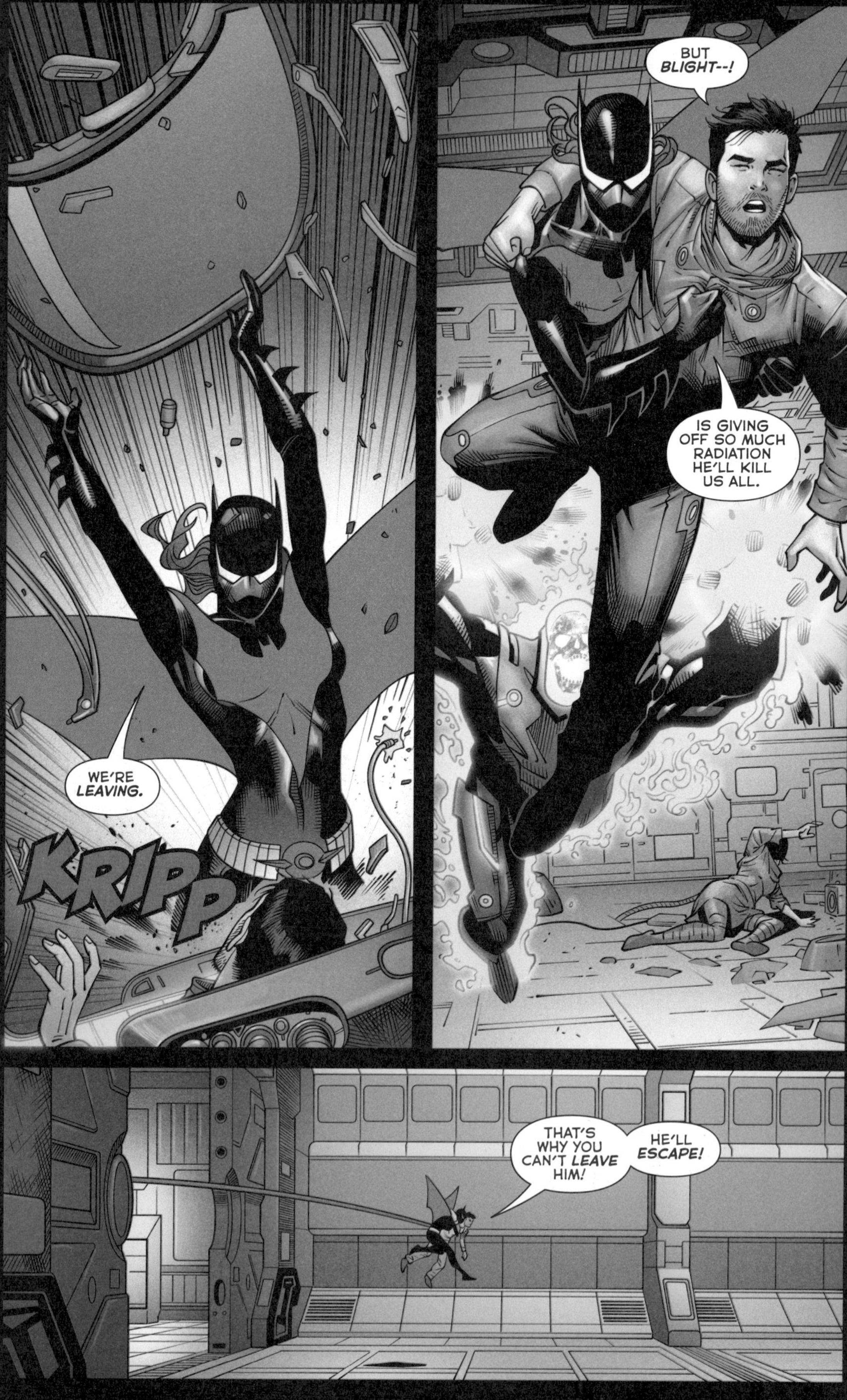
WE'RE LEAVING.
KRIPP
BUT BLIGHT--!
IS GIVING OFF SO MUCH RADIATION HE'LL KILL US ALL.
HE'LL ESCAPE!
THAT'S WHY YOU CAN'T LEAVE HIM!

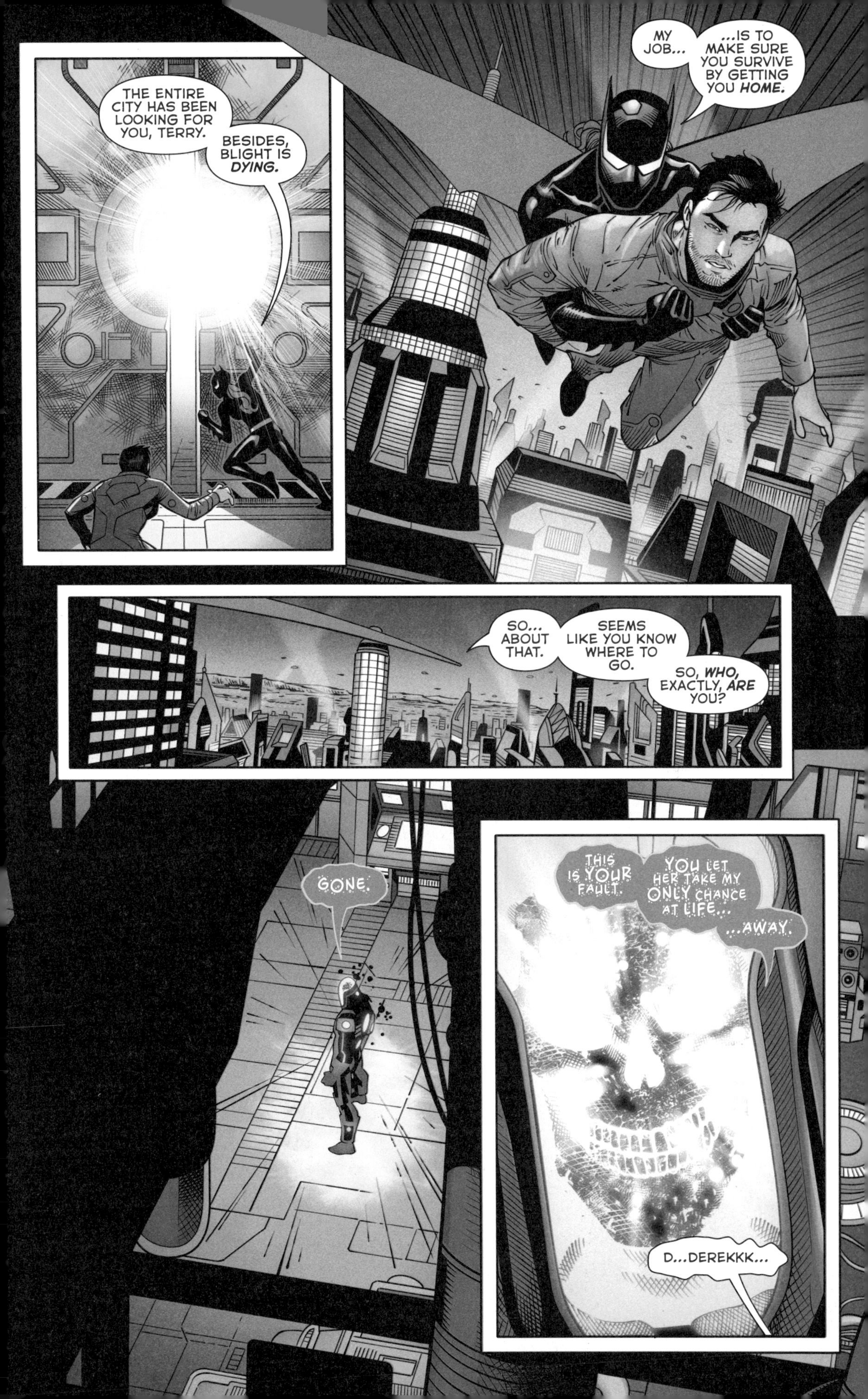
THE ENTIRE CITY HAS BEEN LOOKING FOR YOU, TERRY.
BESIDES, BLIGHT IS *DYING.*
MY JOB...
...IS TO MAKE SURE YOU SURVIVE BY GETTING YOU *HOME.*
SO... ABOUT THAT.
SEEMS LIKE YOU KNOW WHERE TO GO.
SO, *WHO,* EXACTLY, *ARE* YOU?
GONE.
THIS IS YOUR FAULT.
YOU LET HER TAKE MY ONLY CHANCE AT LIFE...
...AWAY.
D...DEREKKK...

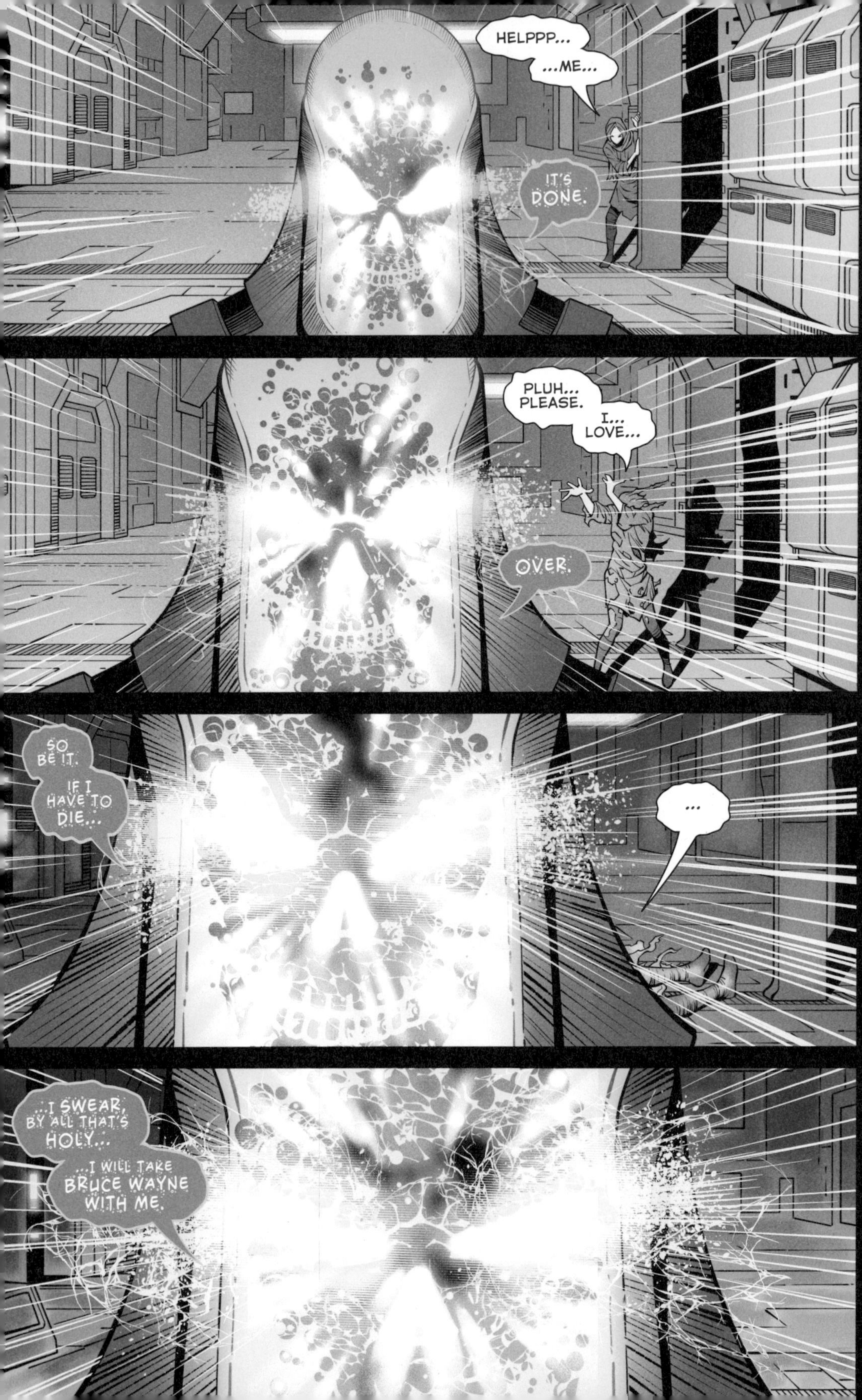
HELPPP...
...ME...
IT'S DONE.
PLUH... PLEASE.
I... LOVE...
OVER.
SO BE IT.
IF I HAVE TO DIE...
...
...I SWEAR, BY ALL THAT'S HOLY...
...I WILL TAKE BRUCE WAYNE WITH ME.

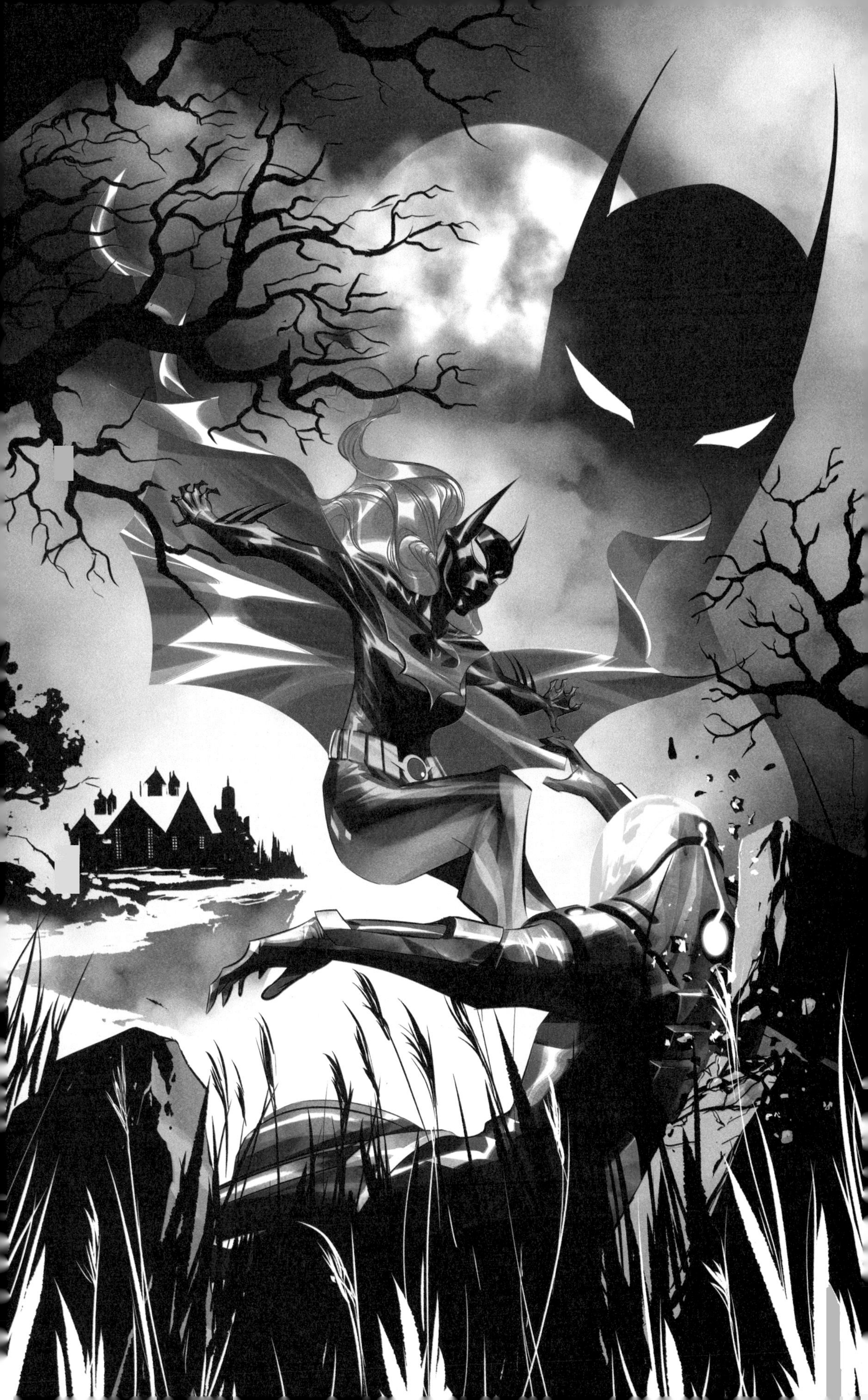

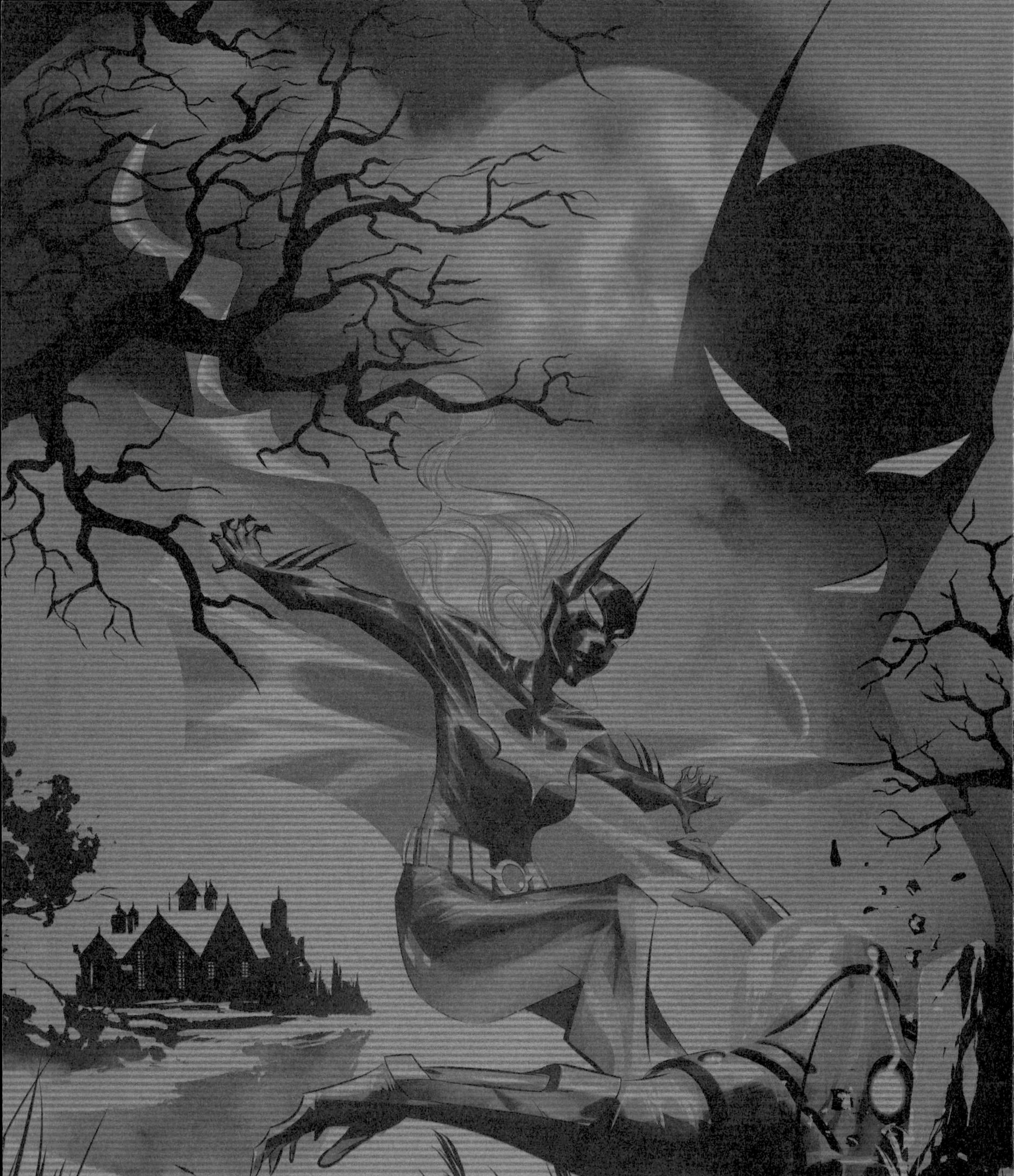

BATMAN
BEYOND

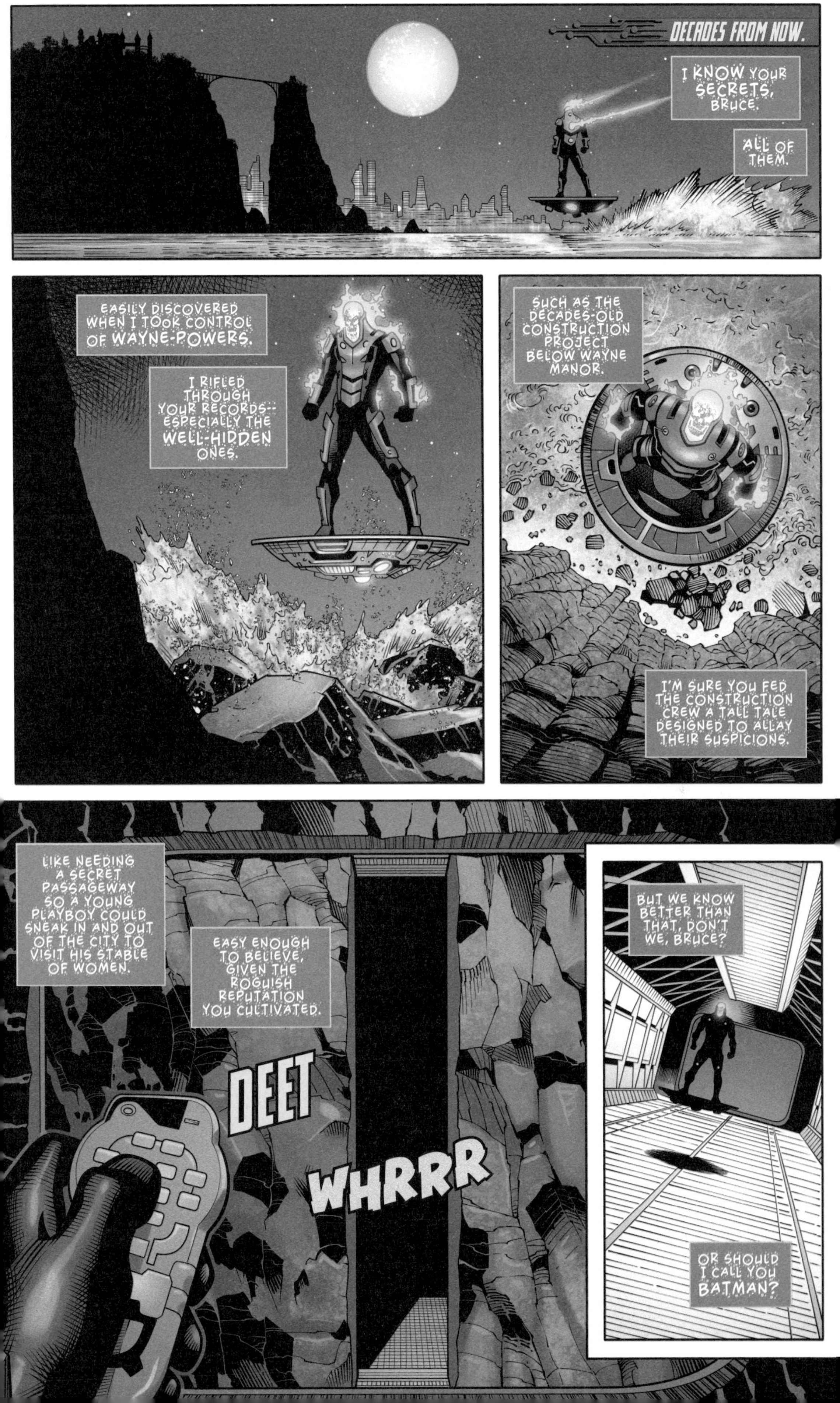
DECADES FROM NOW.
I KNOW YOUR SECRETS, BRUCE.
ALL OF THEM.
EASILY DISCOVERED WHEN I TOOK CONTROL OF WAYNE-POWERS.
I RIFLED THROUGH YOUR RECORDS-- ESPECIALLY THE WELL-HIDDEN ONES.
SUCH AS THE DECADES-OLD CONSTRUCTION PROJECT BELOW WAYNE MANOR.
I'M SURE YOU FED THE CONSTRUCTION CREW A TALL TALE DESIGNED TO ALLAY THEIR SUSPICIONS.
LIKE NEEDING A SECRET PASSAGEWAY SO A YOUNG PLAYBOY COULD SNEAK IN AND OUT OF THE CITY TO VISIT HIS STABLE OF WOMEN.
EASY ENOUGH TO BELIEVE, GIVEN THE ROGUISH REPUTATION YOU CULTIVATED.
DEET
WHRRR
BUT WE KNOW BETTER THAN THAT, DON'T WE, BRUCE?
OR SHOULD I CALL YOU BATMAN?

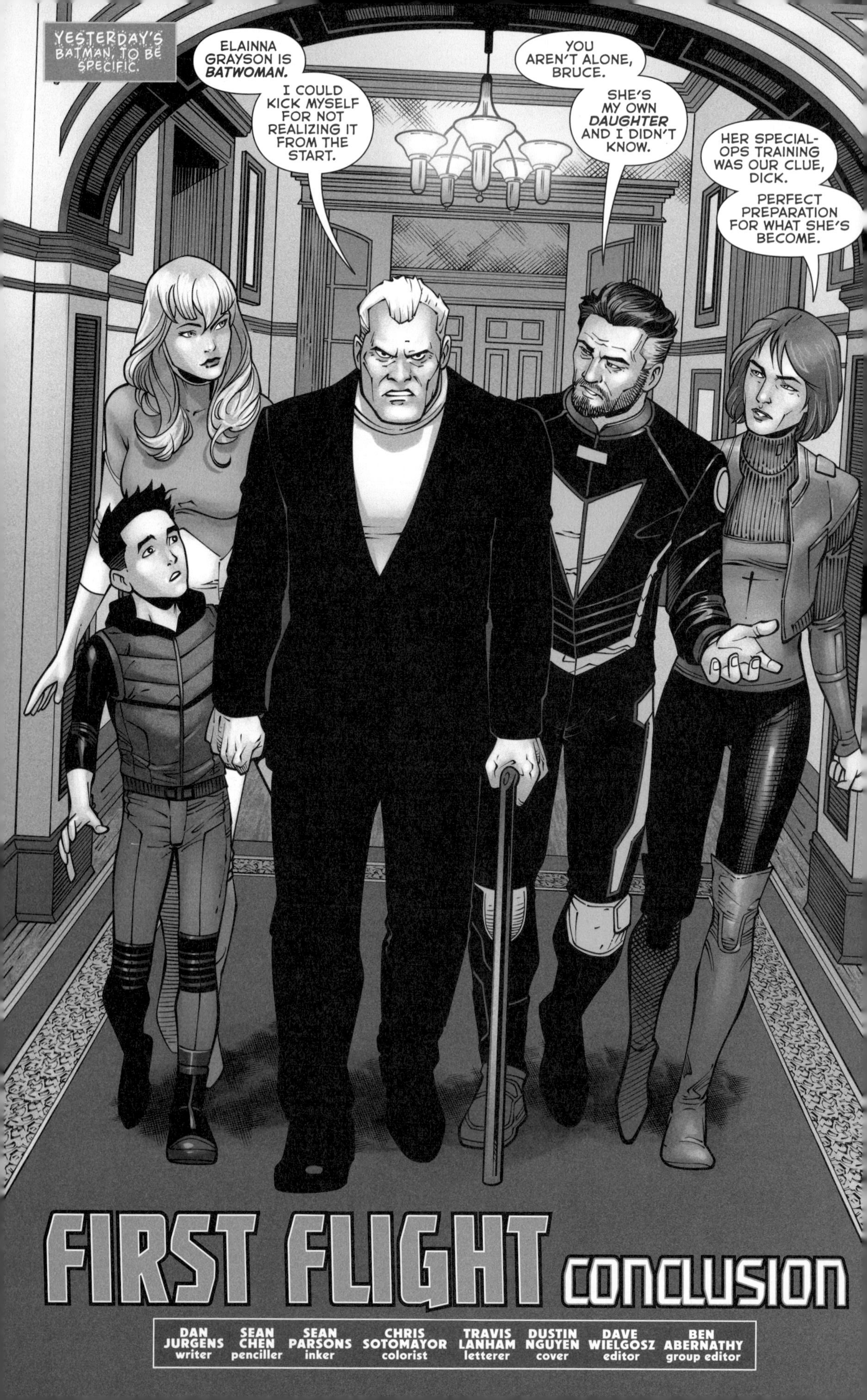
YESTERDAY'S BATMAN, TO BE SPECIFIC.
ELAINNA GRAYSON IS ***BATWOMAN.***
I COULD KICK MYSELF FOR NOT REALIZING IT FROM THE START.
YOU AREN'T ALONE, BRUCE.
SHE'S MY OWN ***DAUGHTER*** AND I DIDN'T KNOW.
HER SPECIAL-OPS TRAINING WAS OUR CLUE, DICK.
PERFECT PREPARATION FOR WHAT SHE'S BECOME.
FIRST FLIGHT CONCLUSION
DAN JURGENS writer
SEAN CHEN penciller
SEAN PARSONS inker
CHRIS SOTOMAYOR colorist
TRAVIS LANHAM letterer
DUSTIN NGUYEN cover
DAVE WIELGOSZ editor
BEN ABERNATHY group editor

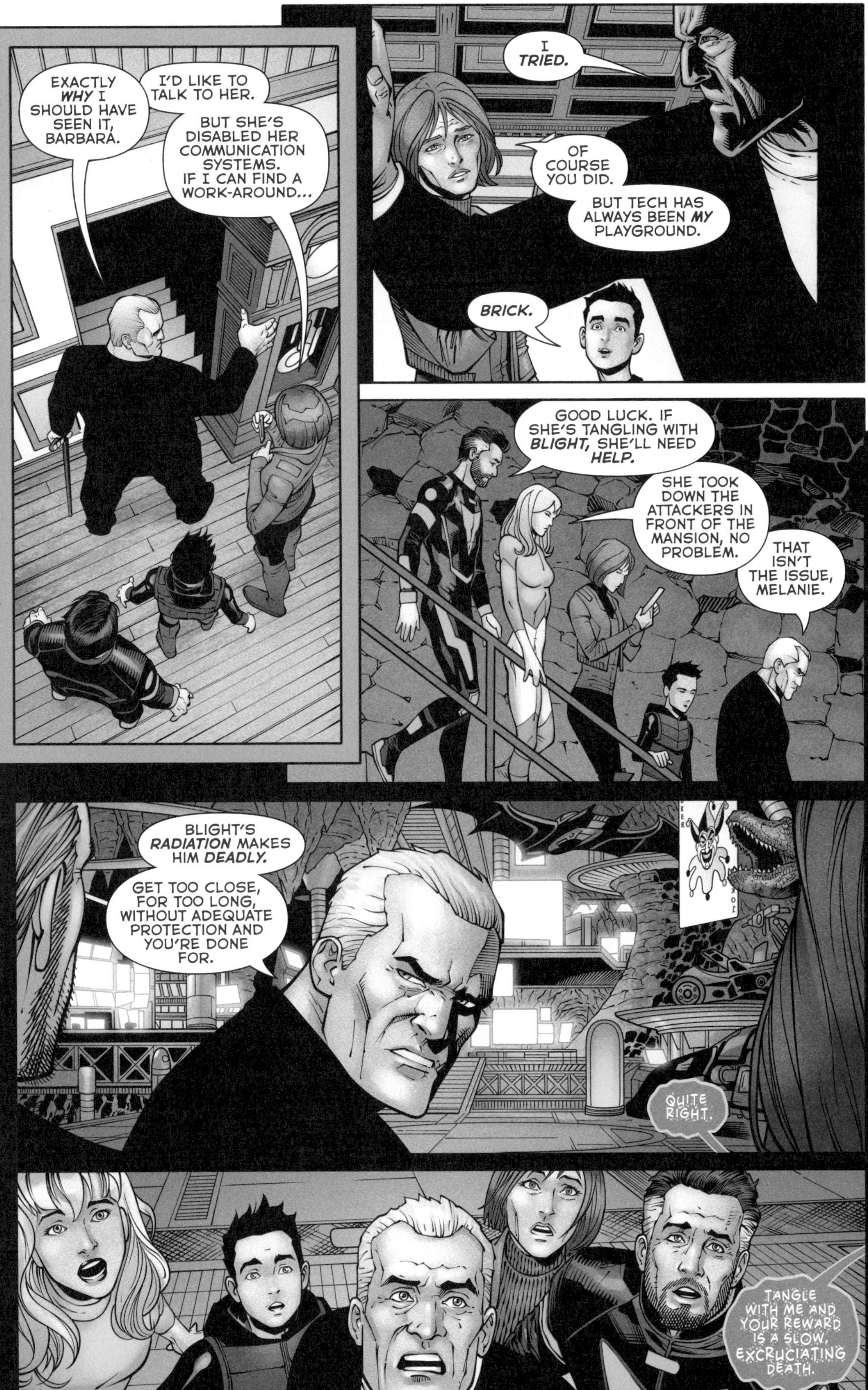

EXACTLY *WHY* I SHOULD HAVE SEEN IT, BARBARA.
I'D LIKE TO TALK TO HER.
BUT SHE'S DISABLED HER COMMUNICATION SYSTEMS. IF I CAN FIND A WORK-AROUND...
I *TRIED.*
OF COURSE YOU DID.
BUT TECH HAS ALWAYS BEEN *MY* PLAYGROUND.
BRICK.
GOOD LUCK. IF SHE'S TANGLING WITH *BLIGHT,* SHE'LL NEED *HELP.*
SHE TOOK DOWN THE ATTACKERS IN FRONT OF THE MANSION, NO PROBLEM.
THAT ISN'T THE ISSUE, MELANIE.
BLIGHT'S *RADIATION* MAKES HIM *DEADLY.*
GET TOO CLOSE, FOR TOO LONG, WITHOUT ADEQUATE PROTECTION AND YOU'RE DONE FOR.
QUITE RIGHT.
TANGLE WITH ME AND YOUR REWARD IS A SLOW, EXCRUCIATING DEATH.

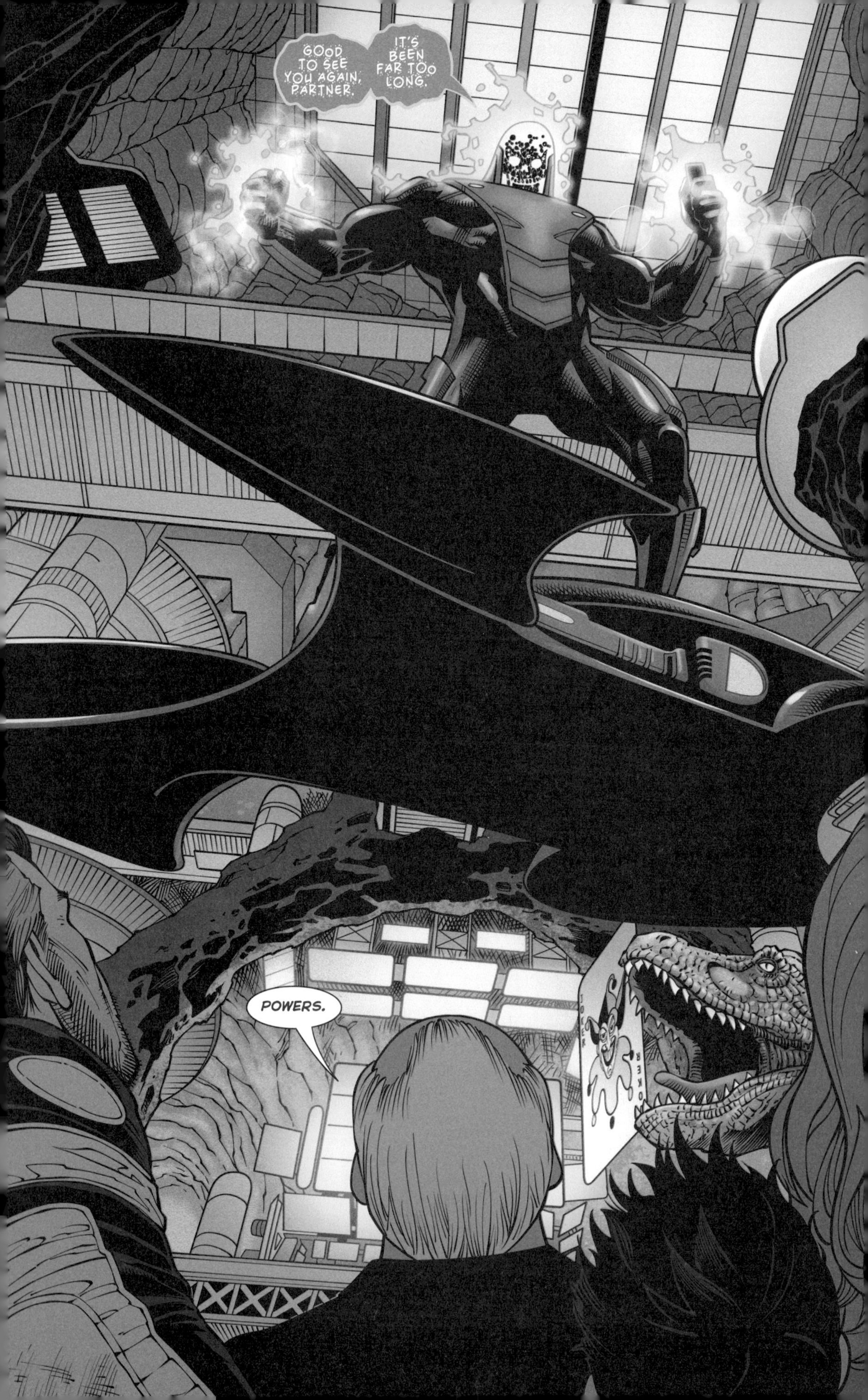
GOOD TO SEE YOU AGAIN, PARTNER.
IT'S BEEN FAR TOO LONG.
POWERS.

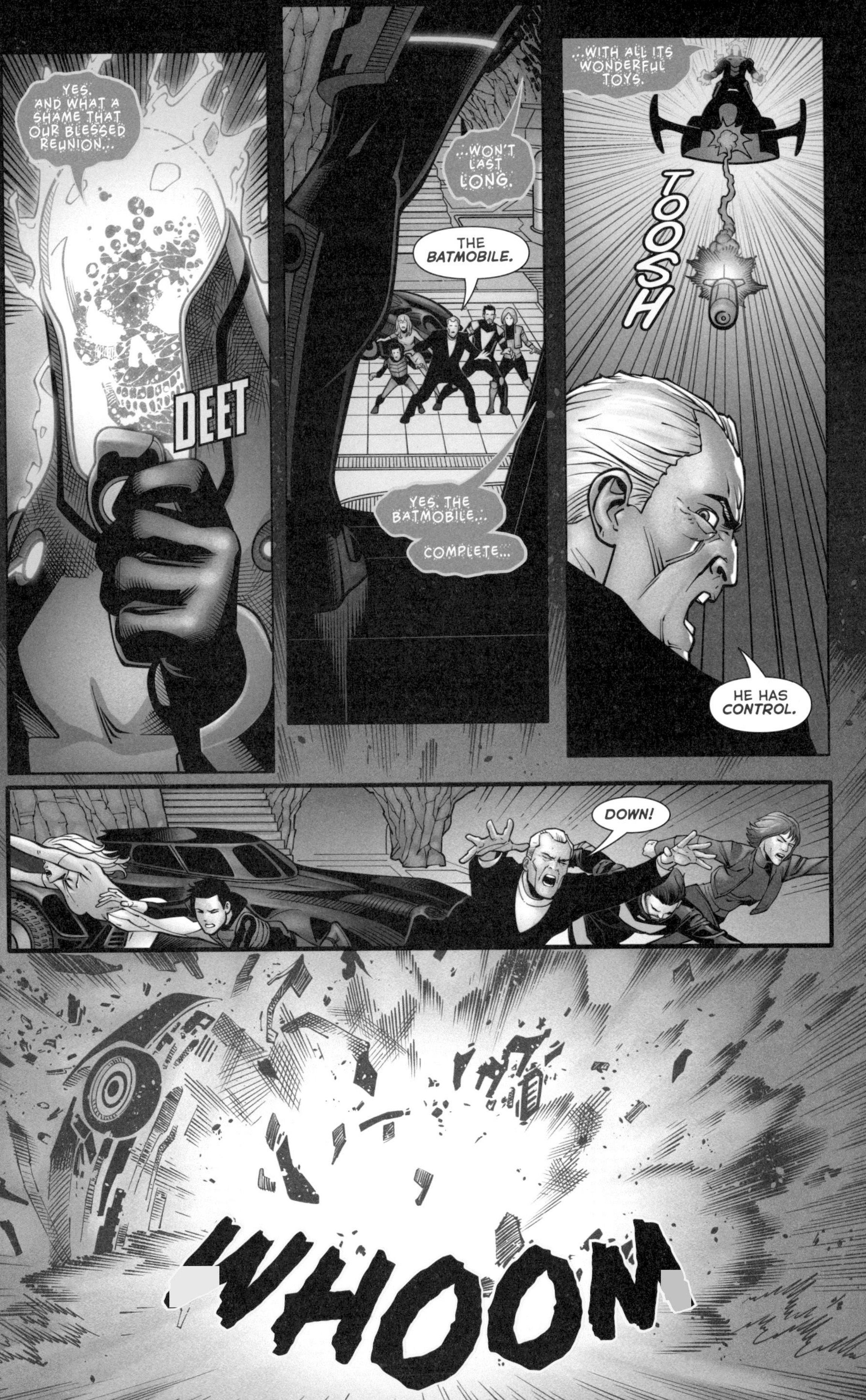
YES. AND WHAT A SHAME THAT OUR BLESSED REUNION...
DEET
...WON'T LAST LONG.
THE BATMOBILE.
YES. THE BATMOBILE...
COMPLETE...
...WITH ALL ITS WONDERFUL TOYS.
TOOSH
HE HAS CONTROL.
DOWN!
WHOOM

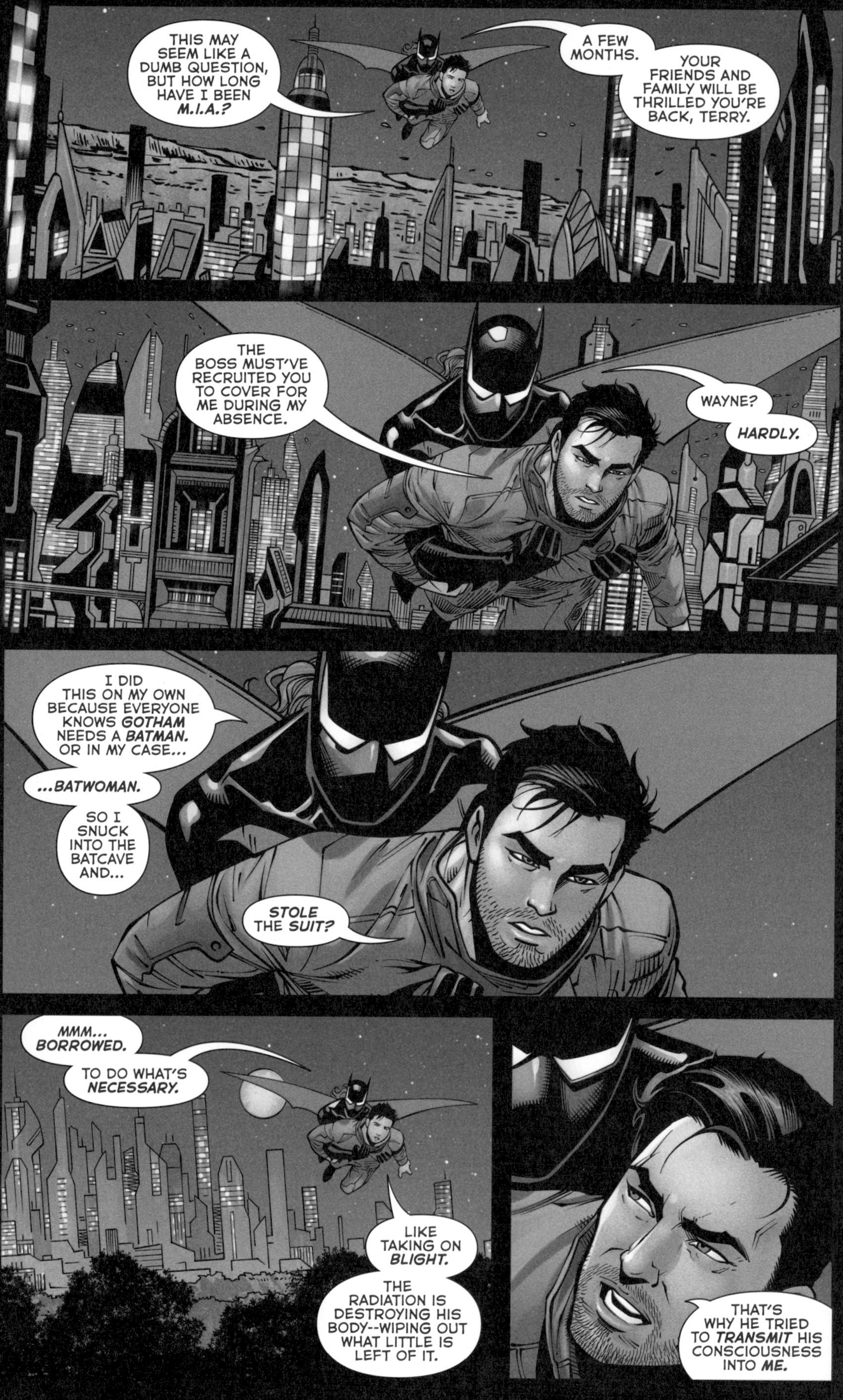
THIS MAY SEEM LIKE A DUMB QUESTION, BUT HOW LONG HAVE I BEEN M.I.A.?
A FEW MONTHS.
YOUR FRIENDS AND FAMILY WILL BE THRILLED YOU'RE BACK, TERRY.
THE BOSS MUST'VE RECRUITED YOU TO COVER FOR ME DURING MY ABSENCE.
WAYNE?
HARDLY.
I DID THIS ON MY OWN BECAUSE EVERYONE KNOWS GOTHAM NEEDS A BATMAN. OR IN MY CASE...
...BATWOMAN.
SO I SNUCK INTO THE BATCAVE AND...
STOLE THE SUIT?
MMM... BORROWED.
TO DO WHAT'S NECESSARY.
LIKE TAKING ON BLIGHT.
THE RADIATION IS DESTROYING HIS BODY--WIPING OUT WHAT LITTLE IS LEFT OF IT.
THAT'S WHY HE TRIED TO TRANSMIT HIS CONSCIOUSNESS INTO ME.

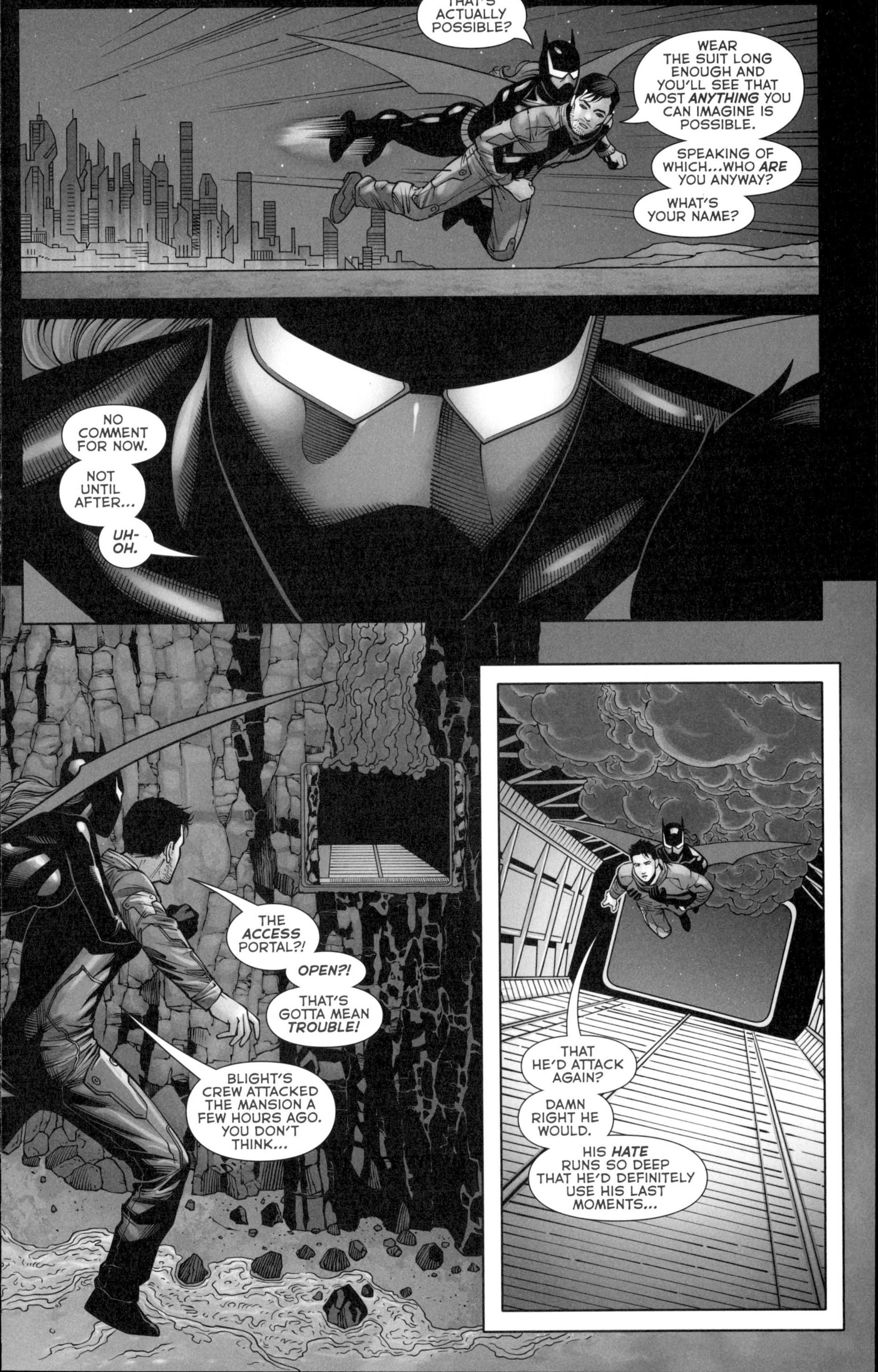
THAT'S ACTUALLY POSSIBLE?
WEAR THE SUIT LONG ENOUGH AND YOU'LL SEE THAT MOST *ANYTHING* YOU CAN IMAGINE IS POSSIBLE.
SPEAKING OF WHICH...WHO *ARE* YOU ANYWAY?
WHAT'S YOUR NAME?
NO COMMENT FOR NOW.
NOT UNTIL AFTER...
UH-OH.
THE *ACCESS* PORTAL?!
OPEN?!
THAT'S GOTTA MEAN *TROUBLE!*
BLIGHT'S CREW ATTACKED THE MANSION A FEW HOURS AGO. YOU DON'T THINK...
THAT HE'D ATTACK AGAIN?
DAMN RIGHT HE WOULD.
HIS *HATE* RUNS SO DEEP THAT HE'D DEFINITELY USE HIS LAST MOMENTS...

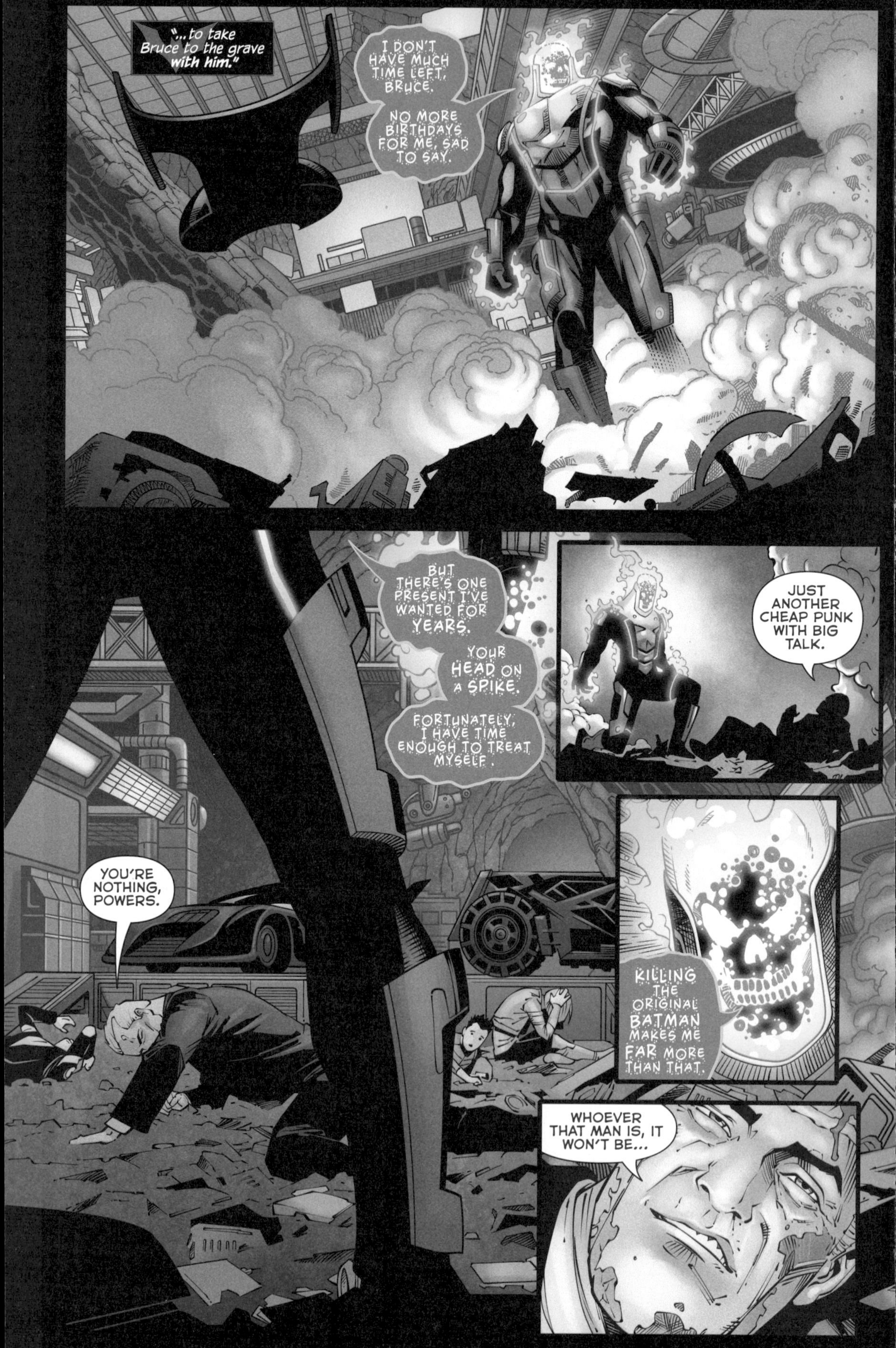
"...to take Bruce to the grave with him."
I DON'T HAVE MUCH TIME LEFT, BRUCE.
NO MORE BIRTHDAYS FOR ME, SAD TO SAY.
BUT THERE'S ONE PRESENT I'VE WANTED FOR YEARS.
YOUR HEAD ON A SPIKE.
FORTUNATELY, I HAVE TIME ENOUGH TO TREAT MYSELF.
JUST ANOTHER CHEAP PUNK WITH BIG TALK.
YOU'RE NOTHING, POWERS.
KILLING THE ORIGINAL BATMAN MAKES ME FAR MORE THAN THAT.
WHOEVER THAT MAN IS, IT WON'T BE...

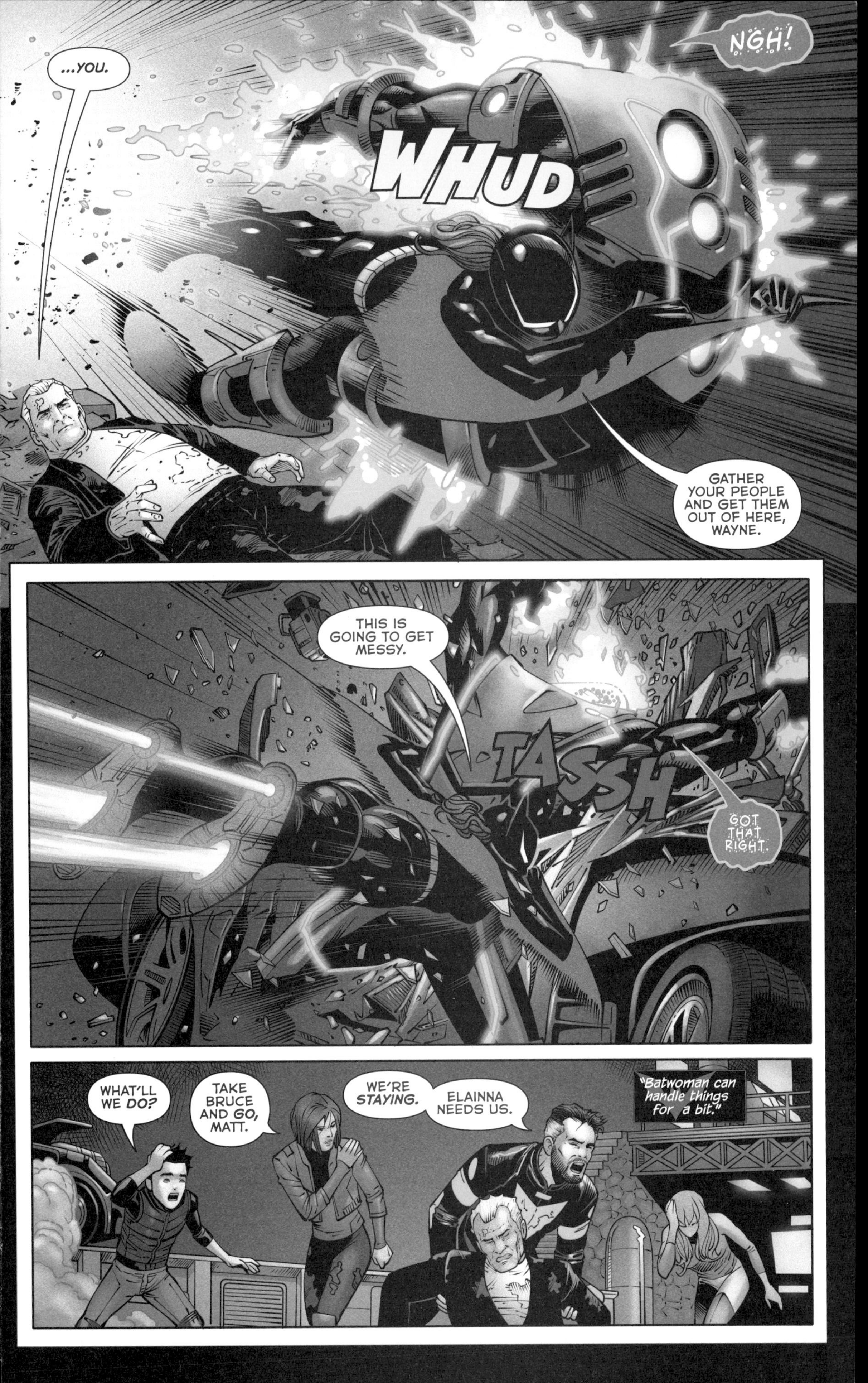

...YOU.
NGH!
WHUD
GATHER YOUR PEOPLE AND GET THEM OUT OF HERE, WAYNE.
THIS IS GOING TO GET MESSY.
TASSH
GOT THAT RIGHT.
WHAT'LL WE DO?
TAKE BRUCE AND GO, MATT.
WE'RE STAYING.
ELAINNA NEEDS US.
"Batwoman can handle things for a bit."

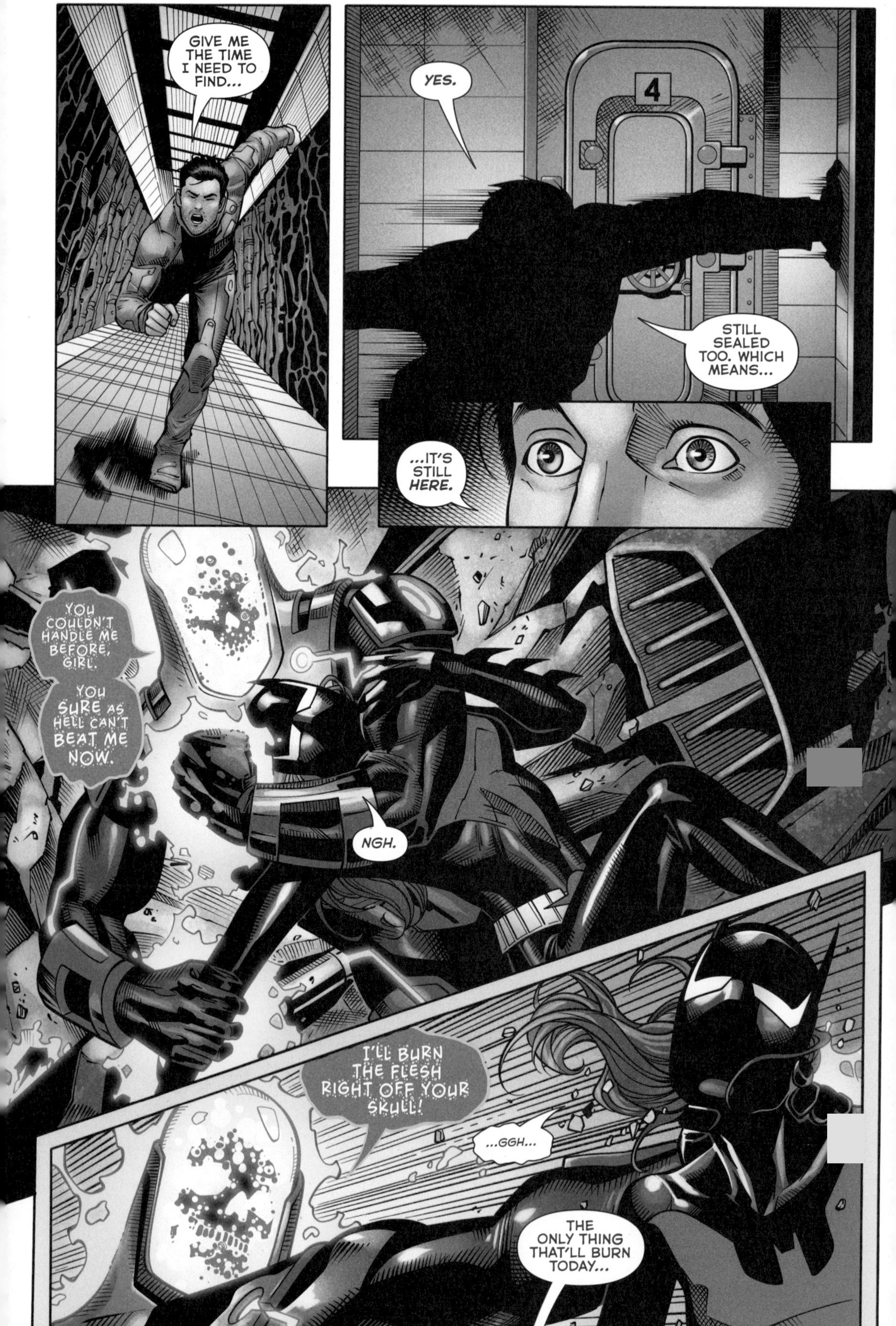
GIVE ME THE TIME I NEED TO FIND...
YES.
STILL SEALED TOO. WHICH MEANS...
...IT'S STILL HERE.
YOU COULDN'T HANDLE ME BEFORE, GIRL.
YOU SURE AS HELL CAN'T BEAT ME NOW.
NGH.
I'LL BURN THE FLESH RIGHT OFF YOUR SKULL!
...GGH...
THE ONLY THING THAT'LL BURN TODAY...

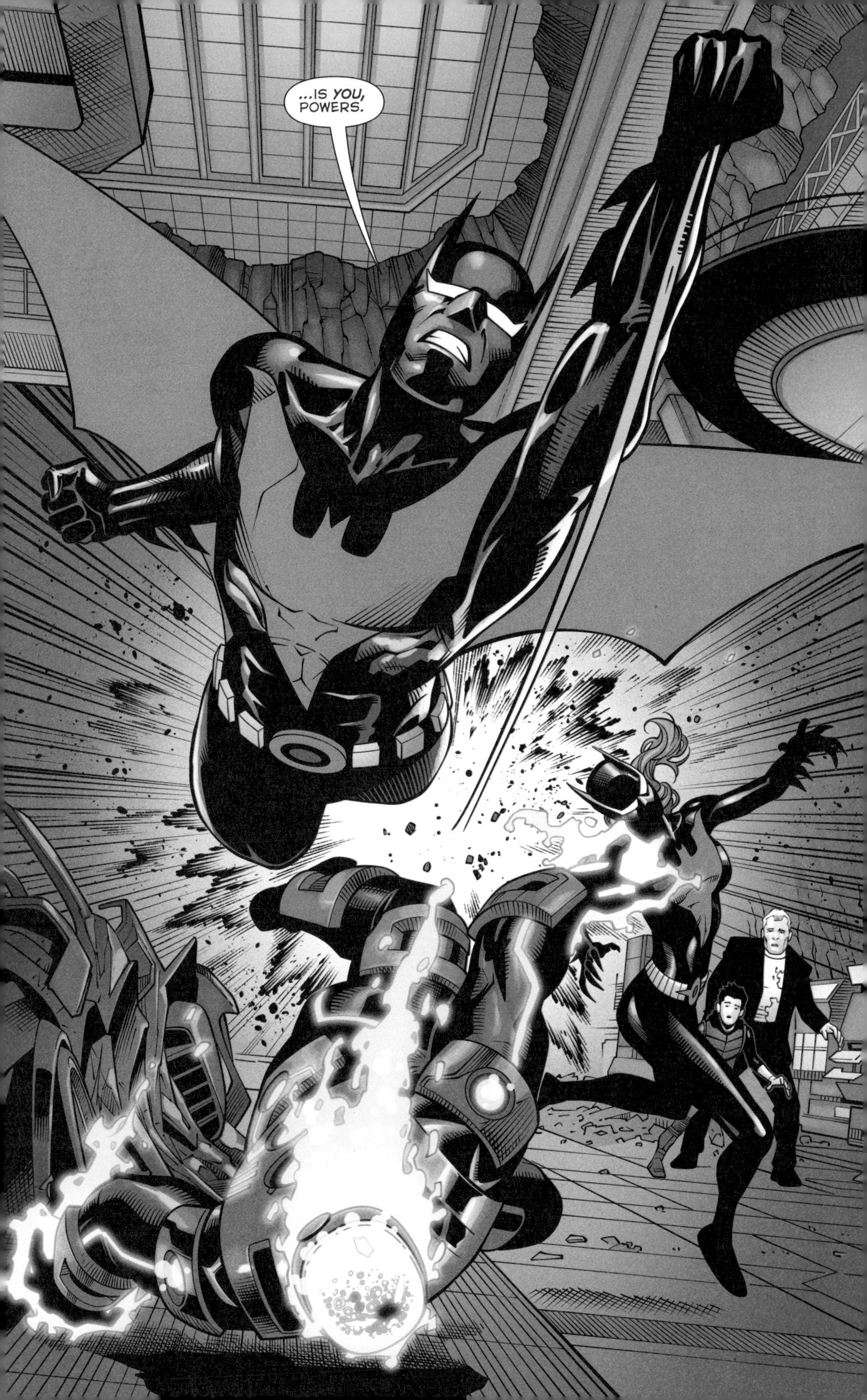
...IS *YOU*, POWERS.

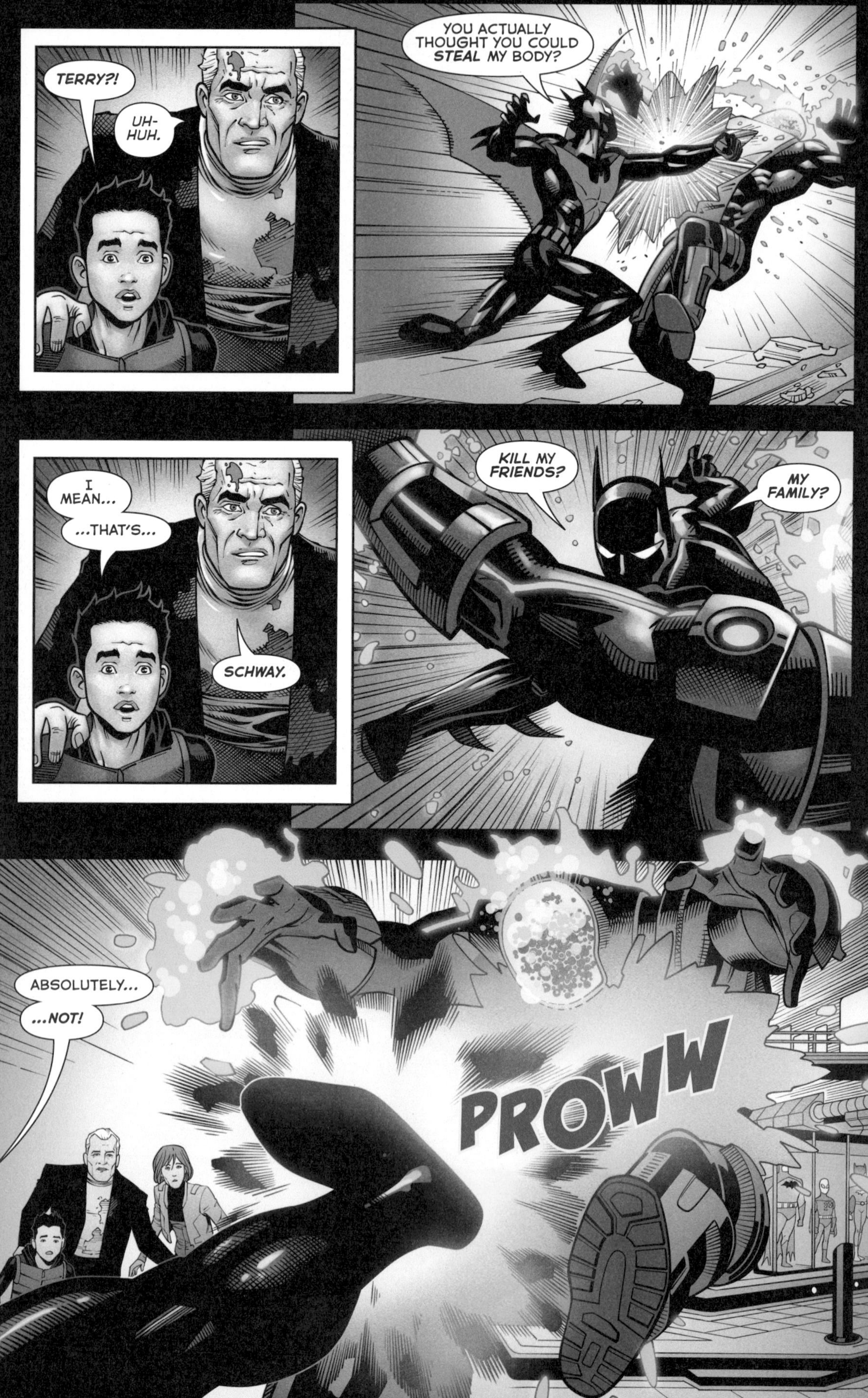
TERRY?!
UH-HUH.
YOU ACTUALLY THOUGHT YOU COULD STEAL MY BODY?
I MEAN...
...THAT'S...
SCHWAY.
KILL MY FRIENDS?
MY FAMILY?
ABSOLUTELY...
...NOT!
PROWW

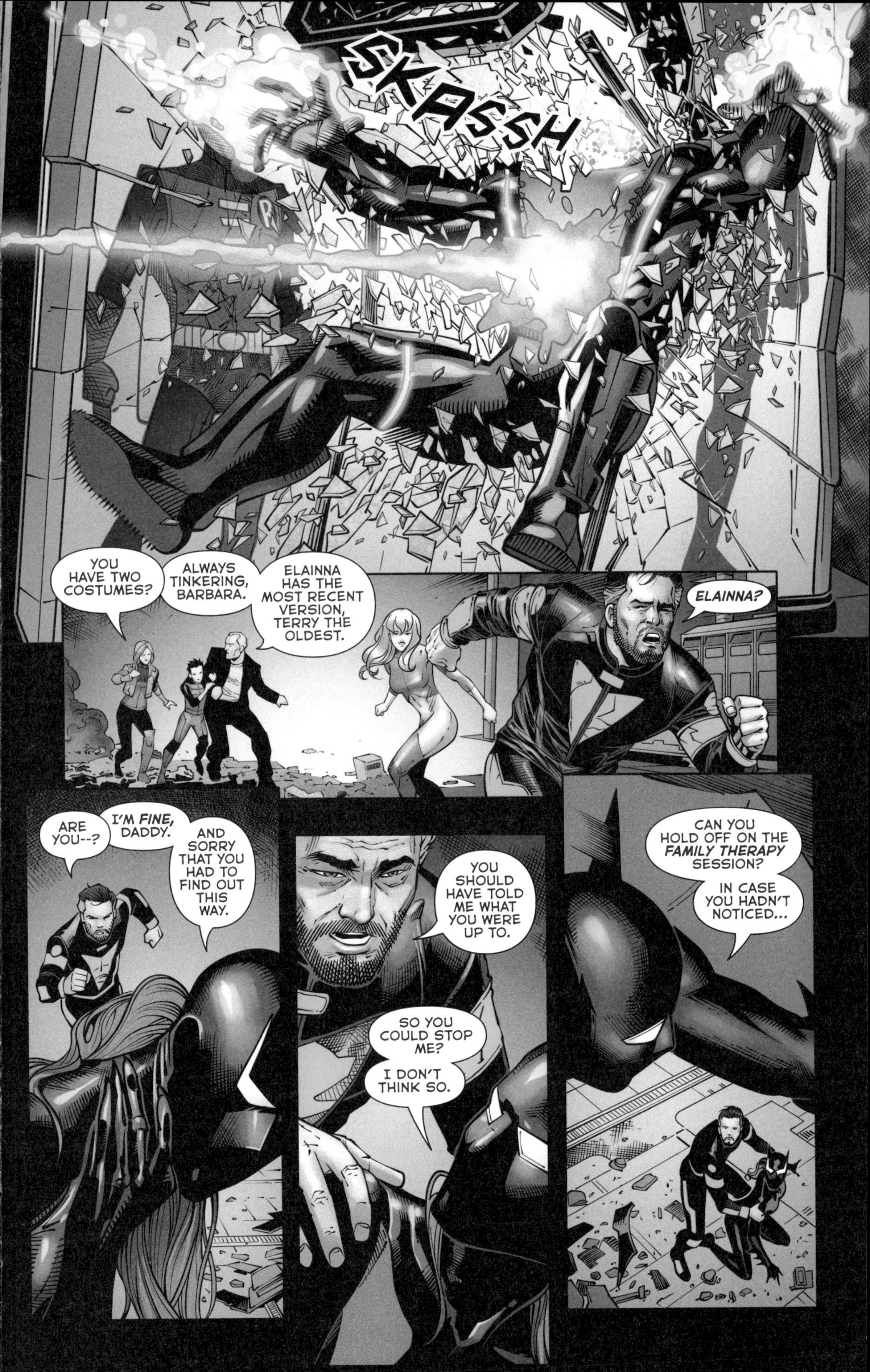
SKASSH
YOU HAVE TWO COSTUMES?
ALWAYS TINKERING, BARBARA.
ELAINNA HAS THE MOST RECENT VERSION, TERRY THE OLDEST.
ELAINNA?
ARE YOU--?
I'M FINE, DADDY.
AND SORRY THAT YOU HAD TO FIND OUT THIS WAY.
YOU SHOULD HAVE TOLD ME WHAT YOU WERE UP TO.
SO YOU COULD STOP ME?
I DON'T THINK SO.
CAN YOU HOLD OFF ON THE FAMILY THERAPY SESSION?
IN CASE YOU HADN'T NOTICED...

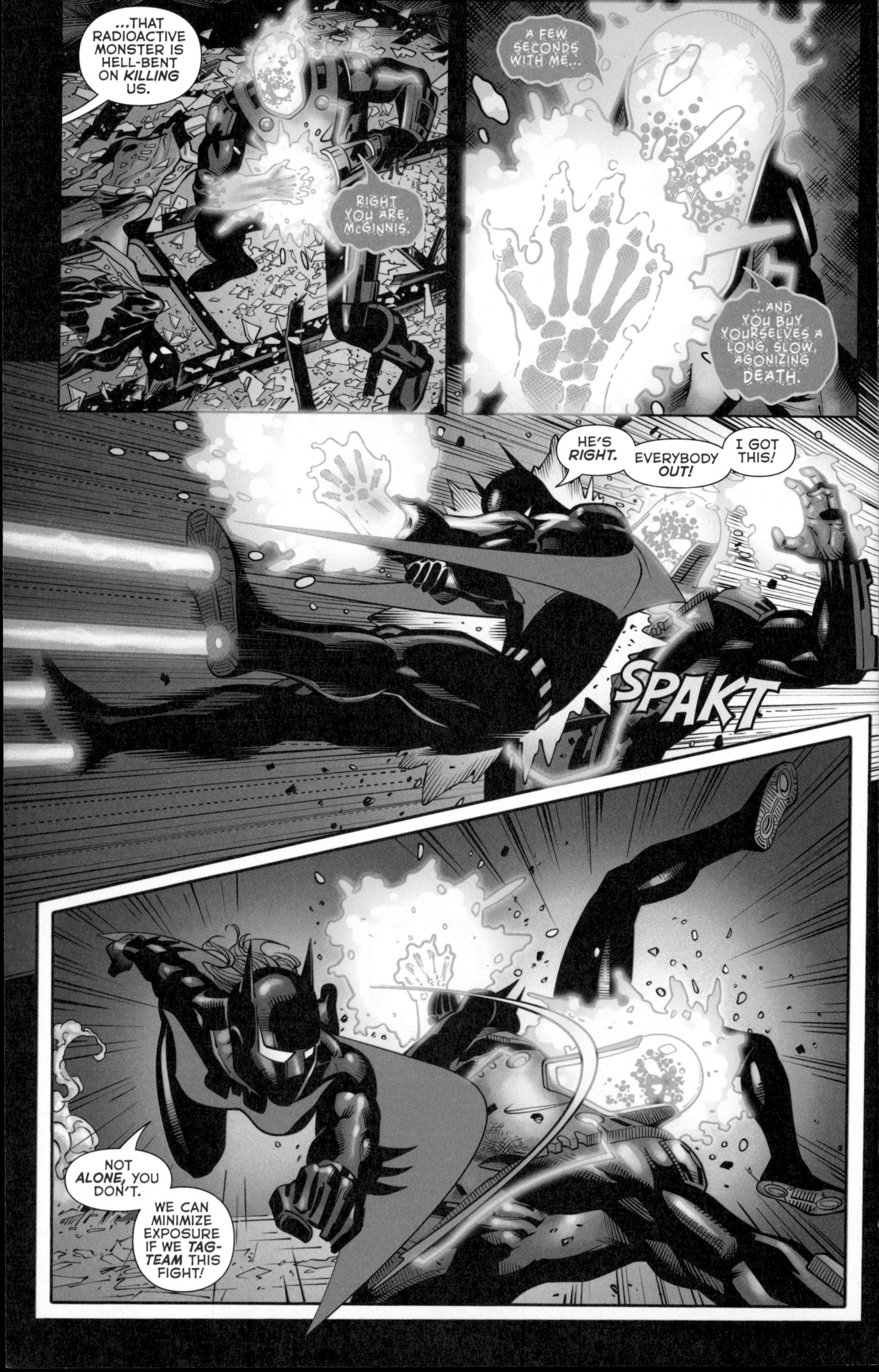
...THAT RADIOACTIVE MONSTER IS HELL-BENT ON *KILLING* US.
RIGHT YOU ARE, McGINNIS.
A FEW SECONDS WITH ME...
...AND YOU BUY YOURSELVES A LONG, SLOW, AGONIZING DEATH.
HE'S *RIGHT.*
EVERYBODY *OUT!*
I GOT THIS!
SPAKT
NOT *ALONE,* YOU DON'T.
WE CAN MINIMIZE EXPOSURE IF WE *TAG-TEAM* THIS FIGHT!

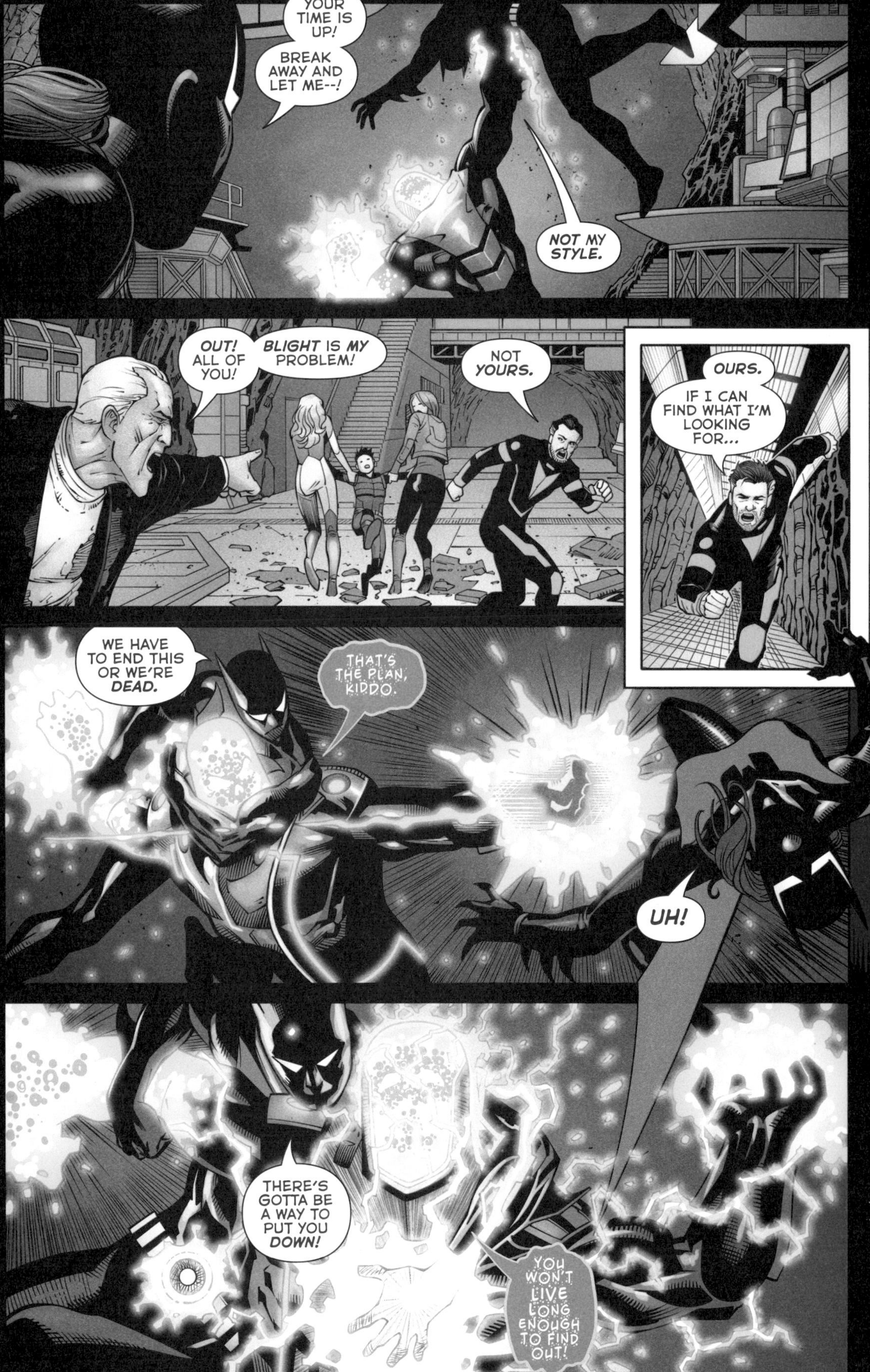

YOUR TIME IS UP!
BREAK AWAY AND LET ME--!
NOT MY STYLE.
OUT! ALL OF YOU!
BLIGHT IS MY PROBLEM!
NOT YOURS.
OURS.
IF I CAN FIND WHAT I'M LOOKING FOR...
WE HAVE TO END THIS OR WE'RE DEAD.
THAT'S THE PLAN, KIDDO.
UH!
THERE'S GOTTA BE A WAY TO PUT YOU DOWN!
YOU WON'T LIVE LONG ENOUGH TO FIND OUT!

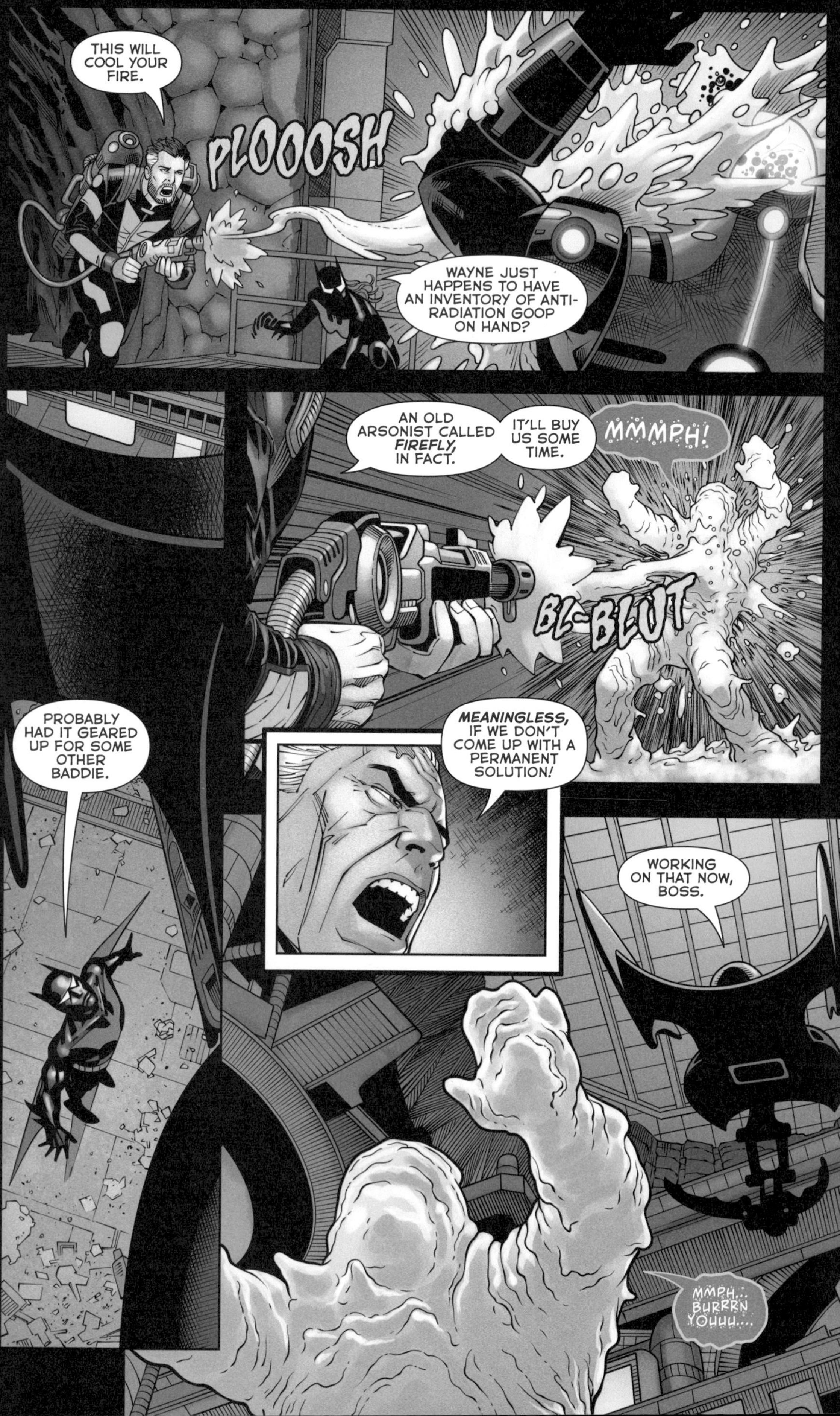
THIS WILL COOL YOUR FIRE.
PLOOOSH
WAYNE JUST HAPPENS TO HAVE AN INVENTORY OF ANTI-RADIATION GOOP ON HAND?
AN OLD ARSONIST CALLED *FIREFLY,* IN FACT.
IT'LL BUY US SOME TIME.
MMMPH!
BL-BLUT
PROBABLY HAD IT GEARED UP FOR SOME OTHER BADDIE.
MEANINGLESS, IF WE DON'T COME UP WITH A PERMANENT SOLUTION!
WORKING ON THAT NOW, BOSS.
MMPH... BURRRN YOUUU....

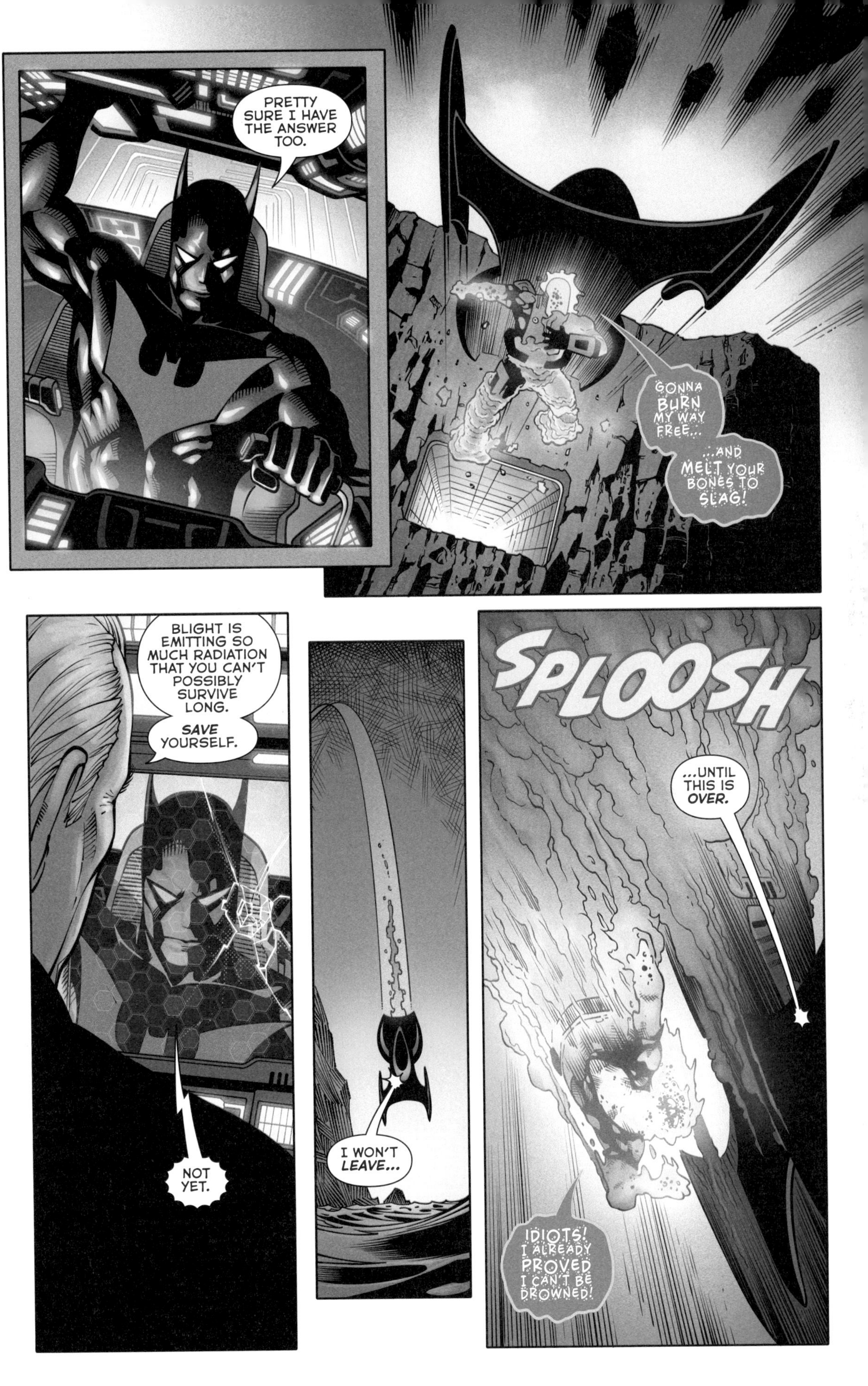
PRETTY SURE I HAVE THE ANSWER TOO.
GONNA BURN MY WAY FREE...
...AND MELT YOUR BONES TO SLAG!
BLIGHT IS EMITTING SO MUCH RADIATION THAT YOU CAN'T POSSIBLY SURVIVE LONG.
SAVE YOURSELF.
NOT YET.
I WON'T LEAVE...
SPLOOSH
...UNTIL THIS IS OVER.
IDIOTS! I ALREADY PROVED I CAN'T BE DROWNED!

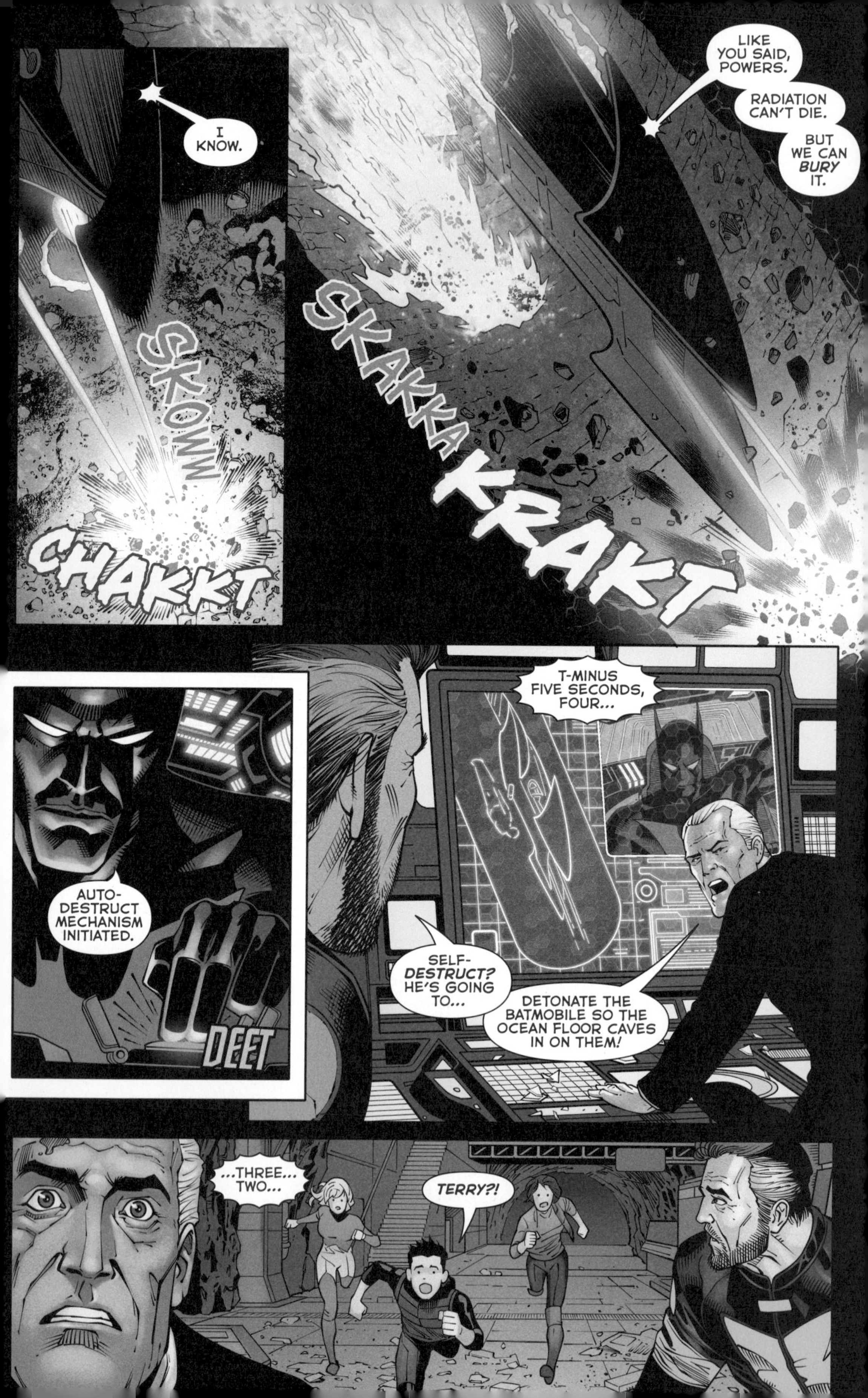
I KNOW.
LIKE YOU SAID, POWERS.
RADIATION CAN'T DIE.
BUT WE CAN *BURY* IT.
SKOWW
CHAKKT
SKAKKA KRAKT
AUTO-DESTRUCT MECHANISM INITIATED.
DEET
T-MINUS FIVE SECONDS, FOUR...
SELF-*DESTRUCT?* HE'S GOING TO...
DETONATE THE BATMOBILE SO THE OCEAN FLOOR CAVES IN ON THEM!
...THREE... TWO...
TERRY?!

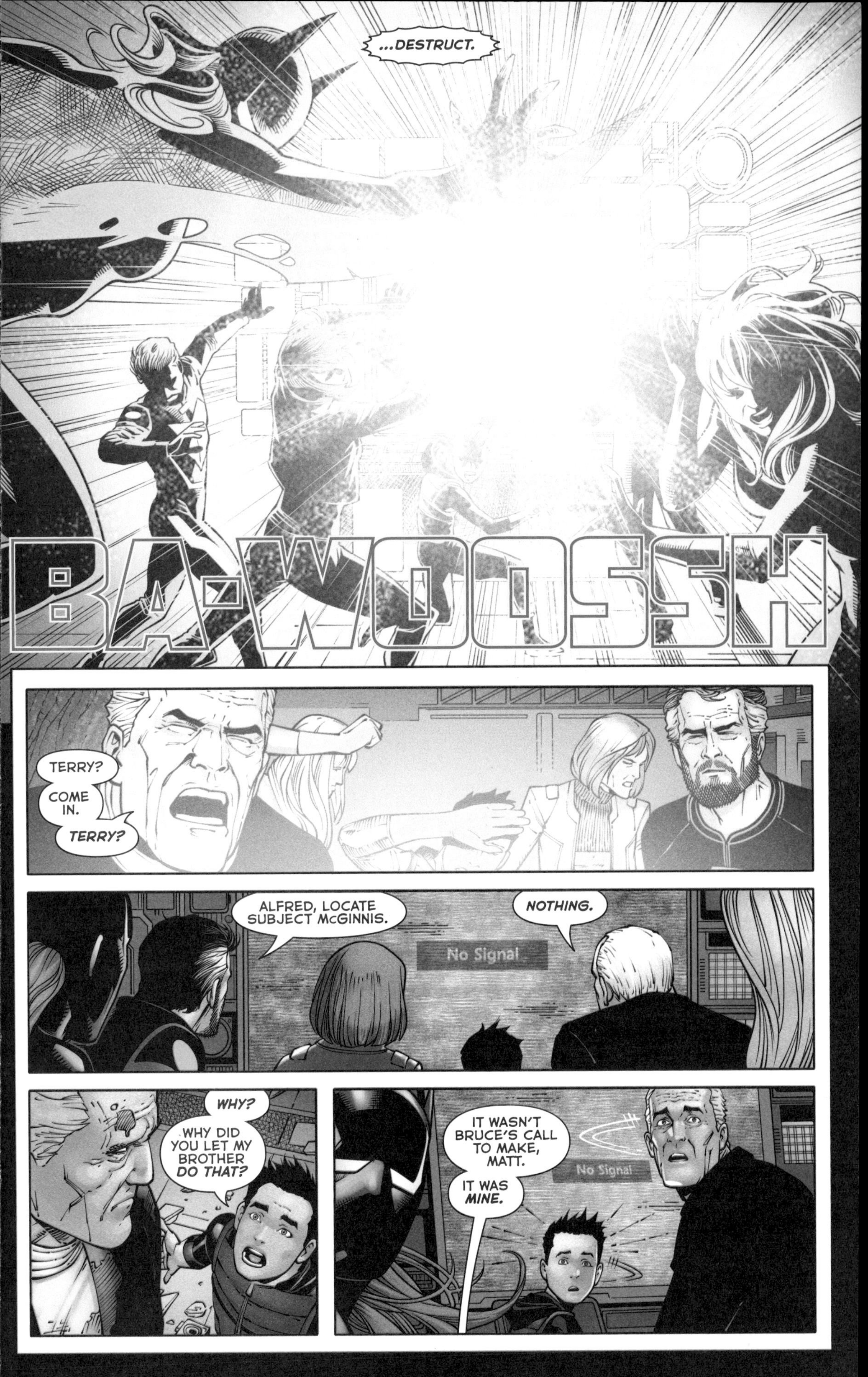
...DESTRUCT.
BA-WOOSSH
TERRY?
COME IN.
TERRY?
ALFRED, LOCATE SUBJECT McGINNIS.
No Signal
NOTHING.
WHY?
WHY DID YOU LET MY BROTHER DO THAT?
No Signal
IT WASN'T BRUCE'S CALL TO MAKE, MATT.
IT WAS MINE.

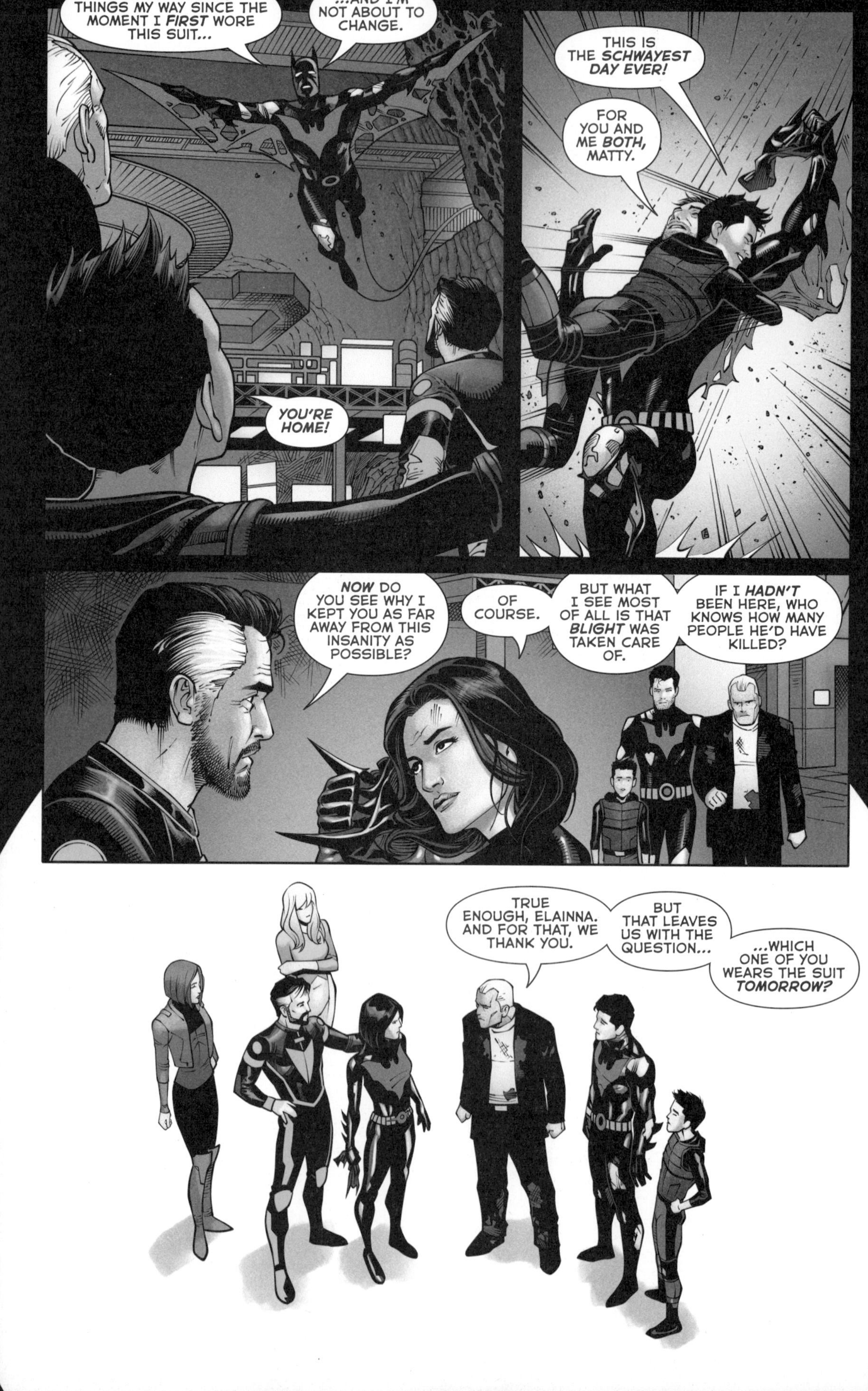
I'VE BEEN DOING THINGS MY WAY SINCE THE MOMENT I *FIRST* WORE THIS SUIT...
...AND I'M NOT ABOUT TO CHANGE.
YOU'RE HOME!
THIS IS THE *SCHWAYEST DAY EVER!*
FOR YOU AND ME *BOTH,* MATTY.
NOW DO YOU SEE WHY I KEPT YOU AS FAR AWAY FROM THIS INSANITY AS POSSIBLE?
OF COURSE.
BUT WHAT I SEE MOST OF ALL IS THAT *BLIGHT* WAS TAKEN CARE OF.
IF I *HADN'T* BEEN HERE, WHO KNOWS HOW MANY PEOPLE HE'D HAVE KILLED?
TRUE ENOUGH, ELAINNA. AND FOR THAT, WE THANK YOU.
BUT THAT LEAVES US WITH THE QUESTION...
...WHICH ONE OF YOU WEARS THE SUIT *TOMORROW?*

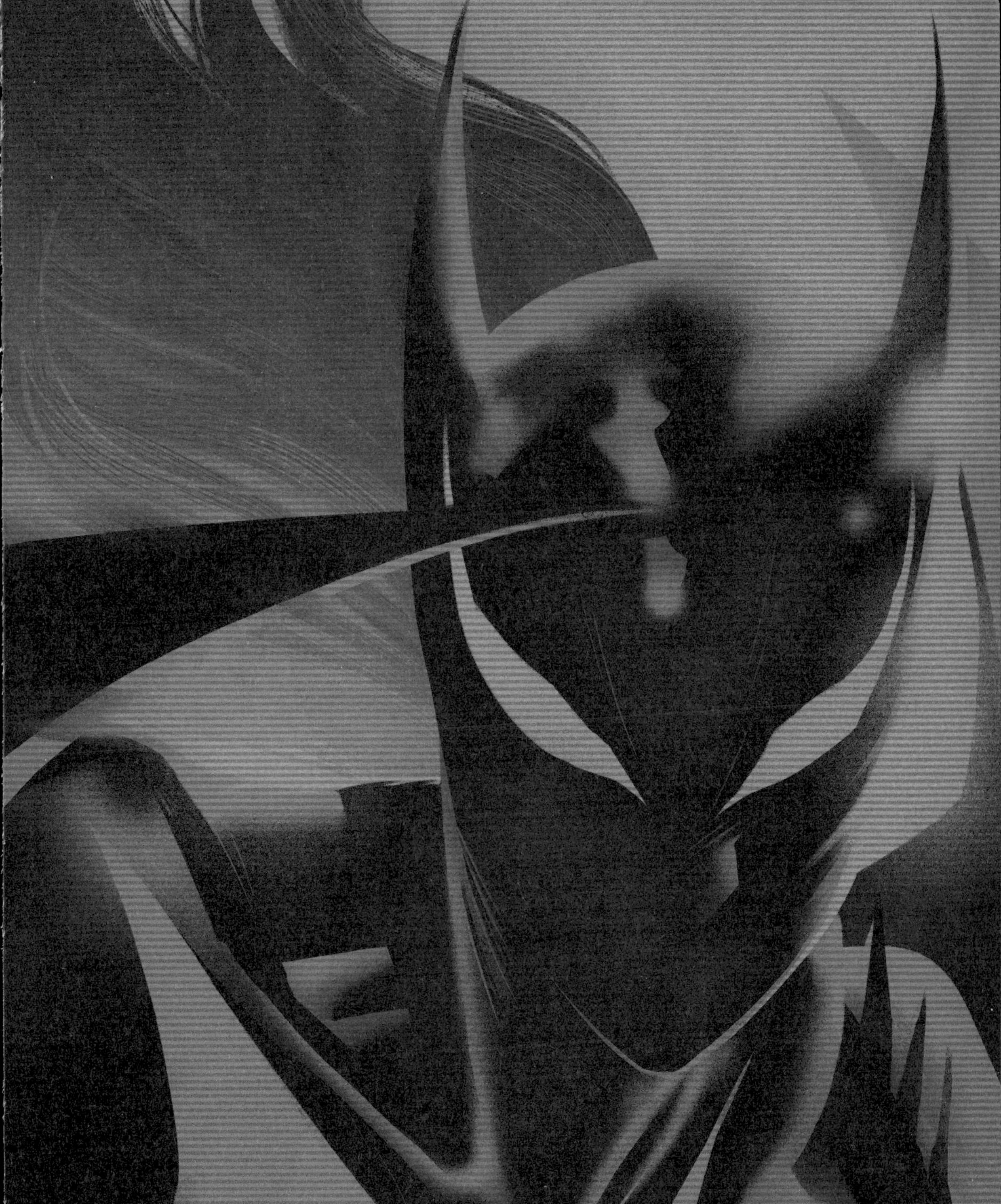

VARIANT COVER GALLERY

Batman Beyond #37-42 variant covers by FRANCIS MANAPUL

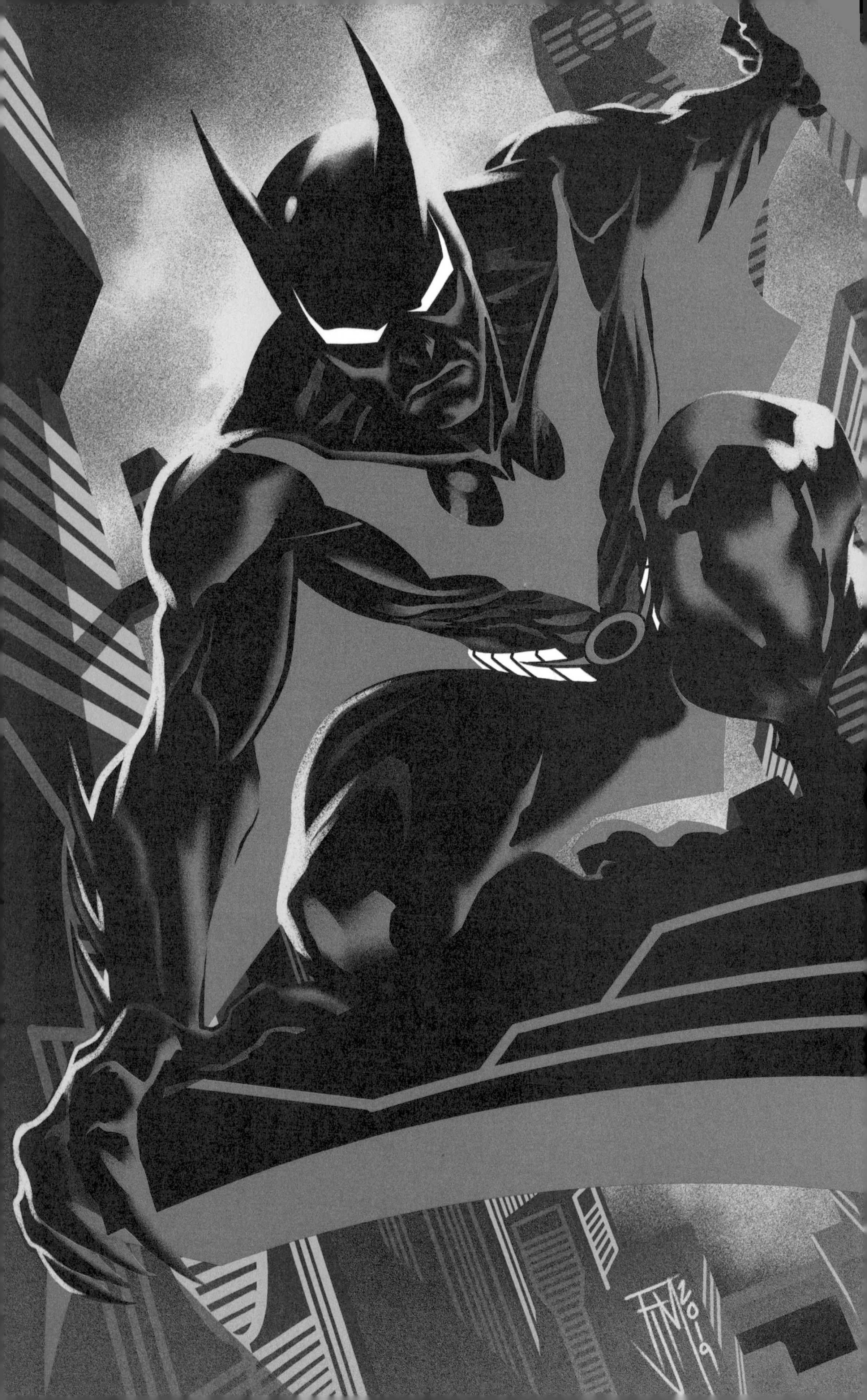

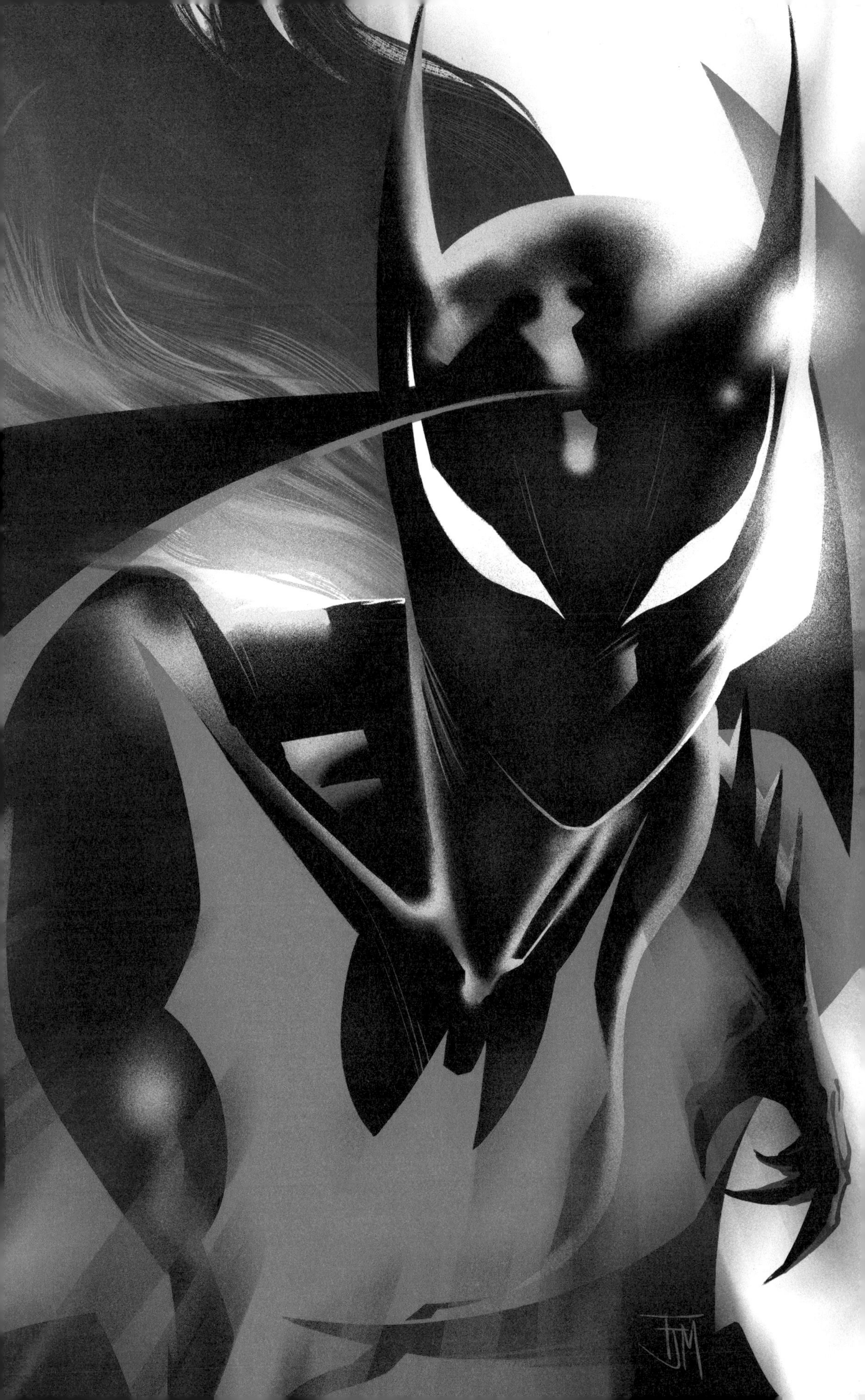

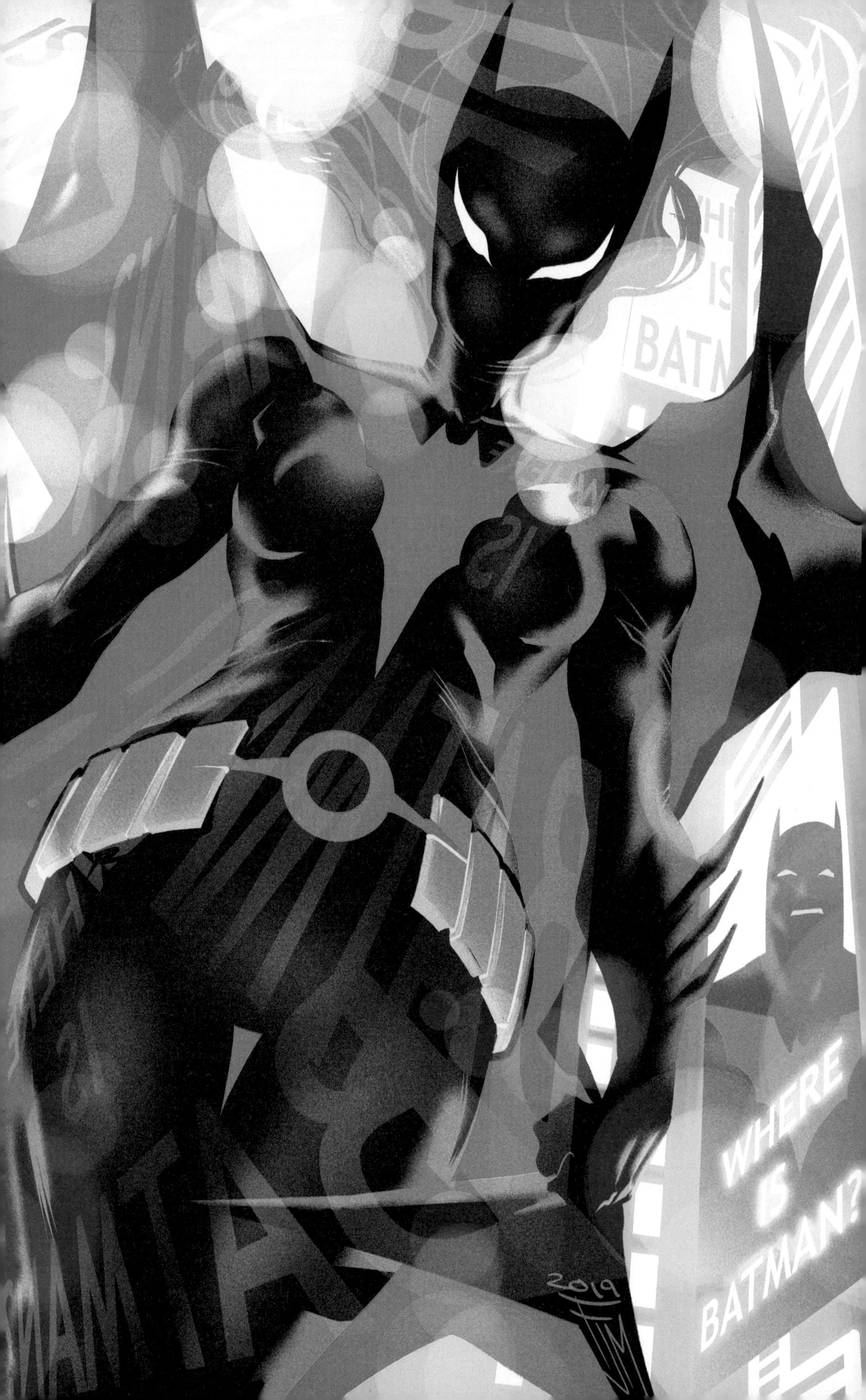
WHERE IS BATMAN?
2019

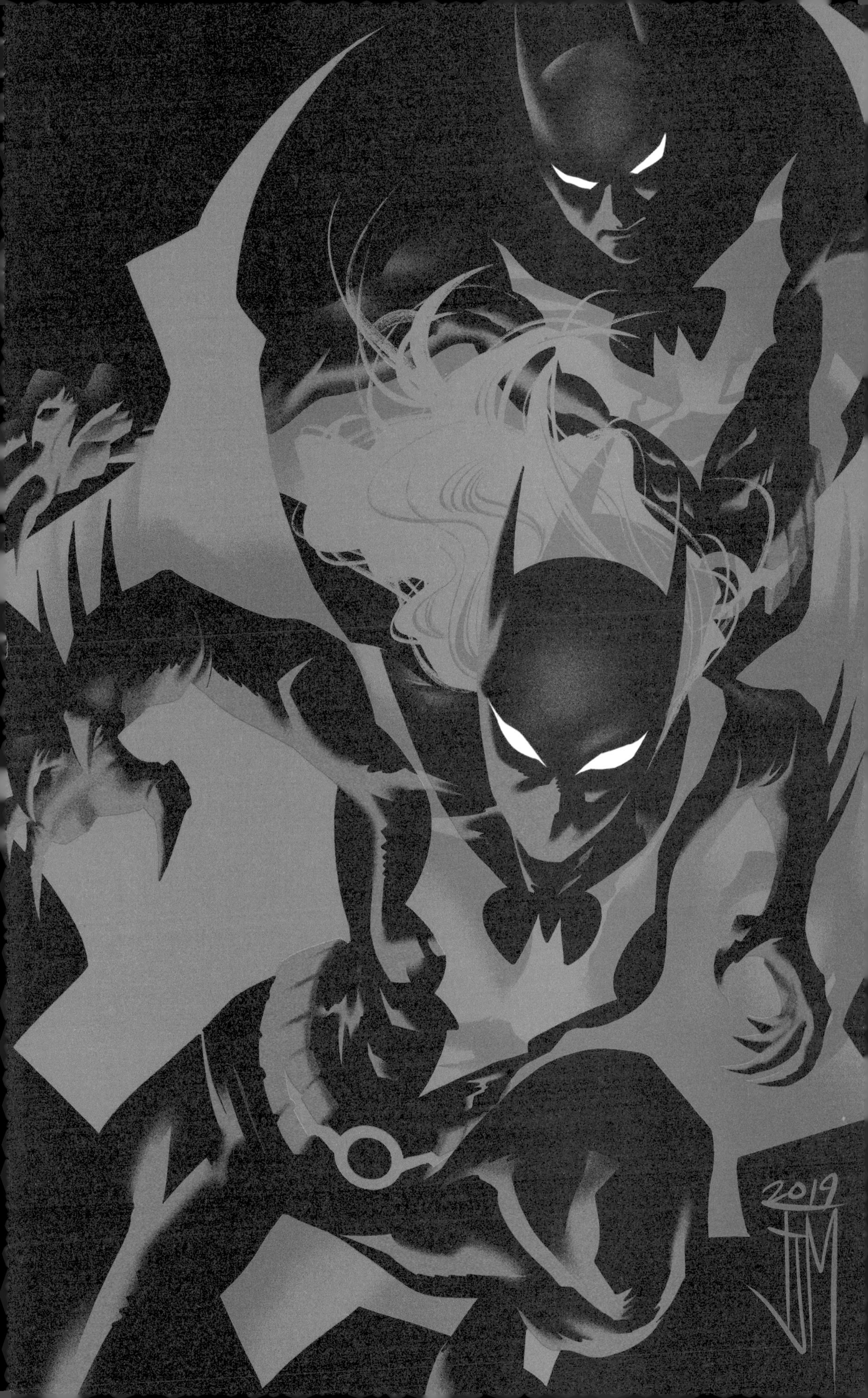

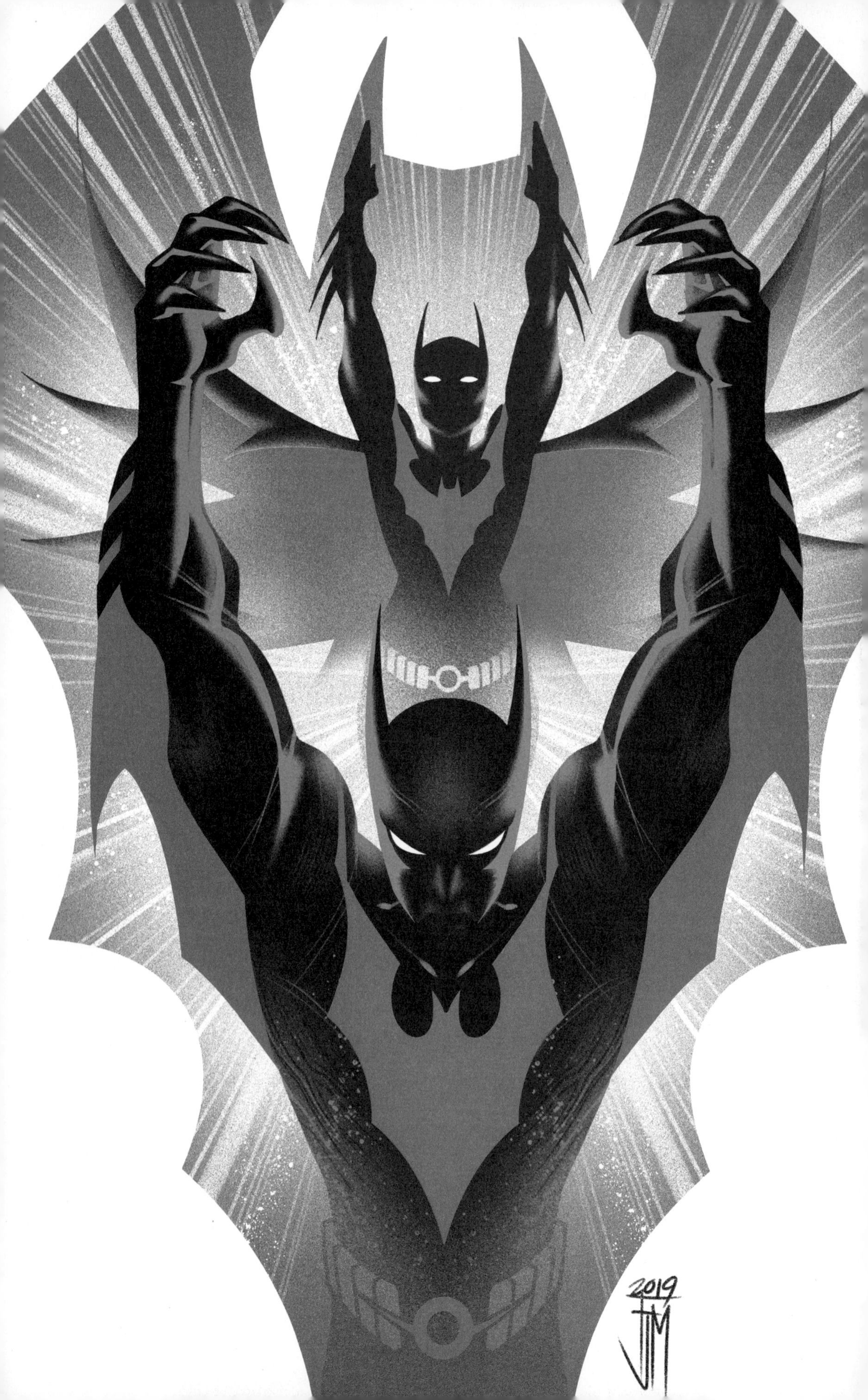
2019

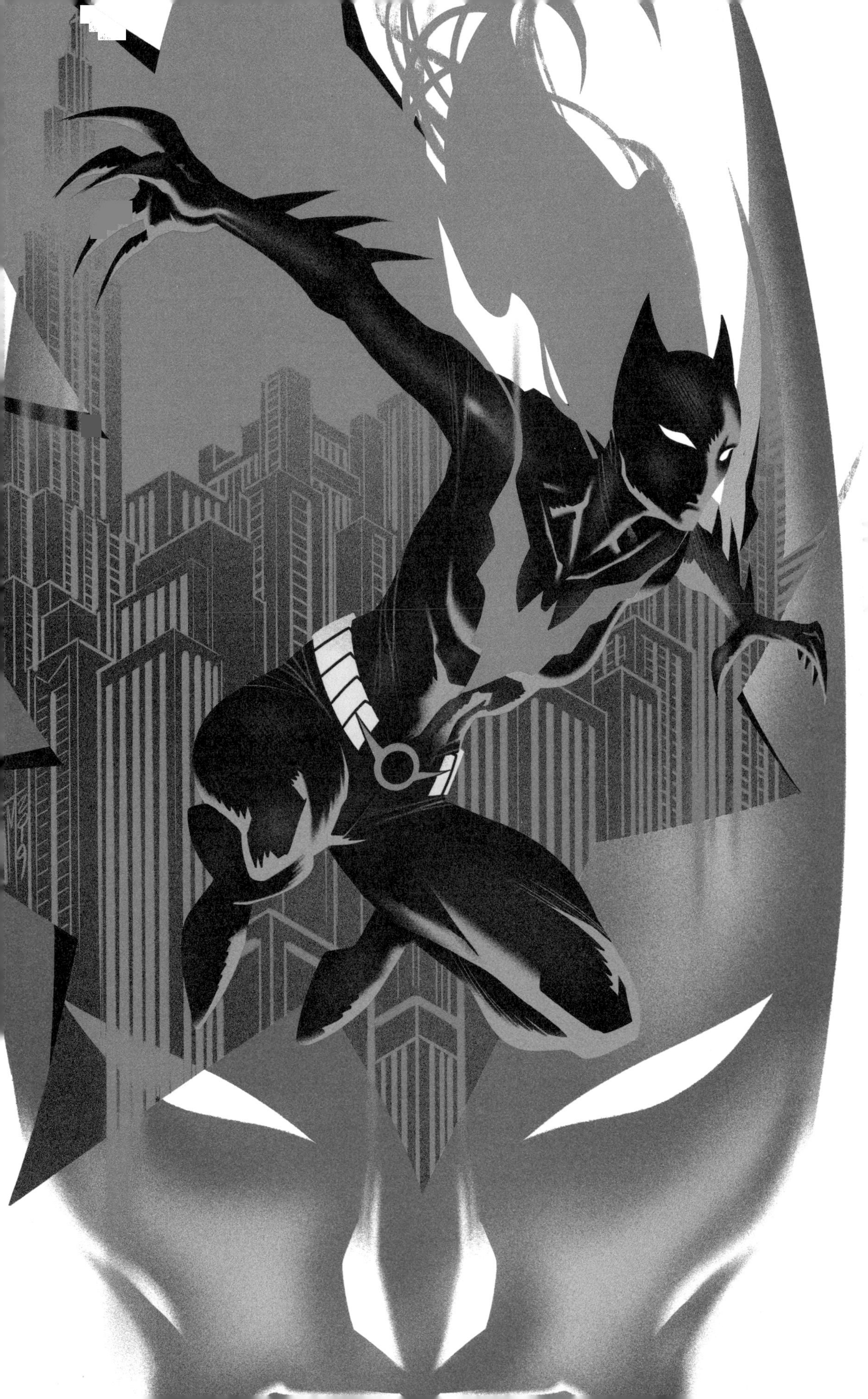

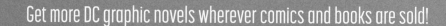